The Silent Cry

Also by Cathy Glass

Damaged
Hidden
Cut
The Saddest Girl in the World
Happy Kids
The Girl in the Mirror
I Miss Mummy
Mummy Told Me Not to Tell
My Dad's a Policeman (a Quick Reads novel)
Run, Mummy, Run
The Night the Angels Came
Happy Adults
A Baby's Cry
Happy Mealtimes for Kids
Another Forgotten Child
Please Don't Take My Baby
Will You Love Me?
About Writing and How to Publish
Daddy's Little Princess
The Child Bride
Saving Danny
Girl Alone

THE MILLION COPY BESTSELLING AUTHOR

CATHY GLASS

The Silent Cry

Alone, there is nothing Kim can do
as her mother's mental health
spirals out of control

Certain details in this story, including names, places and dates,
have been changed to protect the children.

HarperElement
An imprint of HarperCollins*Publishers*
1 London Bridge Street
London SE1 9GF

www.harpercollins.co.uk

First published by HarperElement 2016

1 3 5 7 9 10 8 6 4 2

A catalogue record of this book is
available from the British Library

ISBN 978-0-00-815371-7

Printed and bound in Great Britain by
Clays Ltd, St Ives plc

ACKNOWLEDGEMENTS

A big thank you to my family; my editors, Carolyn and Holly; my literary agent, Andrew; my UK publishers HarperCollins, and my overseas publishers who are now too numerous to list by name. Last, but definitely not least, a big thank you to my readers for your unfailing support and kind words.

PROLOGUE

The room is dark, although it's daylight outside. Strangely dark and eerily quiet. Not a sound when there should be noise. Crying and screaming, that's what she was expecting to hear. And the room seems smaller now too, as though the walls are gradually closing in and crushing her, crushing her to death.

She sits huddled at one end of the sofa, too scared to look around. Scared of what she might see in this unnaturally dark and quiet room that is threatening to squeeze the air out of her and squash her to nothing. Scared, too, of what lies ahead if she stands and goes to the telephone to make that call, and tells them what she's done. They will come and take her baby for sure if she tells them that she has given birth to the devil.

CHAPTER ONE

A FUNNY TURN

Everyone loves a newborn baby and wants a little look. Even those who protest that they are not 'baby lovers' can't resist a peep at the miracle of a new life. I joined the other mothers grouped around the pram in the school playground as we waited with our children for the start of school.

'Congratulations, he's gorgeous,' I said, adding my own best wishes to the many others.

'Thank you,' Laura (the new mum) said quietly, a little bemused by all the attention.

'How old is he now?' I asked.

'Two weeks.'

'Aah, he's adorable.'

'Make the most of every moment,' another mother said. 'They grow up far too quickly.'

My own daughter, Paula, aged thirteen months, was sitting in the stroller and wanted to have a look too, so I unclipped the safety harness and lifted her out so she could see into the pram.

'Baby,' she said cutely, pointing.

'Yes, that's baby Liam,' I said.

'Baby Liam,' she repeated with a little chuckle.

'You were that small once,' I said, and she chuckled again.

'He's my baby brother,' Kim, Laura's daughter, said proudly.

'I know. Aren't you a lucky girl?' I said to her, returning Paula to her stroller.

Kim nodded and touched her baby brother's face protectively, then planted a delicate little kiss on his cheek.

The family had moved into the street where I lived about a year before. Laura and I had got to know each other a little from seeing each other on the way to and from school. My son Adrian, aged five, attended this school but was in a different year to Kim, who was seven. Living quite close to each other I kept meaning to invite Laura in for a coffee and develop our friendship, but I hadn't found the opportunity, what with looking after my own family, fostering and studying for a degree part-time. I guessed Laura had been busy too, especially now she had a baby.

Amid all the oohings and aahings over little Liam the Klaxon sounded the start of school and parents began saying goodbye to their children.

'Bye, love,' I said to Adrian, giving him a kiss on the cheek. 'Have a good day. Make sure you eat your lunch, and have a drink.' He'd only been in school a year and I still fussed over him.

'Bye, Mum. Bye, Paula,' he said, and ran over to join his class who were lining up, ready to go in.

'Bye, little Liam,' Kim said, leaning into the pram again to give her brother one last kiss. She clearly didn't want to leave him. 'See you later. Be a good boy for Mummy.' I smiled.

'Cathy,' Laura said suddenly, clutching my arm. 'I feel a bit hot. I'm going to get a drink of water. Could you stay with the pram, please?'

She turned and walked quickly towards the water fountain situated in an alcove at the far end of the building. Kim looked at me anxiously.

'Don't worry, love. I'll make sure your mum is all right. You go into school.'

She hesitated, but then ran over to join her class, who were going in. I could see Laura at the fountain, leaning forward and sipping the cool water. I thought I should go over in case she was feeling faint. She'd only given birth two weeks before and I could remember how I'd sometimes suddenly felt hot and dizzy in the first few weeks after having both of my children. Pushing Paula's stroller with my right hand and Liam's pram with my left, I steered them across the playground to the water fountain. 'Are you OK?' I asked Laura as we approached.

'Oh, yes, thank you,' she said, straightening and wiping her mouth on a tissue. 'I came over a bit funny. I'm all right now.'

I thought she looked pale. 'Why don't you sit down for a while? The children are going in.' There were a couple of benches in the playground that the children used at playtime.

'No, I'm all right, honestly. I just felt a bit hot and panicky. I think it was all the attention, and it is warm today.'

'Yes, it is warm for May,' I agreed. 'But make sure you don't overdo it.'

She tucked the tissue into her pocket and shook her hair from her face. 'My husband and mother-in-law said it was too soon for me to be out and about. I guess they were right. But I was getting cabin fever staying at home all the time. I needed a change of scenery.' She put her hands onto the pram handle ready for the off.

'Are you going straight home?' I asked. 'I'll walk with you.'

3

'Yes, but there's no need. I'll be fine.'

'I'd like to,' I said. 'I walk by your house on the way to mine.'

'All right. Thanks.' She flicked her hair from her face again and we began across the playground to the main gate. Laura was a tall, attractive woman, whom I guessed to be in her mid-thirties, and she was very slim despite recently giving birth. She had naturally wavy, shoulder-length brown hair, which was swept away from her forehead.

'Is Liam sleeping and feeding well?' I asked, making conversation as we walked.

'Baby,' Paula repeated, pointing to his pram travelling along beside her.

'Yes, that's right,' I said to her. 'Baby Liam.'

'I'm up every three hours at night feeding him,' Laura said. 'But you expect that with a newborn, don't you?'

I nodded. 'It's very tiring. I remember craving sleep in the first few months. If someone had offered me a night out at a top-class restaurant or seven hours unbroken sleep, I would have gone for the latter without a doubt.'

'Agreed,' Laura said with a small smile.

We were silent for a few moments as we concentrated on crossing the road, and then we turned the corner and began up our street. 'How do you like living here?' I asked, resuming conversation.

'Fine. It's nearer Andy's – my husband's – job, and his family. My mother-in-law only lives five streets away.'

'Is that the lady I've seen in the playground, collecting Kim from school?' I asked out of interest.

'Yes. Geraldine. She's very helpful. I don't know what I'd do without her.'

'It's good to have help,' I said. 'My parents help me out when they can, but they live an hour's drive away, and my husband's family are even further away.'

'Yes,' Laura said, looking thoughtful. 'My mother lives over a hundred miles away. You foster, don't you?'

'I do, although I'm taking a few months off at present to finish my degree. After our last foster child left my husband accepted a contract to work abroad for three months, so it seemed a good opportunity to study. The social services know I'm available for an emergency or for respite care, but I'm hoping I won't be disturbed too often.'

'What's respite?' Laura asked, interested.

'It's when a foster carer looks after a child for a short period to give the parents or another foster carer a break. It might just be for a weekend or a week or two, but then the child returns home or to their permanent carer.'

'I see. It's good of you to foster.'

'Not really. I enjoy it. But I must admit I've been struggling recently to study and foster, with Paula being so little. Hopefully I'll now have the chance to complete my dissertation.'

'What are you studying?'

'Education and psychology.'

She nodded. We'd now arrived outside her house, number 53, and Laura pushed open the gate. 'Well, it's been nice talking to you. Cathy, isn't it?'

'Yes – sorry, I should have said.'

'Thanks again for helping me out in the playground. I hope I haven't kept you.'

'Not at all. If ever you want me to collect Kim from school or take her, do let me know. I'm there every day with Adrian.'

'Thanks, that's kind of you, but Geraldine, my mother-in-law, always does it if I can't.'

'OK. But if she can't at any time you know where I am. And perhaps you'd like to pop in for a coffee one day when you're free.'

She looked slightly surprised. 'Oh, I see. That's nice, but I expect you're very busy.'

'Never too busy for a coffee and a chat,' I said with a smile. 'I'll give you my telephone number.' I began delving into my bag for a pen and paper.

'Can you give it to me another time?' Laura said, appearing rather anxious. She began up her garden path, clearly eager to be away. 'Sorry, but I'm dying to go to the bathroom!' she called.

'Yes, of course. I'll see you later in the playground. I can give it to you then.'

'Geraldine will probably be there,' she returned, with her back to me, and quickly unlocking the door. 'Push it through my letterbox.'

'OK. Bye then.'

'Bye!' she called, and going in closed the front door.

'Baby Liam,' Paula said, pointing to the house.

'Yes, that's where he lives,' I said.

'Out!' Paula now demanded, raising her arms to be lifted out of the stroller.

'Yes, you can walk, but remember you always hold my hand.'

I undid the safety harness, helped her out and took her little hand in mine. 'We always hold hands by the road,' I reminded her. I didn't use walking reins but insisted she held my hand.

'Baby Liam,' Paula said again, looking at his house.

'Yes, that's right.' I glanced over. A woman, whom I now knew to be Laura's mother-in-law, Geraldine, was looking out of the downstairs window. I smiled and gave a little wave, but she couldn't have seen me for she turned and disappeared into the room.

'Home,' Paula said.

'Yes, we're going home now.'

We continued haltingly up the street with Paula stopping every few steps to examine something that caught her interest, including most garden gates, walls, fences, lampposts, fallen leaves, every tree in the street and most of the paving slabs. But I knew that the exercise would tire her out and that once home, after she'd had a drink and a snack, she'd have at least an hour's sleep, which would give me the chance to continue researching and writing my dissertation: 'The psychological impact being in care has on a child and how it affects their educational outcome.'

That afternoon, before I set off to collect Adrian from school, I wrote my telephone number on a piece of paper and tucked it into my pocket ready to give to Laura. She wasn't in the playground and for a while it appeared that no one had come to collect Kim, for I couldn't see Geraldine either. The Klaxon sounded for the end of school and the children began to file out, and then Geraldine rushed into the playground at the last minute and went over to Kim. Adrian arrived at my side very excited because his class was going on an outing. He handed me a printed sheet with the details of the outing and a consent form, and I carefully tucked it into my bag. I looked around for Geraldine, but she'd already gone. We joined the other parents and children filing out of the main gate and then crossed the road. As we turned the corner into our street I could see Kim and her grandmother a little way ahead. Kim turned and gave a small wave. We waved back. I was half-expecting Geraldine to turn and acknowledge us, or maybe even wait for us to catch up and fall into conversation, but she didn't. She kept on walking until they arrived at number 53, where she opened the garden gate and began up the path. As we drew level she was opening the front door.

'Excuse me!' I called. She turned. 'Could you give this to Laura, please?' I held out the piece of paper. 'It's my telephone number. I said I'd let her have it. Is she all right now?'

Geraldine nodded, straight-faced, and tapped Kim on the shoulder as a signal for her to collect the paper.

Kim ran down the path and smiled at me as she took the paper. 'Thank you,' she said politely.

'Say hi to your mum,' I said.

'I will.'

With another smile she ran back up the path to her grand-mother, who'd now opened the front door and was waiting just inside, ready to close it. I smiled at her but she didn't return the gesture, and as soon as Kim was inside she closed the door. With her short grey hair and unsmiling features Geraldine came across as stern. I was slightly surprised by her coldness, and it crossed my mind that she'd very likely seen me that morning through the front-room window and, for whatever reason, had chosen to ignore me.

CHAPTER TWO

VERY CONCERNED

I saw Geraldine in the playground every day for the rest of that week – in the morning when she took Kim to school, and in the afternoon when she collected her – but she didn't acknowledge me or make any attempt to start a conversation. Neither did she have anything to do with any of the other parents waiting in the playground, which was unusual. It was a relatively small school, and friendly, so that eventually most people started chatting to someone as they waited for their children. But Geraldine didn't; she hurried into the playground at the last moment and out again, aloof and stern-looking. By Friday, when Laura still hadn't reappeared, I began to wonder if she was ill. She'd had a funny turn earlier in the week, on her first outing with Liam – perhaps she'd been sickening for something and was really poorly. Although Geraldine apparently didn't want anything to do with me, Laura hadn't been so hostile, and given that we lived in the same street and our children attended the same school I felt it would be neighbourly of me to ask how she was. If you are feeling unwell and someone asks after you it can be a real pick-me-up. So on Friday afternoon when Geraldine collected Kim from school I intercepted her as she hurried out of the playground.

'I was wondering how Laura was,' I said. 'I'm Cathy. I live in the same street.'

'Yes, I know who you are,' she said stiffly. 'Laura is fine, thank you. Why do you ask?' Which seemed an odd question.

'When I last saw Laura she wasn't feeling so good. She came over a bit hot and wobbly. I wondered if she was all right now.'

'Oh, that. It was nothing,' Geraldine said dismissively. 'It was far too soon for her to be going out and she realizes that now.'

I gave a small nod. 'As long as she's not ill.'

'No, of course not,' she said bluntly.

'Good. Well, if she ever fancies a change of scenery and a coffee, she knows where I live.'

'Oh, she won't be up to that for a long while,' Geraldine said tartly. 'I've told her she's not to go out for at least another four weeks, possibly longer. That's the advice we had after giving birth.' Taking Kim by the arm, she headed off.

Not go out for another four weeks! You could have knocked me down with a feather. Wherever had she got that from? It was nearly three weeks since Laura had given birth and as far as I knew there was no medical advice that said a new mother had to wait seven weeks before going out, unless Geraldine was confusing it with postpartum sex, but even then seven weeks was excessive if the birth had been normal. More likely, I thought, Geraldine was suffering from empty-nest syndrome and she liked being the centre of the family and having Laura rely on her. It would make her feel needed, and if that suited Laura, fine. It was none of my business. I'd been reassured that Laura wasn't ill, and I had my family to look after and work to do.

* * *

It was the weekend and the weather was glorious, so Adrian, Paula and I spent most of Saturday in the garden, where the children played while I read and then did some gardening. On Sunday my parents came for the day and after lunch we were in the garden again. In the evening after they'd gone, my husband, John, telephoned from America where he was working. He'd got into the habit of telephoning on a Sunday evening when it was lunchtime where he was. We all took turns to speak to him and tell him our news. Even little Paula 'spoke' to him, although she was bemused by the workings of the telephone and kept examining the handset, trying to work out where the voice was coming from, rather than holding it to her ear.

On Monday the school week began again, and as the weather was fine we walked to and from school. I only used my car for school if it was raining hard or if I had to go somewhere straight after school. Geraldine continued to take Kim to school and collect her, and continued to ignore me and all the other parents. Perhaps she was just shy, I thought, although she had a standoffish, austere look about her. Each time I passed Laura's house, number 53, which was four times a day (on the way to and from school), I glanced over. But there was never any sign of Laura or baby Liam, so I assumed Laura was making the most of having Geraldine in charge and was relaxing indoors or in the back garden. Sometimes Paula pointed to the house and, remembering that Liam lived there, said, 'Baby.' If she was out of her stroller and walking, she tried the gate – and most of the others in the street!

On Thursday afternoon, once we'd returned home from school, we hadn't been in long when the telephone rang. It was a social worker asking if I could do some respite and look after a little boy, Darrel, aged three, for that night and all day Friday. His mother, Shelley, a young, single parent, had to go into hospital as a day patient and the person who was supposed to have been looking after Darrel had let her down at the last minute. She had no one else she could ask at such short notice, and I said I'd be happy to help and look after Darrel.

'Shelley's a young mum but she's a good one,' the social worker said. 'She'll bring Darrel to you at about six o'clock this evening. She said she'd bring everything he needs, but she's fretting that she's run out of meatless sausages. She's a vegetarian and she's bringing up Darrel the same. Apparently he loves meatless sausages for lunch, but she hasn't got time to go into town and buy more. I've told her you'll be able to cook him something else vegetarian.'

'Yes, of course I will, but tell her I'll see if I can get some of the sausages. If she's not bringing Darrel until six, I've got time to pop down to our local supermarket. I'm sure I've seen some there.'

'Oh, you are good. I'll tell her. It's the first time Darrel has been away from her overnight and she's getting herself into a bit of a state. It's understandable.'

'Yes,' I agreed.

'She has to be at the hospital at eight o'clock tomorrow morning and she should be discharged later that afternoon. If she does have to stay overnight or doesn't feel up to collecting Darrel on Friday evening can he stay with you for a second night?'

'Yes, of course.'

'Thank you. I'll phone Shelley now and reassure her, and give her your contact details.'

'I'll see her about six then.' We said goodbye and I hung up. I hadn't been told what was wrong with Shelley and I didn't need to know. But I could appreciate why she was anxious at being separated from her son and was fretting because he would miss his favourite food. I'd seen the meatless sausages in the freezer cabinet at the supermarket a few weeks before when I'd been looking for something else. I just hoped they'd still have some in stock. But it's strange the way things work out sometimes, as if it's meant to be, for had I not offered to go to the supermarket I would probably have remained ignorant of what was really going on in Laura's house.

'Sorry,' I said to Adrian and Paula. 'We've got to pop down to the shop.'

Adrian pulled a face. 'We've only just got in and I wanted to play in the garden.'

'You can play as soon as we return,' I said. 'We won't be long. We're looking after a little boy tonight and he likes a special type of sausage. I want to see if I can buy some.'

Adrian was growing up with fostering, as was Paula, so it didn't surprise him that a child could suddenly appear and join our family. It was when they left that he didn't like it. Neither did I, but as a foster carer you have to learn to accept that the children leave you, and you take comfort from knowing you've done your best to help the child and their family, and then be ready for the next child.

'Can I have an ice cream from the shop then?' Adrian asked cannily.

Usually the answer would have been, 'No, not before your dinner,' but given that he was having to come out again and go shopping rather than playing in the garden, I thought a little reward was in order.

'Yes, a small one that won't spoil your dinner,' I said.

'Yippee, ice cream!' Adrian said.

'Ice cream,' Paula repeated.

'Yes, you can have one too.'

As Adrian put on his trainers I fitted Paula's shoes and then lifted her into the stroller, which I kept in the hall.

The local supermarket was at the bottom of my street, to the right, on the same road as the school. While it wasn't suitable for a big shop it was very useful for topping up, and I often popped in if we were running short on essentials. If they didn't have the sausages in stock I would tell Shelley I'd tried and then ask her what else Darrel liked to eat. I was sure I'd be able to find something else he liked. Although he was only staying with me for a day or so, it was important the experience was a good one for him and his mother, and that included meeting his needs and accommodating his likes and dislikes where possible. I would also ask Shelley about Darrel's routine, and I'd keep to it as much as possible to minimize the disruption to him. Even so, despite everything I was going to do, he was still likely to be upset – a three-year-old left with strangers. Had this not been an emergency respite placement he could have come for a visit beforehand to meet us, so it wouldn't be so strange for him.

As we walked down the street Adrian asked, 'Will Darrel go to my school?'

'No, he's not old enough for school yet,' I said.

'Oh, yes, of course,' Adrian said, with an embarrassed grin. 'I knew that really. I am a muppet.'

'Muppet,' Paula repeated.

'You're a muppet,' Adrian said, teasing his sister and ruffling her hair.

'Muppet,' she said again, giggling.

'You're a muppet,' Adrian said again. And so we continued down the street with the word 'muppet' bouncing good-humouredly back and forth between the two of them.

'So how do we cross the road safely?' I asked Adrian as we arrived at the pavement edge.

'Think, stop, look and listen, and when it's all clear walk, don't run, across the road,' he said, paraphrasing the safety code that they'd been taught at school.

'Good boy.'

We waited for the cars to pass and then crossed the road and went into the supermarket. I took a shopping basket and we went straight to the freezer cabinet. To my relief they had three packets of meatless sausages; I took one and placed it in the basket. Adrian then spent some time selecting ice creams for him and Paula and put those in the basket too. Paula reached out and began whining, wanting her ice cream straight away. 'I have to pay for it first and take off the wrapper,' I said.

We headed for the checkout. As we turned the corner of the aisle we saw Kim with a shopping basket on her arm, looking at a display of biscuits. 'Hello, love,' I said. 'Are you helping your mum?'

'Yes,' she said, a little self-consciously. I glanced around for Laura but couldn't see her. 'Where is she?' I asked her. 'I'll say hello.'

'She's at home,' Kim said.

'Oh, OK. Tell her I said hi, please.'

Kim smiled and gave a small nod.

I wasn't going in search of her grandmother, whom I assumed was in one of the other aisles, to say hello, so we continued to the checkout. There was a woman in front of us and as we waited another joined the small queue behind us. Then, as we stepped forward for our turn, I saw Kim join the queue. The cashier rang up our items and placed them in a carrier bag, which I hung on the stroller. I paid and before we left I looked again at Kim and smiled – she was still waiting in the queue, without her grandmother.

Outside the shop I parked the stroller out of the way of the main door and gave Adrian his ice cream, and then removed the wrapper from Paula's. I glanced through the glass shop-front and saw that Kim was now at the till. 'Surely Kim isn't here alone?' I said out loud, voicing my concerns.

Adrian shrugged, more interested in his ice cream.

I threw the wrappers in the bin but didn't immediately start for home.

'Can we go now?' Adrian asked impatiently. 'I want to play in the garden.'

'Yes, in a minute.'

I watched as Kim packed and paid for her shopping and then came out. 'Are you here alone?' I asked her.

She gave a small, furtive nod, almost as if she'd been caught doing something she shouldn't.

'We can walk back together,' I suggested.

She gave another small nod and we crossed the pavement and waited on the kerb. I was surprised and concerned that Kim was by herself. She was only seven, and while there is no law that states a child of seven shouldn't go out alone I thought it was far too young. She wasn't in sight of her house, she was by herself and she'd had to cross quite a busy road. A foster child certainly wouldn't have been allowed to make this journey alone at her age, and neither would I have allowed my own children to do so.

'Is your mother all right?' I asked Kim as we began up our street. I wondered if there had been an emergency, which had necessitated Kim having to buy some items.

'Yes, thank you,' she said politely.

'Where's your gran?' I asked, trying not to sound as though I was questioning her.

'At her house,' Kim replied.

'And you've been doing some shopping for your mother?' She nodded. 'Do you often do the shopping?' I asked after a moment, for she appeared quite confident in her role.

'Yes, sometimes, since Mum had Liam.'

'Does your gran not do the shopping then?'

'Sometimes, but Mum doesn't always like the things Gran buys.'

So why not ask her to buy the things she does like? I thought but didn't say.

'And your mum didn't want to walk down with you?' I asked as we walked.

'She's got a bad headache. She's in bed, and Dad won't be home until later.'

'Oh dear.' I could see Kim looking enviously at Adrian's and Paula's ice creams and I wished I'd thought to buy her one. 'So who's looking after Liam?' I asked.

'He's in the pram, asleep. I wanted to bring him with me, but Mum wouldn't let me. If she's not up later I can make him a bottle,' Kim added proudly. 'I know what to do.'

I smiled and hid my concerns. This wasn't making sense. If Geraldine liked to help, why wasn't she helping the family now when they needed her? Laura was in bed, unwell, and Kim's father wasn't home. Why not phone Geraldine and ask for help? She only lived five streets away. We were drawing close to Laura's house now.

'What time does your dad get in from work?' I asked her. 'Do you know?'

'I think it's usually about seven-thirty or eight,' Kim said.

That was three hours away. 'Does he know your mum is unwell and you had to go to the shop?' We'd arrived at her garden gate.

'No,' Kim said, and opened the gate. If I hadn't been expecting Shelley and Darrel, I would have gone in and asked Laura if there was anything I could do.

Kim paused on the other side of the gate as she looped the carrier bag over her arm and took a front-door key from her purse.

'Kim, will you please tell your mother I said hello and to phone me if there is anything I can do? She has my telephone number.'

'Yes. Thank you,' Kim said sweetly, and then hesitated. With a slightly guilty look she said, 'You won't tell Dad or Gran you saw me, will you?'

'No, but is there a reason?'

'They wouldn't like it,' Kim said. With a little embarrassed smile she turned and continued up the path to her front door.

I watched her open the door and go in. There was no sign of Laura. The door closed and we continued on our way home.

'Why is Kim doing the shopping?' Adrian asked, having heard some of the conversation.

'Her mother isn't feeling well.'

'Would I have to do the shopping if you weren't well?' he said through a mouthful of ice cream.

'No. You're too young.'

'So who would do the shopping while Dad's away if you were ill?'

'I'd ask Sue [our neighbour], or another friend, or Nana and Grandpa. But don't you worry, I'm not going to be ill.' I knew Adrian was anxious about his father working away, and he occasionally asked who would do the jobs his dad usually did, like cutting the grass, or about other 'what if' scenarios, and I always reassured him.

I paused to wipe ice cream from Paula's mouth and hands, as it was melting faster than she could eat it, and then we continued up the street towards home. Perhaps it was from years of fostering that I instinctively sensed when a child might be hiding something, and I felt that now with Kim. What she might be hiding I didn't know, but I had a nagging doubt that something wasn't right in her house. I decided that the following week, at the first opportunity, I would make a neighbourly call and knock on Laura's door – unless, of course, she was in the playground on Monday, which I doubted.

CHAPTER THREE

LULLABY AT BEDTIME

We'd just finished dinner that evening when the doorbell rang, and Adrian and Paula came with me to answer the door. Although it was still light outside I checked the security spyhole before opening it.

'I'm Shelley and this is Darrel,' the young woman said, with a nervous smile.

'Yes, I've been expecting you, love. Come in.'

'This is the lady I told you about,' Shelley said, bending down to Darrel. He was standing beside her, holding her hand, and now buried his face against her leg, reluctant to come in.

'He's bound to be a bit shy to begin with,' I said.

'I know. I understand how he feels,' Shelley said, clearly anxious herself. 'Look, Darrel, Cathy has children you can play with.'

'This is Adrian and this is Paula,' I said.

But Darrel kept his face pressed against his mother's leg as she gently eased him over the doorstep and into the hall. I closed the front door. Adrian, two years older than Darrel and more confident on home territory, went up to him and touched his arm. 'Would you like to come and play with some of my toys?' he asked kindly.

'That's nice of you,' Shelley said, but Darrel didn't look up or release his grip on his mother.

Then Paula decided that she, too, was shy and buried her face against my leg.

'Do you want to leave your bags there?' I said to Shelley, pointing to a space in the hall. 'I'll sort them out later.'

She was carrying a large holdall on each shoulder and, unhooking them, set them on the floor. She was also carrying a cool bag. 'Could you put these things in the fridge, please?' she said, handing me the cool bag. 'There's a pot containing his porridge for breakfast. I made it the way he likes it, with milk, before we came, so you just have to heat it up.'

'OK, that's fine, thank you.'

'And there's some yoghurt in there as well, and diced fruit in little pots. He has them for pudding and snacks. I've also put in a pint of full-cream milk. He prefers that to the semi-skimmed. I give him a drink before he goes to bed. I forgot to tell the social worker that and I didn't know if you had full-cream milk here.'

'I've got most things,' I said, trying to reassure her. 'But it's nice for Darrel to have what you've brought.'

'Oh, the sausages!' Shelley exclaimed.

'Yes, I got some. Don't worry.'

'Thank you so much. I am grateful.' Then, bending down to Darrel again, she said, 'Cathy has got your favourite sausages. Isn't that nice?'

But Darrel kept his face pressed against his mother, and Shelley appeared equally nervous and anxious.

'Try not to worry. He'll be fine soon,' I said. 'Come and have a seat in the living room, while I put these things in the fridge.'

Shelley picked him up and held him tightly to her. I thought he was probably sensing her anxiety as much as he was nervous and shy himself. I showed them into the living room. Adrian went in, too, while Paula, slightly unsettled, came with me into the kitchen. At her age it was more difficult for her to understand fostering.

'Baby?' she asked as I set the cool bag on the work surface and unzipped the lid.

'No, Darrel is older than you. He's three. He's sleeping here for one night. You can play with him.'

I began putting the contents of the cool bag into the fridge as Paula watched. Shelley seemed to have thought of everything, and I recognized the love, care, concern and anxiety that had gone into making up all these little pots so that Darrel had everything he was used to at home. Each pot was labelled with his name, what the pot contained and when he ate the food – so, for example: *Darrel's porridge, breakfast, around 8 a.m.*, and *Darrel's apple and orange mid-morning snack, around 11 a.m.* Once I'd emptied the cool bag I returned to the living room with Paula and placed the bag near Shelley. 'All done,' I said.

'Thank you so much,' she said gratefully. Darrel was sitting on her lap, with his face buried in her sweater. 'I've written down his routine,' she said, passing me a sheet of paper that she'd taken from her bag.

'Thanks. That will be useful.' I sat on the sofa and Paula sat beside me. Adrian was on the floor, playing with the toys and glancing at Darrel in the hope that he would join in.

'I'm sure he'll play with you soon,' I said. Then to Shelley: 'Would you and Darrel like a drink?'

'No, thank you, we had one before we left. He had warm milk, and he has one before he goes to bed too. I put the milk in the bag.'

'Yes, I saw it, thanks. Although I've got plenty of milk here. Has he had his dinner?'

'Yes, and I gave him a bath this morning so there is no need for him to have one this evening. I thought it would be better for him if I did it rather than him having to have a bath in a strange house. No offence, but you know what I mean.'

I smiled. 'Of course. Don't worry. I'll keep to your routine. I'll show you both around the house before you leave, so it won't be so strange.'

'Thank you.'

I guessed Shelley was in her early twenties, so she could only have been seventeen or eighteen when she'd had Darrel, but she obviously thought the world of him, and, as the social worker had said, she was a good mother. She was slim, average height, with fair, shoulder-length hair and was dressed fashionably in jeans and layered tops. She had a sweet, round face but was clearly on edge – she kept frowning and chewing her bottom lip. I knew Darrel would pick up on this. Paula, at my side, was now chancing a look at Darrel as if she might be brave enough to go over to him soon. Shelley saw this. 'Come and say hello to Darrel,' she said. 'He's just a bit shy, like me.'

But Paula shook her head. 'In a few minutes,' I said.

'I think I've packed everything Darrel needs,' Shelley said. 'His plate, bowl, mug and cutlery are in the blue bag in the hall. I've put in some of his favourite toys and Spot the dog. He's the soft toy Darrel takes to bed. Darrel is toilet trained, but he still has a nappy at night. I've put some nappies in the black bag, but he only needs one. I didn't have room to bring his step stool, but he needs that to reach the toilet.'

'Don't worry. I have a couple of those,' I said. 'They are already in place in the bathroom and toilet.'

'Thanks. I've put baby wipes in the blue bag too. His clothes and night things are in the black bag, but I couldn't fit in his changing mat.'

'Don't worry,' I said again. 'I have one of those too. In fact, I have most things children need.'

'Oh, yes, of course, you would have,' Shelley said with a small, embarrassed laugh. 'You have children and you foster. Silly me.'

She was lovely but so anxious. 'I promise I'll take good care of Darrel and keep him safe,' I said. 'He'll be fine. How did you get here with all those bags and Darrel?'

'On the bus,' she replied.

'I wish I'd known. I could have come and collected you in the car.'

'That's kind, but we're pretty self-sufficient. I like it that way. You can't be let down then.' She gave another nervous little laugh and I wondered what had happened in her past to make her feel that way.

Toscha, our lovable and docile cat, sauntered into the room and went over to Adrian.

'Oh, you've got a cat!' Shelley exclaimed. For a moment I thought she was going to tell me that Darrel was allergic to cat fur and it could trigger an asthma attack, which was true for some children. Had this not been an emergency placement I would have known more about Darrel, including facts like this. Thankfully Shelley now said excitedly, 'Look at Cathy's cat, Darrel. You like cats. Are you going to stroke her?' Then to me: 'Is she friendly?'

'Yes, she's very friendly. She's called Toscha.'

Toscha was the prompt Darrel needed to relinquish his grip on his mother's jersey. He turned and looked at the cat and then left her lap and joined Adrian on the floor beside Toscha. Paula then forgot her shyness and slid from the sofa to join them too.

'Toscha likes being stroked,' I said. Which was just as well, as three little hands now stroked her fur and petted her while she purred contentedly. Now Darrel was less anxious I could see Shelley start to relax too. With a small sigh she sat back in her chair.

'I know I shouldn't worry so much,' she said. 'But coming here brought back so many memories.'

I smiled, puzzled. 'Oh yes? What sort of memories?'

'Going into a foster carer's home for the first time. I was in care for most of my life and I had so many moves. I hated having to move. New people and new routines. It was so scary. I felt scared most of my early life. I thought I'd got over all of that, but bringing Darrel here today brought it back.' Which I thought explained at lot of Shelley's apprehension and anxiety. 'I'd rather die than let my little boy lead the life I had,' she added.

'He won't,' I said. 'You'll make sure of it. You're doing a great job. Your social worker told me what a fantastic mum you are. I'm sorry your experiences in care weren't good. It was wrong you had to keep moving, very wrong, but try not to worry about Darrel. He'll be fine here with me and you'll see him again tomorrow.' My heart went out to her. Whatever had the poor child been through?

'Thank you,' she said quietly. 'I worry about him so much. He's all the family I have. I nearly wasn't allowed to keep him when he was a baby. I had to prove to the social services that I could look after him.'

'And you've done that,' I said firmly. 'Admirably.' But I could see she was worried, and I understood why she had overcompensated. 'Do the social services still have any involvement with you and Darrel?' I asked, which again would have been something I'd known if the placement had been planned.

'Not since Darrel was eighteen months old,' Shelley said. 'That's when their supervision order stopped. It was a great relief. I was going to cancel my hospital appointment tomorrow when my friend let me down and said she couldn't look after Darrel. But I knew I'd have to wait ages for another appoint-ment and my teeth really hurt. I've got two impacted wisdom teeth and they're taking them out under general anaesthetic tomorrow. I was really nervous when I phoned the social services to ask for help. I hung up twice before I spoke to anyone. Then I got through to my old social worker and told her what had happened. She was lovely and asked how Darrel and I were. She said she'd see what she could do to arrange something for Darrel so I didn't have to cancel my appointment.'

I nodded sympathetically, and not for the first time since I'd started fostering I realized just how alone in the world some people are. 'So who is collecting you from hospital tomorrow?' I asked.

'No one. I'll get a cab here.'

'I can come and collect you,' I offered.

'That's nice of you, but I'll be fine, and I don't know what time I'll be discharged.'

'You could phone me when you know and I'd come straight over. The hospital isn't far.'

She gave a small shrug. 'Thanks. I'll see how it goes.' And I knew that given her comment about being self-sufficient she'd have to be feeling very poorly before she took up my offer of help.

Toscha had sauntered off and the children were now playing with the toys I'd set out. It was after six-thirty and at some point Shelley would have to say goodbye to Darrel and leave, which would be difficult for them both. The sooner we got it over with the better, and then I could settle Darrel before he went to bed.

'I'll show you around the house before you go,' I said to Shelley.

Her forehead creased and she looked very anxious again. 'I was thinking, if you don't mind, is it possible for me to stay and put Darrel to bed? Once he's asleep I'd go, and he wouldn't be upset.'

Each fostering situation is different, and foster carers have to be adaptable to accommodate the needs of the child (or children) they are looking after, and also often the parents too. There was no reason why she couldn't stay.

'Yes, that's fine with me,' I said. 'But we will need to explain to Darrel what is happening. Otherwise he'll wake up in the morning expecting to find you here, and be upset when you're not.'

'Darrel, love,' Shelley said, leaving her chair and going over to kneel on the floor beside him, 'I've got something to tell you.'

He stopped playing and looked at her, wide-eyed with expectation and concern.

'It's nothing for you to worry about,' she reassured him. 'But you remember I explained how you would be sleeping here for one night while I went into hospital?'

Darrel gave a small nod.

'Well, I am not going to leave you until after you are asleep. Then, in the morning when you wake up, Cathy will be here to look after you until I come back. I'll be back as soon as I can tomorrow. All right, pet?'

'Yes, Mummy,' he said quietly.

'Good boy.' She kissed his cheek.

I thought Shelley had phrased it well, and at three years of age Darrel would have some understanding of 'tomorrow'.

'Shall we have a look around the house now?' I suggested. 'You can see where you will be sleeping,' I said to Darrel.

'Yes, please,' Shelley said enthusiastically, standing. Darrel stood, too, and held her hand. He looked at Adrian and Paula, now his friends.

'Yes, they will come too,' I said. They usually liked to join in the tour of the house I gave each child when they first arrived, although obviously there was no need, as they lived here. 'This is the living room,' I began. 'And through here is the kitchen and our dining table where we eat.'

As we went into the kitchen Darrel exclaimed, 'There's the cat's food!' and pointed to Toscha's feeding bowl.

'That's right,' I said, pleased he was thawing out a little. 'It's empty now because Toscha has had her dinner.'

'I've had my dinner,' Darrel said.

'I know. Your mummy told me. What did you have? Can you remember?'

'Stew,' he said. 'With dumplings.'

'Very nice. Did you eat it all up?'

'Yes.'

'He's a good eater,' Shelley said. 'He's likes my bean stew. I learned to make it from a recipe book. I put in lots of vegetables and he eats it all.'

'Very good,' I said, impressed, and thinking I should make stew and dumplings more often.

We went down the hall and into the front room. Given that Darrel was only young and here for one night, I didn't go into detail about what we used the rooms for; I was just showing him around so he was familiar with the layout of the house and would hopefully feel more at home.

'We'll bring the bags up later,' I said as I led the way upstairs. We went round the landing to Darrel's room.

'It's not like my room at home,' he said, slightly disappointed as we went in.

I smiled. 'I'm sure your bedroom at home is fantastic, and it'll have all your things in it, but this will be fine for tonight.'

'Yes, thank you, Cathy,' Shelley said, frowning at Darrel. 'It's very nice.'

I then briefly showed them the other rooms upstairs, including the toilet and bathroom where the step stools were already in place. I made a point of showing Darrel where I slept so that if he woke in the night he knew where to find me. It helped to reassure the child (and their parents), although in truth I was a light sleeper and always heard a child if they were out of bed or called out in the night.

'Thank you very much, Cathy,' Shelley said, and we began downstairs.

We returned to the living room and the children played with the toys again. Shelley sat on the floor with them and joined in, childlike and enthusiastic in her play. She carefully arranged the toy cars and play-people in the garage and sat the attendant behind the cash desk. I thought that, like many children from neglected and abusive backgrounds, she'd probably missed out on her childhood and had grown up fast to survive. After a while she left the children to finish their game and joined me on the sofa. I took the opportunity to explain to her that I would have to take Darrel with me to school in the morning when I took Adrian. I said that if he couldn't manage the walk there and back I had a double stroller I could use.

'He'll be fine walking,' Shelley said. 'It's not far, and he walks everywhere with me. I don't have a car and I sold his stroller six months ago as I needed the money.' I appreciated it must be difficult for her financially, bringing up a child alone.

It was nearly seven o'clock and I said I usually took Paula up for her bath and bed about this time.

'It's nearly Darrel's bedtime too,' Shelley said. 'Can I give him his drink of warm milk now?'

'Yes, of course. I'll show you where everything is in the kitchen.'

Leaving the children playing I took Shelley into the kitchen, showed her around and then left her to warm Darrel's milk, while I took Paula upstairs to get ready for bed.

'Baby bed?' Paula asked.

'Darrel will be going to bed soon,' I said, guessing that was what she meant. My reply seemed to satisfy her, for she chuckled.

I gave Paula a quick bath, put her in a clean nappy and then, after lots of hugs and kisses, tucked her into her cot bed. 'Night, love,' I said, kissing her soft, warm cheek one last time. 'Sleep tight and see you in the morning.'

Paula grinned, showing her relatively new front teeth, and I kissed her some more. I said 'Night-night' again and finally came out, leaving her bedroom door slightly open so I could hear her if she didn't settle or woke in the night, although she usually slept through now.

Downstairs Darrel had had his milk and Shelley was in the kitchen, washing up his mug while Darrel played with Adrian in the living room. Shelley looked quite at home in the kitchen and I asked her if she'd like a cup of tea, but she said she'd like to get Darrel to bed first. We went into the living room where she told Darrel it was time for bed. 'Say goodnight to Adrian,' she said.

'Goodnight,' Darrel said politely, and kissed Adrian's cheek. Adrian looked slightly embarrassed at having a boy kiss him, but of course Darrel was only three.

'I'm sorry,' Shelley said, seeing Adrian's discomfort. 'He always kisses me when we say goodnight.'

'It's fine,' I said. 'As Mrs Clause says in *Santa Clause: The Movie*, "If you give extra kisses, you get bigger hugs!"'

'That's lovely,' Shelley said, clasping her hands together in delight. 'I'll have to remember that – "If you give extra kisses, you get bigger hugs!"'

Adrian grinned; he loved that Christmas movie and the saying, as I did.

Shelley and I carried the holdalls upstairs and into Darrel's room, with Darrel following. Having checked she had everything she needed, I left Shelley to get Darrel ready for bed and went downstairs. I'd got into the routine of putting Paula to bed first and then spending some time with Adrian. He usually read his school book, then we'd play a game or just chat, and then I'd read him a bedtime story and take him up to bed. It was our time together, set aside from the hustle and bustle of him having a younger sister and fostering. Now, as I sat on the sofa with my arm around him, we could hear Shelley moving around upstairs while she saw to Darrel.

'It's strange having another mummy in the house,' Adrian said.

'Yes, it is,' I agreed. 'But it's rather nice.' It was touching and reassuring to hear another mother patiently and lovingly tending to the needs of her child.

Once I'd finished reading Adrian his bedtime story, he put the book back on the shelf and then went over to say good-night to Toscha as he did every night. She was curled on her favourite chair and he gently kissed the top of her furry head once and then twice. 'Remember, Toscha,' he said. '"If you give extra kisses, you get bigger hugs!"'

'That's right,' I said. 'Although I'd be very surprised if she got up and hugged you.' Adrian laughed loudly.

'Mum, you are silly sometimes.'

We went upstairs and while Adrian went to the toilet I checked on Paula. She was fast asleep, flat on her back, with her arms and legs spread out like a little snow angel. I kissed her forehead and crept out, again leaving her door slightly open. Shelley was in Darrel's room now and through their open door I could hear her telling him that she would only go once he was asleep, and then she'd come back for him as soon as possible the next day. There was anxiety in her voice again, and I hoped it wouldn't unsettle Darrel, for it could take hours before he went to sleep.

I ran Adrian's bath and waited while he washed – even at his age I didn't leave him unattended in the bath for long. I also washed his back, which he often forgot about. Once he was out, dried and dressed in his pyjamas, I went with him to his room. Following our usual routine, he switched on his lamp and I switched off the main light, then I sat on his bed while he snuggled down and settled ready for sleep. He often remembered something he had to tell me at this time that couldn't wait until the morning. Sometimes it was a worry he'd been harbouring during the day, but more often it was just a general chat – a young, active boy delaying the time when he had to go to sleep. But tonight we heard Shelley talking quietly to Darrel in the room next door.

'Will Darrel still be here when I come home from school tomorrow?' Adrian asked.

'I don't think so. His mother is hoping to collect him in the early afternoon.'

'He's nice, isn't he?' Adrian said.

'Yes, he's a lovely little boy, just like you.'

Adrian smiled and I stroked his forehead. 'Time for sleep,' I said.

Then we both stopped and looked at each other in the half-light as the most beautiful, angelic voice floated in from Darrel's room. Shelley was singing him a lullaby and her soft, gentle voice caressed the air, pitch perfect and as tender and innocent as a newborn baby – it sent shivers down my spine. First Brahms's 'Lullaby' and then 'All Through the Night':

'Sleep, my child, and peace attend thee,
All through the night,
Guardian angels God will send thee,
All through the night ...'

By the time she'd finished my eyes had filled and I swallowed the lump in my throat. It was the most beautiful, soulful singing I'd ever heard, and I felt enriched for having been part of it.

CHAPTER FOUR

SHELLEY

'You've got a lovely voice,' I said to Shelley when she finally came downstairs from settling Darrel for the night.

'Thank you. I wanted to become a professional singer, but that won't happen now.'

I was in the living room with the curtains closed against the night sky, reading the sheet of paper Shelley had given to me on Darrel's routine. 'Would you like that cup of tea now?' I asked her.

'Yes, please. Shall I make it?'

'No, you sit down,' I said, standing. 'You've had a busy day. Milk and sugar?'

'Just milk, please.'

'Would you like something to eat now too?' I asked. 'It's a while since you had dinner.'

'A biscuit would be nice, thank you,' Shelley said. 'I usually have one with a cup of tea when I've finished putting Darrel to bed.'

I went through to the kitchen, smiling at the thought of Shelley's little evening ritual, not dissimilar to my own, of putting the children to bed first and then sitting down and relaxing with a cup of tea and a biscuit. I guessed parents everywhere probably did something similar.

I made the tea, set the cups and a plate of biscuits on a tray and carried it through to the living room. 'Help yourself to biscuits,' I said, putting the tray on the occasional table and passing her a cup of tea.

'Thank you. You've got a nice home,' she said sweetly. 'It's so welcoming and friendly.'

'That's a lovely compliment,' I said, pleased.

'Do you find it hard with your husband working away?' Shelley asked, taking a couple of biscuits.

'I did to begin with,' I said. 'But we're in a routine now. And my parents will always help out if necessary.'

'I wish I had parents,' she said.

'Where are they?' I asked. 'Do you know?' It was clear that Shelley wanted to talk, so I felt it was all right to ask this.

'My mum's dead, and I never knew my dad. I think he's dead too,' she said without self-pity.

'I am sorry.'

She gave a small shrug. 'It was a long time ago. It happened when I was a child. They were both heavy drug users. It was the drugs that killed my mum and I think my dad too. I remember my mum from when I was little, but not my dad. I never saw him. I have a photo of my mum at home. I keep it by my bed. But even back then you can see she was wasted from the drugs. When the kids at secondary school started boasting that they'd been trying drugs I used to think: you wouldn't if you saw what they did. My mum was only twenty-six when she died, but she was all wrinkled and wizened, and stick thin.'

'I am sorry,' I said again. 'You've had a lot to cope with in your life. And it must be difficult bringing up a child completely alone. Although you are doing a good job,' I added.

Shelley gave a small nod and sipped her tea. 'I was a week off my eighteenth birthday when I had Darrel,' she said, setting the cup on the saucer. 'All my plans had to be put on hold. I had great plans. I wanted to be something. Go to college and study music and try to become a professional singer. I thought I'd get a good job, buy a house and a car, and go on holidays like other people do. But that's all gone now. I know other young single mums and, although we all love our children, if we're honest we'd do things differently if we had our time over again – get a job and training first, meet someone, set up home and then have a family. You can't do that if you have a child.'

'It is difficult,' I agreed. 'You're not in touch with any of your foster carers?'

'No. I was moved so often I can't even remember most of their names. Some of them were nice, others weren't. The only one I really felt was like a mother to me was Carol. I was with her from when I was fourteen to when I was seventeen. She was so nice. She helped me through a really bad time. But when I was seventeen the social worker said I had to go and live in a semi-independence unit ready for when I left care. Carol tried to stay in touch – she phoned and put cards through my door – but I never got back to her.'

'That's a pity. Why not?'

Shelley shrugged. 'Not sure. But I was dating then and I sort of put my trust in him.'

'Have you thought about trying to contact Carol now?' I asked. 'I'm sure she'd be pleased to hear from you.'

'It's been over three years,' Shelley said.

'Even so, I still think she'd be pleased if you did get in touch. I know I am when a child I've fostered leaves and we lose contact, and then they suddenly phone or send a card or arrive at my door. Foster carers never forget the children they look after, but once the child has left the social services don't tell us how you are doing.'

'I didn't realize that,' Shelley said, slightly surprised. 'I'll think about it.' She took another biscuit.

'Are you sure I can't make you something proper to eat?' I asked.

'No, really, I'm fine. I must go soon.' But she didn't make any move to go and I was happy for her to sit and talk. 'When I found out I was pregnant,' she continued, 'Darrel's father had already left me. I told the social worker getting pregnant was an accident, but it wasn't a complete accident. I mean, I didn't plan on getting pregnant – I wanted to go to college – but neither did I take any precautions. I was pretty messed up at the time, and I sort of thought that having a child would give me the family I'd never had. I wanted to be loved and needed.'

'We all want that,' I said. 'It's such a pity you weren't found a forever family. I don't understand why the social services didn't look for an adoptive family for you, with both your parents dead.'

'They did,' Shelley said in the same matter-of-fact way. 'I was adopted. But it didn't work out.'

'Didn't work out?' I asked, dismayed. 'Adoption is supposed to be for life. In law, an adopted child is the same as a birth child.'

'I know. They even changed my surname to theirs. I was with them for two years, from when I was nine. But then the woman got pregnant. They thought they couldn't have kids and when the baby was born they were all over it and I was pushed out. That's what it felt like. So I started playing up and being really naughty. I remember doing it because I felt like no one loved me, so they put me back into care.'

'That's awful,' I said. 'I am so sorry to hear that.' It was such a sad story, but Shelley didn't appear bitter.

'That's life,' she said with a dismissive shrug. Draining the last of her tea, she returned the cup and saucer to the tray. 'I'd better be going. Thanks for listening. I hope I haven't kept you.'

'Of course not. I've enjoyed having your company. And please don't worry about Darrel. I'll take good care of him. I hope the operation goes well.' The clock on the mantelpiece showed it was nearly ten o'clock. 'Shelley, I don't really want you going home on the bus alone at this time. Can I call a cab? I'll pay for it.'

'That's kind of you. I'm not usually out this late,' she said with a small laugh. 'I'm usually at home with Darrel. But is it safe for a woman to be alone in a cab? I mean, you read bad stuff in the papers.'

'It's a local firm I know well,' I said. 'They have at least one lady cab driver. Shall I see if she's free?'

'Yes, please. I'll pop up to the loo while you phone them.'

I called the cab firm and the controller said they had a lady driver working that night, so I booked the cab. He said she would be with us in about fifteen minutes. Shelley had been right to be concerned, a young woman alone in a cab, but I was confident she'd be safe using this firm or I wouldn't have suggested it. I heard her footsteps on the landing, but before she came downstairs she went into Darrel's room. A few moments later she returned to the living room. 'He's fast asleep,' she said, joining me on the sofa. 'He should sleep through, but he'll wake early with a sopping wet nappy. I'm trying to get him dry at night, but it's difficult.'

'You could try giving him his last drink in the evening earlier,' I suggested. 'Perhaps with his dinner, or just after. That's what I did with Adrian and the children I've fostered who were still in nappies at night. After all, what goes in must come out!'

She smiled. 'Yes, very true. I'll give it a try.'

I told her the cab was on its way and, taking out my purse, I gave her a twenty-pound note to pay the fare.

'It won't be that much,' she said. 'I'll give you change.'

'No. It's OK. Buy yourself something.'

'Thank you. That is kind.'

We continued chatting, mainly about Darrel and being a parent, until the doorbell rang. I went with her to the front door and opened it. The lady driver said she'd wait in her cab.

'Good luck for tomorrow,' I said to Shelley. 'And phone me if you change your mind about a lift back from the hospital.'

'All right. Thanks for everything,' she said, and gave me a big hug. 'How different my life would have been if I'd been fostered by you,' she added reflectively.

I felt my eyes fill. 'Take care, love, and see you tomorrow.'

I waited with the door open until she was safely in the cab, and then I closed and locked it for the night. Shelley's unsettled past was sadly not a one-off. Too many children are bounced around the care system (for a number of reasons) and never have a chance to put down roots and have a family of their own. These young people often struggle in adult life, and feeling unloved can lead to drink and drugs or abusive relationships. Since I started writing my fostering memoirs I've been heartbroken by some of the emails I've received from young men and women with experiences similar to Shelley's. Far more needs to be done to keep children in the same foster family or adoptive home so that they grow up and meet the challenges of adulthood with the confidence and self-esteem that comes from being loved and wanted.

Before I went to bed I checked all three children were asleep, leaving their bedroom doors ajar so I would hear them if they called out. I never sleep well when I have a new child in the house. I'm half listening out in case they wake and are upset. As it happened, Darrel slept through, but I woke with a start at six o'clock when I heard him cry, 'Mummy!'

I was immediately out of bed and going round the landing in my dressing gown. The poor little chap was sitting up in bed, his round face sad and scared. 'Where's Mummy?' he asked.

'She's gone to the hospital to have her tooth made better,' I said, sitting on the edge of the bed. 'I'm Cathy. Do you remember coming here yesterday? You're staying with me while Mummy is at the hospital, then she'll come and collect you.'

But he wasn't reassured. His face crumbled and his tears fell. 'I want my mummy.'

'Oh, love, come here.' I put my arm around him and held him close. It was only natural for him to be upset, waking in a strange bed and being separated from his mother for the first time.

'It's all right,' I soothed, stroking his head. 'I'll look after you until Mummy comes back.'

'I want my mummy,' he sobbed. 'Where's my mummy?'

I felt so sorry for him. 'She's not here, love. She's at the hospital. You'll see her later.'

But he wouldn't be consoled. 'Mummy! Mummy!' he called out with rising desperation. I knew it was only a matter of time before he woke Adrian and Paula.

Sure enough, a moment later Adrian's feet pitter-pattered round the landing and he came into Darrel's room in his pyjamas, looking very worried.

'It's OK,' I reassured him and Darrel. 'Darrel will be fine soon.'

'Don't be upset,' Adrian said, coming over to Darrel and gently rubbing his arm. 'We'll look after you. You can play with my best toys in my bedroom if you like.'

'Wow. Did you hear that, Darrel?' I said to him. 'Adrian says you can play with his best toys.' He kept them in his bedroom out of harm's way, as Paula at thirteen months was still rather clumsy.

The offer to play with an older boy's best toys was too good to refuse, and far more comforting than my well-meant words of reassurance. Darrel's tears stopped and he climbed out of bed. 'I have to take my nappy off first,' he said to Adrian.

I knew from Shelley's notes that she used baby wipes to clean Darrel in the morning, and then he went to the toilet. So once he was clean and dry, he stayed in his pyjamas and went into Adrian's room where Adrian had already set out some toys for them both to play with. With the boys occupied and Paula still asleep, I took the opportunity to shower and dress. By the time I'd finished Paula was awake and jumping up and down in her cot wanting to be 'Out! Out!' so I got her dressed. I took her with me into Adrian's room, thanked him for looking after Darrel and left him to dress while I helped Darrel in his room. Aged three, Darrel could mostly dress himself but needed some help, especially with his socks, which are difficult for young children – he kept getting them on with the heel on top.

By the time we arrived downstairs for breakfast Adrian was Darrel's best friend and he wouldn't let him out of his sight. I had to push his chair right up close to Adrian's at the table so they were touching, and he chatted away to Adrian. I warmed up the porridge Shelley had made for him and poured it into a bowl. Before Darrel began eating he asked Adrian if he'd like some. 'Mummy won't mind,' he said cutely.

'That's OK, you have it,' Adrian said. 'I've got wheat flakes.' In truth, Adrian had gone off porridge and didn't eat it at that point.

Paula was sitting on her booster seat at the table, opposite Darrel, and was far more interested in watching him than she was in feeding herself. He was a new face at the table and she didn't understand why he was there. I was sitting beside her and kept filling her spoon from her bowl of hot oat cereal and reminding her to eat. Darrel finished his porridge and I gave him the fruit his mother had prepared. He gave us a grape each, which we thanked him for and ate. 'Very nice,' I said.

Mindful of the time ticking by, I shepherded everyone upstairs and into the bathroom to brush their teeth and wash their faces. It was quite a logistical exercise getting three small children ready to leave the house on time, but eventually they were all in the hall with their jackets done up and their shoes on. Paula wanted to walk, but there wasn't time, so I told her she could walk on the way back from school and lifted her into the stroller and fastened her safety harness before she had a chance to protest. Outside she wanted to hold Darrel's hand as he walked beside her stroller and he was happy to do so, finding the novelty of a little one quite amusing. The boys talked to each other as we walked and Darrel told Adrian he would be starting school in September when he was four.

We arrived in the school playground with a few minutes to spare and I glanced around for any sign of Kim, but she wasn't there. The Klaxon sounded for the start of school and Adrian began saying goodbye to us all. Although I'd already explained to Darrel that Adrian would have to go to school, I don't think he understood the implications, for he suddenly looked very sad. 'Don't leave me,' he said. I thought he was going to cry.

Adrian looked at me anxiously. 'You go in,' I said. 'Don't worry. Darrel will be fine.' It was possible they might see each other at the end of school, but I couldn't promise, as that would depend on what time Shelley was discharged from hospital and came to collect Darrel.

Saying goodbye, Adrian ran over to line up with his class and I turned to Darrel. 'I could do with your help,' I said to distract him. 'Paula's going to walk back and she obviously likes holding your hand. When I let her out of the stroller could you hold one of her hands, please, and I'll hold the other? She doesn't understand about road safety yet, so it's important she holds our hands.'

Darrel rose to the occasion. 'I'm good at helping,' he said proudly, looking less sad. 'I help my mummy.'

'Excellent.'

I undid Paula's harness and helped her out of the stroller. As I did I saw Geraldine rush into the playground with Kim. Neither of them looked at me as they were concentrating on getting Kim into school on time. I still intended to call on Laura the following week if she didn't appear in the playground. With Darrel on one side of Paula and me on the other, we made our way out of the main gate and began our walk home. It was a slow walk – very slow – but it didn't matter, as it kept Darrel occupied and distracted him from worrying about his mother. He found Paula's habit of stopping every few steps to examine something in detail very funny. 'What's she looking at now?' he said, laughing. 'It's a twig, Paula!' Or, 'It's another stone. You are funny.' It was nice to see him happy, and Paula was enjoying his company, although I don't think she understood why her behaviour was amusing. At one point Geraldine overtook us on the opposite said of the street, although she didn't look in our direction.

Paula paused as usual outside number 53 and rattled the garden gate. 'Baby,' she said, recognizing the house.

'Yes, baby Liam lives there,' I said. I glanced at the windows, but there was no sign of anyone.

She took another couple of steps up the street and then stopped to examine a weed that was sprouting between the paving slabs.

'It's a weed,' Darrel said. 'There are lots of them!'

And so we continued our meandering journey home.

CHAPTER FIVE

A VERY STRANGE PHONE CALL

Once home, I kept Darrel and Paula entertained with various games and activities, and then at eleven o'clock I gave both children a drink and a snack, before putting Paula in her cot for a little nap. While she slept I read to Darrel from books he chose from our bookshelves, and then we had a few rounds of the card game Snap, which he was learning to play. He asked about his mummy a couple of times and I reassured him that she was being well looked after and he'd see her before too long, so he wasn't upset. I knew from Shelley's notes that he had his lunch at about 12.30 p.m., so once Paula was awake I got her up and cooked vegetarian sausages, mash and peas for us all. I'd just set the food on the table when the doorbell rang.

'Mummy?' Darrel asked.

'I think it's a bit early yet,' I said. 'Stay here and I'll check.'

Leaving the children at the table, I went down the hall to answer the door. To my surprise it was Shelley, looking very pale, with one side of her face swollen and a bloody tissue pressed to her lips.

'Oh, love,' I said, concerned and drawing her in. 'Whyever didn't you phone me to collect you? I hope you haven't come on the bus.'

'I got a cab,' she mumbled, stepping in and barely able to speak. 'I used the rest of the money you gave me.' It obviously hurt her when she spoke.

'Have you taken something for the pain?' I asked.

She nodded. 'Paracetamol.'

'Mummy!' Darrel cried, having heard his mother's voice. He left the table and ran into the hall but stopped dead when he saw her swollen face.

'It's all right,' I reassured him. 'Mummy's mouth is sore, but she'll be better soon. I think she needs looking after.' I took her hand and led her down the hall and into the living room. As we passed Darrel she managed a wonky smile, but he looked very concerned. 'Mummy's going to have a quiet sit down while you have your lunch,' I said, settling her on the sofa.

'Thank you,' she said, sitting back with a small sigh.

'Can I get you anything?' I asked.

'A glass of water, please.' She winced as she spoke and put her hand to her face.

'You sit there and I'll fetch it,' I said. Then to Darrel, 'Come with me. We'll leave Mummy to have a rest.'

He hesitated.

'Go on, love,' Shelley said. 'Good boy.'

He slipped his hand into mine and I took him to the dining table, where Paula was still seated and making a good attempt to feed herself using her toddler fork and spoon. 'Good girl,' I said, returning the peas to her plate.

Darrel picked up his knife and fork and began eating, while I went into the kitchen and poured Shelley a glass of water. I added a straw to make drinking it a little easier, then took the glass through to the living room.

'Thank you,' she said gratefully, and gingerly took a few sips before handing it back to me. She sighed and rested her head back on the sofa.

'Would you like to go upstairs for a lie down?' I suggested.

'I'll just sit here for a bit if that's all right.'

'Yes, of course.' I set her glass of water on the coffee table within her reach and also a box of tissues. 'Do you want anything else?' I asked. She shook her head and her eyelids began to close. 'Call me if you need anything,' I said. She nodded and I came out closing the door behind me so the children and I wouldn't disturb her. I thought a sleep would do her good; having an anaesthetic can leave you feeling very tired.

'Mummy is having a rest,' I said to Darrel as I returned to the table. 'She'll be all right soon, so you have your lunch and when she wakes we'll tell her what a good boy you've been.'

He looked concerned but continued eating. Paula dropped a lump of mashed potato in her lap and tried to pick it up. She laughed as it squashed between her fingers, which made Darrel smile too. He ate all his meal and Paula ate her mash and peas but left some of the sausage. It was the first time she'd had a vegetarian sausage, so it was a new taste and texture for her, but at least she'd tried it. Darrel had one of the yoghurts his mother had brought for his pudding and Paula had a fromage frais. Once they'd finished I went into the living room to check on Shelley. She was fast asleep with her head resting on the sofa back and her mouth slightly open. I crept out and quietly closed the door. I suggested to Darrel that the three of us play something at the table so we wouldn't disturb his mother. 'Do you like Play-Doh?' I asked him. I'd never met a child who didn't.

'I have Play-Doh at my house,' he said enthusiastically.

I cleared the dishes from the table, covered it with a protective plastic tablecloth and took out the Play-Doh set. Once they were both occupied I went into the kitchen, where I could still see them, and cleared up, then I joined in their play at the table. Darrel was concentrating on feeding blue Play-Doh through the toy machine and creating different shapes. Some of it came out as long, thin strands like spaghetti and he pretended to eat it, which made Paula laugh.

I checked on Shelley again, but she was still fast asleep. If necessary I could leave her sleeping and take Darrel with me when I collected Adrian from school, but that wasn't for another hour. When Darrel and Paula had tired of the Play-Doh we packed it away and I showed Darrel the toy cupboard and let him choose something else to play with. He picked a jigsaw puzzle of a farmyard scene and I took out an early-years puzzle for Paula. The three of us sat at the table assembling the puzzles. When Darrel had completed his I praised him and he packed it away and took out another one. Five minutes later I heard the door to the living room open and then Shelley came in carrying her empty glass of water. 'How are you feeling, love?' I said. Darrel looked at her anxiously.

'A bit better now, thanks,' she said, trying to raise a smile. 'I need to take a couple more paracetamol. Can I have another glass of water, please?'

'Yes, of course. Sit down. I'll get it.'

She sat at the table and as I poured the water I could see Darrel looking at her anxiously. It's difficult for a child to see their usually strong parent compromised and vulnerable. 'That's a good puzzle,' she said, trying to divert his attention. 'See if you can finish it before we go.'

I handed her the glass of water and she took two tablets. 'Could you manage something to eat now?' I asked. 'Soup? I could break up some bread to put in. That would be easy to eat.'

'Oh, yes, please,' she said gratefully. 'I couldn't have anything before the operation and I am hungry. But are you sure I'm not keeping you?'

'Not at all. I don't have to collect Adrian for three-quarters of an hour, and you're more than welcome to stay here while I get him. I can take you home in the car after.'

'The doctor said I mustn't have anything too hot,' she added as I went into the kitchen. 'Because of the stitches.'

'Stitches?' Darrel asked, worried.

'Yes, to help make my mouth get better,' Shelley said, reassuring him.

She sat at the table and watched the children playing as I warmed some cream of tomato soup, buttered some bread and cut it into small chunks to dunk in the soup. I carried it through and set in on the table with a spoon.

'Thank you,' Shelley said again. 'You are kind to me.' Bless her, I thought. She was such a sweet kid. I wished I could have done more for her.

I played with the children while she ate, and once she'd finished she thanked me again and then to my horror said: 'I feel well enough to go and get the bus now.'

'There's no way you're going home on the bus,' I said, dismayed. 'If you don't want to wait until I return from collecting Adrian, when I can take you in the car, then I'll call a cab.'

'I'd really like to get home and get settled, and then have an early night,' she said, which I could understand.

'OK, I'll call a cab then,' I said, standing. Without waiting for further protest I went to the phone in the living room and booked the cab with a lady driver, then, returning to Shelley, I gave her money for the fare. Needless to say, she thanked me profusely.

While Shelley stayed with the children I quickly went round the house gathering together Darrel's belongings and packing them into his bags, which I put in the hall. Fifteen minutes later the cab arrived and the driver helped Shelley with the bags while I took Darrel and Paula to the car. Shelley and Darrel climbed into the rear of the cab and Shelley fastened their seatbelts. 'Thank you so much,' she said again.

'You're welcome, love. Take care.'

'Say goodbye and thank you to Cathy,' she told Darrel.

'Bye, and thank you,' he said adorably.

'We've all enjoyed having you to stay,' I said.

'Thanks for everything, and thank Adrian for playing with Darrel,' Shelley said.

'I will.'

I closed the cab door and Paula and I waved until the cab was out of sight. Although Darrel was obviously pleased to be going home, Paula looked sad. But goodbyes are part of fostering, and it was important that Paula was included in this, for a good farewell is as important as welcoming a child when they first arrive. Yet I'll admit I felt sad too. Even if a child is only with you a short while, as Darrel had been, they touch your life and you don't forget them. I would remember Darrel and Shelley in the years to come and wonder how they were doing. If I saw them again then that would be a huge bonus, but it couldn't be guaranteed, and as a foster carer I had to accept that.

* * *

I returned indoors with Paula and then it was time to collect Adrian from school. I persuaded her into the stroller with the promise that she could walk some of the way back. As we waited in the playground I saw Geraldine arrive in good time and then as usual stand alone, separate from the other parents, as she waited for school to end. The Klaxon sounded and Adrian ran out amid the hubbub and excitement of Friday afternoon and the start of the weekend. But as he neared I could see him looking for Darrel.

'He's just gone home with his mother,' I said. 'They said to say goodbye and thank you for looking after Darrel.'

'Oh, OK,' he said. 'Pity I couldn't have said goodbye.'

'I know.' Then I distracted him by talking about the busy weekend we had coming up. We were going to visit my parents on Saturday and then Adrian had been invited to a friend's football birthday party on Sunday. I reminded him that the present needed wrapping and the card had to be written and suggested we did it that evening.

Once we'd crossed the road and entered our street I let Paula out of the stroller. There was no sign of Geraldine and Kim ahead of or behind us. Perhaps they'd stopped off at the shop. However, as we passed number 53 I saw that their front door was wide open. I glanced in but couldn't see anyone in the hall. We continued our slow, faltering walk past and then a few steps further up I heard a loud bang as a door slammed shut behind me. I instinctively turned. A middle-aged man in a suit and tie was storming down the front garden path of Laura's house. He was clearly annoyed – his face was set and his body tense as he thrust a fob at the car parked in the kerb outside their house. He jumped in, immediately started the engine and the car tyres screeched as it pulled away and sped past us.

'That car's going far too fast,' Adrian remarked.

'Yes, it is,' I agreed.

I had no idea what Laura's husband looked like – I barely knew her – and if it was her husband and they'd had an argument then it was none of my business. Or was it? How many neighbours when interviewed after a tragic domestic incident exonerate themselves by saying that the family seemed pleasant but kept themselves to themselves. I already had some concerns about Laura, and perhaps as a result of fostering and having to piece together snippets of information from children who were trying to tell me what they had been through (they rarely tell the full story all in one go), I'd become more adept at looking at the wider picture. But on the other hand you can't jump to conclusions and phone the social services just because you have a suspicion that all is not well in a family. You need some evidence.

Half an hour later, after we'd arrived home, the telephone rang. I wasn't thinking about Laura at that moment and I didn't make the connection when I heard a female voice say rather loudly, 'Is that Cathy?'

'Yes?' I said tentatively.

'You don't recognize me, do you? It's Laura from number 53.'

'Oh, hello. How are you?' I was completely thrown. It didn't sound like her at all.

'I'm fine,' she said. 'Really good. I thought I'd give you a ring. Do you remember you left your phone number with my mother-in-law and said to phone for a chat?'

'Yes, of course.' But it was an odd time to phone for a chat. Most parents with a young family were occupied at this time making dinner or seeing to their children. 'Is everything all right?'

'Yes, fine, good. How are you? I haven't been going to school. Geraldine's been taking and collecting Kim. She says I have to rest. My husband Andy says so too. They agree about most things. So I'm doing what I'm told. Like a good girl. That's why you haven't seen me. But I'm fine. We're all fine …' And her words continued, fast and furious, fired at me in short, staccato sentences and not 'chatty' at all. She sounded hyper, agitated. 'So Geraldine, my mother-in-law, is looking after us all,' she continued. 'Me, Kim, Andy and little Liam. She's doing a great job.'

'How is Liam?' I asked, forcing a gap.

'He's fine. Well, like a baby. Eating, sleeping, crying. But Geraldine takes care of that. Many thanks to Geraldine, I say. She's a natural with children. I think some people are, don't you?'

'Is Geraldine with you now?' I interjected.

'Who?'

'Geraldine. Your mother-in-law. Is she with you now?'

'Yes, of course. Why do you ask? She's here most days while Andy is at work. Andy is my husband. Sometimes she stays after he comes home to make sure he has his dinner. But that's mothers for you. They never stop fussing over their little boys. Although what would I know? Kim is a girl. But Geraldine is great. In fact, it was she who suggested I phone you. She thought I should.'

'Why?'

'Oh, you know. For a chat. To tell you I'm OK. In fact, we're all OK. Me, Andy, Liam and Kim. We're doing fine. I believe you saw Kim at the shop? She's a good girl, helps me out sometimes. But we won't mention that, will we?' And she gave a small, high-pitched laugh.

'Is there anything I can do?' I asked.

'No, nothing you can do.'

'I was thinking of popping in to see you next week.'

'Oh, I see. Well, you can if you like, but really there's no need. I'm fine. We all are. Couldn't be better.'

'What day suits you?' I began.

'Not sure. Have to go now. Bye.' The line went dead.

I stood for a moment, completely bemused, then slowly returned the handset to its cradle. It was one of the strangest telephone calls I'd ever received. Whatever was all that about? Why had she phoned? I had no idea. The Laura I'd spoken to while walking back from school had been quiet, shy and a little withdrawn, whereas this Laura was gushy and completely over the top. It didn't sound like the same person. I didn't think she was drunk, although she had sounded confused and had repeated herself. But Geraldine was with her, presumably helping her, so I put Laura out of my thoughts for the time being and concentrated on my family.

After dinner I played some games with the children and then began Paula's bath and bedtime routine. Later, when she was asleep, I lay propped on Adrian's bed and we had our little chat before he settled for the night. He suddenly asked, 'I wonder what Darrel is doing now.'

'I expect he's asleep,' I said.

'Do you think his mummy sings to him every night?'

'Yes, although maybe not tonight, as her mouth is sore.'

'What's that tune called?' Adrian asked. 'The one that goes like this.' He began humming one of the lullabies Shelley had sung.

'Brahms's "Lullaby",' I said. 'It is beautiful, isn't it?'

'Yes. I wish you could sing it like Shelley,' Adrian said.

'So do I.' I smiled. 'She's got a lovely voice. Perhaps we could hum it together? Let's try.'

I put my arm around him and in the light of the lamp we began humming the haunting melody of the lullaby, which has become a classic for children everywhere. It didn't sound too bad at all. And I hoped that the sentiment in our tune carried through the night air and touched Shelley and Darrel, so that they knew we were thinking about them.

'Night, Shelley and Darrel,' Adrian said as we finished. 'Night, Mum.'

'Night, love. Sleep tight.'

'Love you.'

'Love you more.'

CHAPTER SIX

USELESS

On Monday morning I was going to ask Geraldine if it would be convenient for me to pop in and see Laura on the way back from school, but she left the playground before I had a chance to speak to her. Laura's phone call on Friday had played on my mind over the weekend and I wanted to just say hi to her and make sure she was all right. I decided I'd stop by anyway, and if it wasn't convenient I could arrange to go back another time. I bought a bunch of flowers for Laura from the local supermarket and once we'd crossed the road I let Paula out of her stroller to walk. It was 9.40 by the time we arrived outside number 53.

'Baby,' Paula said as I opened their gate.

'Yes, that's right. We are going in to see if we can visit baby Liam and Laura,' I said. Paula grinned.

I parked the stroller to one side of the porch and, holding Paula's hand, pressed the doorbell. It was answered almost immediately by Geraldine, who didn't seem unduly surprised to see me.

'Laura's up, but not dressed,' she said rather brusquely.

'Would you give these flowers to her, please?' I said, assuming from her comment that it wasn't convenient for me to go in.

'You can give them to her yourself,' she said equally bluntly.

'Are you sure? I don't want to intrude.' But Geraldine was already holding the door wider for us to go in.

'She's in the living room,' Geraldine said in the same terse manner and nodding down the hall. 'Sorry about the telephone call on Friday. Laura wasn't herself.'

'Oh. That's OK,' I said, surprised that she'd mentioned it. 'How is she now?'

'Fine,' she said, and led the way down the hall and into the living room. Laura was sitting on the sofa in her dressing gown breastfeeding Liam, and she did appear fine.

'Lovely to see you,' she said, looking up and smiling.

'Baby,' Paula said.

'He's gorgeous,' I said. 'Absolutely beautiful.'

'Thank you. Hi,' Laura said to Paula. Paula hid her face shyly against my leg.

'A few flowers for you,' I said, offering the colourful bouquet.

'That is kind of you. Thank you,' Laura replied easily.

'I'll put them in a vase,' Geraldine said, stepping forward. I passed her the flowers. 'Would you like a coffee?' she asked.

'Only if you are making one.'

'I don't drink coffee,' she replied curtly.

'I'd like one,' Laura said.

Geraldine gave a stiff nod and went out of the room.

'Are you sure you don't mind me dropping by like this?' I asked Laura.

'No, of course not. I'm pleased to see you. I wasn't going anywhere. Sit down, and thanks for the flowers.'

'You're welcome.'

I slipped off my jacket, took Paula's jacket off and draped them over the back of a chair. As I sat down Paula scrambled onto my lap.

'He is a beautiful baby,' I said.

'He looks like his dad,' Laura said.

'I can see you in him too. He's got your nose and chin.'

She smiled. 'Mum said that as well.' Laura seemed more like her old self – the person I'd walked back from school with – quietly spoken, pleasant, unassuming and a little on the shy side. Liam stopped feeding and she began to wind him, gently rubbing his back until he burped. Paula giggled.

'So how are you doing?' I asked Laura.

'OK. Sorry about last Friday. I nearly phoned back to apologize. I'd had a blazing argument with Andy, and Geraldine said you'd seen it all. I was in a right state when I phoned you, but I'm fine now.'

'No worries. We all have family upsets.'

'I suppose so. Although I'm rather sensitive at present and tend to take things personally and get upset. But I'm fine now. How are you? How's the fostering? Geraldine said she saw you in the playground with a little boy.'

'Yes, he's gone home now. He was just with me for a day and a night to help out his mother.'

Laura nodded. As we talked we could hear Geraldine moving around in the kitchen and then go down the hall. Presently she came in with two cups of coffee and a plate of digestive biscuits on a tray, which she placed on the coffee table.

'Thank you,' I said.

She gave a stiff nod. 'I've put the flowers in the front room,' she said to Laura. 'If he's finished, I'll put him in his cot.'

59

Laura wrapped the shawl around Liam and carefully passed him up to Geraldine, who carried him out of the room.

'He sleeps now,' Laura said. 'Help yourself to coffee and biscuits.'

I moved Paula from my lap and onto the seat beside me so I could drink my coffee. She was still shy and kept close but pointed to the biscuits. I passed her one. There weren't any toys in the room; I guessed Kim probably kept hers in her bedroom and Liam wasn't really old enough for toys yet.

Laura took a sip of her coffee and then leant back on the sofa with a small sigh. 'I guess it's normal to feel exhausted when you've had a baby.'

'Absolutely,' I said. 'I was. Up every three hours at night for feeding, and all the hormones rushing around.'

'Yes, those hormones,' she said with another sigh. 'Andy says it's the hormones.'

'But Geraldine is a big help?' I asked.

'Yes.' She glanced at the door as though checking Geraldine couldn't hear, and then lowered her voice. 'I know this sounds really ungrateful, but sometimes I resent her being here. I mean, I need her help, but I wish she wasn't so bloody right the whole time. I guess that's mother-in-laws for you.'

I smiled understandingly.

'Did you feel low after you'd had your babies?' Laura now asked, looking at Paula.

'I was very tired, but thankfully I didn't get the baby blues,' I said. She took another sip of her coffee but kept her eyes down. 'Why? Are you feeling depressed?' I asked.

She gave a small nod and set her cup carefully in the saucer. 'Sometimes, then at other times I'm as high as a kite. Irrational and ridiculously happy. Do you think that's the hormones too?'

'It could be. Have you seen a doctor?'

'No. I'm not ill, just a bit down. That's why Geraldine spends so much time here.'

I nodded. 'And you don't think you should see the doctor or tell the midwife? They might be able to suggest something to help.'

'No. I'll be OK. I got over it last time with Kim. I guess it's the luck of the draw. Geraldine never had it with any of hers, but my mother did.' She stopped, as Geraldine could be heard in the hall and then came into the room.

'You're not overdoing it, are you?' she said to Laura, and I wondered if she'd overheard.

'No!' Laura said, with the briefest flash of resentment.

'I think it's time you showered and dressed,' Geraldine said to her.

'In a moment,' Laura replied. 'There's no rush. It's not as if I have to be anywhere.'

I thought it was time to go. 'I'll be making a move then,' I said. Geraldine hovered as I quickly finished my coffee and then returned the cup and saucer to the tray. 'Thanks for the coffee,' I said to her and, standing, I took our jackets from the chair back.

'Will you come again soon?' Laura asked, with a plea in her voice.

'Yes. I'd like to. When is convenient?' I helped Paula into her jacket.

'Any day. I'll be here. Every day if you like,' Laura said with a small laugh.

'But we do have things to do,' Geraldine said flatly, looking at her.

'What about Thursday or Friday afternoon?' I suggested.

'Yes, Thursday,' Laura said quickly. 'I'll look forward to it.'

'You can come to me if you wish,' I said, putting on my jacket.

'Best if you come here,' Geraldine said. 'One o'clock on Thursday should be convenient.'

I looked at Laura for confirmation and she nodded resignedly.

'I'll see you Thursday then,' I said. I assumed I wouldn't be seeing Laura in the playground before then.

Leaving her sitting on the sofa, I took Paula's hand and we went down the hall. Geraldine saw us out.

'Thank you for the flowers,' she said before she closed the door.

I lifted Paula into the stroller and fastened her safety harness. 'Baby,' she said.

'Yes, baby Liam is having a sleep,' I said.

'Bye,' she said.

'Good girl.'

I pushed the stroller down the front garden path and onto the pavement. I feel there is a fine line between assisting someone in a positive way when they need help, and completely taking over, so the person loses confidence and comes to rely too heavily on their caregiver. It was something I was aware of in fostering and strove to avoid. While I was sure Geraldine meant well in looking after her family, from what I'd seen she was doing far too much for Laura and had taken over, dominating her and making decisions for her. True, I hadn't taken an immediate liking to the woman, but that may have been a personality clash. What concerned me now was that she appeared to have reduced

Laura to a childlike state so that she relied on her for everything, and Laura was starting to resent this, understandably. I liked Laura – she was the type of person I'd want to be friends with – and clearly she'd wanted me to visit again. It was a pity I couldn't persuade her to visit me on Thursday. I felt that not only would the change of scenery have done her good, but it would also have given her a break from her mother-in-law.

When I collected Adrian from school that afternoon Geraldine made a point of nodding in my direction but didn't speak. I returned a pleasant smile. She left the playground as soon as she had Kim, and they were nowhere in sight when we began the slow walk up our road. At home I found a message on the answerphone from Shelley's social worker, thanking me for looking after Darrel at such short notice. She said she'd spoken to Shelley that morning and her mouth felt a lot better now. I was grateful she'd found the time in her busy work schedule to let me know. Not all social workers would have done that and it was very thoughtful of her. Adrian, who'd heard the message, was also pleased Shelley was feeling better.

'So she'll be able to sing to Darrel tonight,' he said.

'Yes, I'm sure she will.'

With no foster child to look after, I made the most of any free time I had to continue writing my dissertation – when Paula had her morning nap, and also in the evening when she and Adrian were in bed. The subject of my dissertation, education and children in care, was a subject I felt passionately about, as so many children in the care system failed to reach their full academic potential. I was exploring the reasons why this should be so and what could be done to reverse the trend. It was a big subject, although one that had received surprisingly little research and had only seldom been addressed. I worked on my dissertation again on Thursday morning while Paula had her nap. After lunch I put some of her toys in the 'baby bag', together with her trainer cup and a change of nappy, and explained to her that we were going to see baby Liam and his mother, Laura.

'Lawwah,' Paula said, making a good attempt at pronouncing her name.

'Yes, Laura.'

'Lawwah, Lawwah,' she repeated, and then broke into fits of giggles. I kissed her cheek.

It was a fine, sunny day, so we didn't need our jackets. I let Paula walk down the street to number 53, but I took the stroller nonetheless. I didn't know how long I'd be staying at Laura's, so I wasn't sure if I'd have time to return home first or if I'd have to go straight to school to collect Adrian.

'Baby,' Paula predictably said as I pushed open the garden gate.

'Yes, we are going to see baby Liam and Laura.'

'Lawwah, Lawwah,' she said, chuckling.

I parked the stroller on one side of the porch, unhooked the baby bag and then pressed the doorbell, but no one answered. I waited and pressed the bell again. 'She did say Thursday,' I said out loud, wondering if I'd got the wrong day.

'Fursday,' Paula repeated, not knowing what I meant.

The door suddenly opened and Geraldine stood before me, looking uncharacteristically flustered. 'I was going to phone you to cancel, but I couldn't find your number.'

'Oh. Do you want me to come back another day? Laura has my phone number.'

'I know, but she wouldn't give it to me – I mean, she couldn't find it,' she quickly corrected herself.

I wasn't sure if I was being admitted or not. Paula stood beside me, holding my hand.

'Well, you may as well come in now you're here, I suppose,' Geraldine said tersely, opening the door wider. 'Or she won't be pleased. But best keep your visit short. Laura hasn't been up long.'

'Oh dear. Is she ill?' I asked, concerned and feeling this was the most likely explanation for someone staying in bed all morning. She didn't reply, so I helped Paula over the doorstep and into the hall.

'She's in the living room,' Geraldine said.

She turned and I followed her down the hall with some apprehension, not knowing what to expect. I sensed an atmosphere, although I wasn't sure why. Laura was sitting on the sofa, gazing into space. I thought she looked pale and tired, and had possibly been crying. There was no sign of Liam.

'Hello,' I said, smiling as we entered.

'I'll leave you to it then,' Geraldine said stiffly, and went out, leaving the living room door wide open.

'Are you all right?' I asked, going over to Laura.

She shook her head, but didn't speak. Standing, she crossed to the living-room door and pushed it shut so hard it slammed. Paula jumped; it made me start too. She returned to the sofa and burst into tears.

'Oh, love, what's wrong?' I asked, going over and sitting beside her.

'Everything,' she sobbed. 'Everything.' Paula stood close to me, looking very worried

'It's OK,' I reassured Paula. 'You can play with your toys while I look after Laura.' I quickly took the toys I'd brought with us from the bag and settled her on the floor, close by my feet. I put my arm around Laura's shoulder and tried to comfort her as she silently wept. I was half expecting Geraldine to reappear – she must have heard the door slam – but she didn't.

'It's all right,' I said to Laura.

I held her until she was calmer and then she took out a packet of tissues she had tucked beside her on the sofa. 'Sorry,' she said, peeling a tissue from the packet and wiping her eyes. 'I'm having a bad day.' Fresh tears formed.

'I understand,' I said, gently rubbing her arm. 'Is there anything in particular upsetting you? Anything I can help you with?' I appreciated how easily things can get on top of you if you are tired and feeling low; even the ironing can seem like an insurmountable task.

She shook her head. 'No. If only it was that simple.' She twisted and pulled at the tissue. 'I feel so useless the whole time. I can't seem to do anything right. I get stressed about the simplest of things, even making a cup of tea or answering the phone, so I don't do anything, because I can't cope. I feel tired the whole time and I can't be bothered to move. Last night I lay in bed listening to Liam crying to be fed, but I didn't have the energy to get up and feed him. Andy had to get up and bring him to me, and then, when he'd finished feeding, he changed him and settled him back in his cot. We agreed I'd do the night feeds, as he has to go to work, but I couldn't. I just couldn't. Then this morning when Geraldine arrived at seven he told her.'

'She arrives that early?' I asked, slightly surprised.

'Yes, that's when Andy has to leave for work. They make sure one of them is here with me the whole time.' She gave a small sob and Paula looked up at her. I threw her a reassuring smile. 'I know I'm useless,' Laura said. 'But Andy and his mother don't help. They talk about me behind my back, and she tuts when I do something wrong. Or maybe it's me being oversensitive, I don't know. I'm sorry, I shouldn't be going on at you like this – you haven't come here to hear this – but I'm so miserable I don't know what to do.' She wiped away more tears.

'It's all right,' I soothed. 'Don't feel embarrassed. We all feel down sometimes, but I am concerned. Have you seen a doctor yet?'

'No. It will pass eventually. It did last time. I just have to get a grip. That's what Geraldine says: "Get a grip."' She sniffed.

'I'm not sure that's the best advice,' I said. 'Sometimes we need help getting over these things. And there may be a physical reason why you're feeling low. A friend of mine developed a thyroid problem after having her second child. She felt really low, with no energy, and she lost her appetite. She worried for weeks before she saw her doctor. He sent her for tests and the thyroid problem showed up. She was put on medication and within a week she was back to her old self. I really think you should see your doctor.'

Laura shrugged despondently. 'I don't know. I'd have to phone the doctor to make the appointment, and I struggle making decisions about anything right now. I couldn't even decide which babygrow to dress Liam in this morning. I mean, how daft is that? It was a choice between white or blue, and I panicked and froze. I just stood there, with him not dressed and getting cold. Then Geraldine heard him crying and came in. She wasn't pleased. She said I should have called her sooner. She dressed him while I went back to bed. I like being in bed, asleep. It's nice being unconscious. I think they like it too. I'm such a burden. I'm sure they'd all be better off without me. Sometimes I think I should do them a favour and kill myself.'

CHAPTER SEVEN

UPSET

I looked at Laura, more concerned than ever now. This was more than feeling down or having a bad day. It sounded to me as though she could be severely depressed.

'I really think you should see a doctor,' I said again. 'I don't understand what's stopping you. You could be suffering from postnatal depression.'

'Yes, I could be,' she said. 'But I don't want it on my medical records. I got through it before with Kim without the doctor, and I will again.'

'How long did it take then?' I asked.

'Not sure. I think I was back to normal when Kim was a year old.'

'A year!' I said, astonished and dismayed. 'That's far too long to be feeling like this. And why should it matter if it's on your medical records? Lots of people suffer from depression at some time in their lives. I remember reading that it was as much as twenty per cent of the population. Shall I make the appointment for you if you don't feel up to doing it yourself? I could phone now from here and you could decide when you wanted to go.' I thought this might help, as everything seemed such an effort for Laura right now, which of course was a sign of depression.

'No, it's OK,' she said. 'I can tell my doctor at my six-week check-up. I think it's the week after next. I'll tell her then.'

'Will you definitely tell her?' I asked.

She nodded.

I couldn't really say any more. Laura was an adult and as such I had to respect that she could make her own decisions, although I was no less worried. 'Have you been out of the house at all?' I asked.

'Not since I was taken ill in the playground. That shook my confidence.' Her eyes welled again.

'Oh, love,' I said, touching her arm.

'Don't worry, I'm not always this low,' she said. 'I'm having a bad day. Some days I'm almost normal, whatever that is.' She gave a small, stilted laugh and wiped her eyes. 'But how rude of me. I haven't offered you a drink. Let's go into the kitchen and make a drink now. I told Geraldine I wanted to do it this time.' She immediately stood.

I took Paula by the hand and we went with Laura into the kitchen. Her house had a similar layout to mine, with the living room and kitchen at the rear, overlooking the garden. 'You've got a lovely garden,' I said. 'Is it your work?'

'It used to be. But I haven't touched it this year. Andy's been keeping it tidy. What would you like to drink? Tea or coffee?'

'I don't mind. Whatever you're making.'

She tensed. 'Could you tell me, please, to make it easy? I don't know what I want.'

'Coffee, please,' I said.

'Good. I'll have the same,' she said, relieved. 'Now, first the mugs.' She turned to the sink, took a mug from the draining board and began drying it on a tea towel. Slowly, carefully, as

70

if it took all her concentration. She set it down and began drying the next.

'Shall I fill the kettle?' I asked, trying to be helpful

'Oh, yes, good idea. You do that, while I find the coffee.' Clearly making coffee was no longer second nature to her, as it is for most of us.

I filled the kettle and plugged it in as Laura placed the dry mugs on a tray and then opened one of the cupboards and took out a jar of instant coffee. She was like a child asked to perform a task by their mother – meticulous and wanting to get it right. But I saw her hands tremble as she spooned a teaspoon of coffee into each mug. Even a simple task like this appeared to cause her anxiety.

'I don't know what biscuits we have,' she said, now looking in the cupboards. 'Geraldine's been buying them.'

'I'll just have a coffee,' I said. 'No biscuit for me, thank you.'

'Are you sure?'

'Yes, I've been eating too many.' I smiled.

'Do you take milk?' she asked intensely.

'Yes, please.'

With the same profound concentration she opened the fridge door, took out the milk and set it on the work surface beside the tray. A plume of steam rose from the spout of the boiling kettle before the sensor switched it off. I kept Paula at my side, away from the boiling water, as Laura carried the kettle to the mugs and then carefully poured in the hot water and returned it to its stand. She added the milk. All her movements were slow, controlled and precise.

'Ready,' she said with a small sigh, and returned the milk to the fridge.

She carefully picked up the tray and Paula and I followed her back into the living room where she set it on the coffee table. I was going to ask Laura if I could fill Paula's trainer cup with water, but she flopped on the sofa and, throwing her head back, began crying again.

'What's wrong?' I asked, very concerned and going to her.

'I've spilt some,' she said, pointing to the tray.

I glanced at the tray; there was a tiny slop of coffee on it, really small. 'It doesn't matter,' I said. 'I can wipe it up if it's bothering you.'

But, of course, in Laura's fragile state it did matter, a lot, and her tears fell silent and uncontrollable. My heart went out to her. To be so wretched and upset over something so small was pitiful. 'It doesn't matter, really,' I said, trying to reassure her. 'Shall I fetch some kitchen towel and wipe it up?' I thought this might help.

She shook her head but wouldn't be consoled. It was heart-breaking to see a grown woman reduced to this state over something so trivial. Paula must have felt it too for she climbed onto my lap and wanted a cuddle. I sat with one arm around Laura and the other around Paula.

'I'm sorry,' Laura said through her tears. 'I've upset your daughter now.'

'Don't worry. It's you I'm concerned about.' More tears fell.

Geraldine must have heard, for she came in. 'I think it's best if you go,' she said.

I nodded. My presence didn't seem to be doing Laura any good, but I thought I should hear from Laura that she wanted me to leave.

'Shall I go?' I asked her gently. 'And come back another time?'

'Yes, I'm so sorry. I'll have a sleep now.' Fumbling for the packet of tissues, she stood and walked quickly from the room calling 'Sorry!' again as she left.

I looked at Geraldine. Her face had finally lost its stern, almost condescending expression and she looked worried. 'It's a pity you've had to see her like this,' she said. 'But she'll feel better after she's had a lie down.'

I didn't point out that Laura had been in bed all morning and had only just got up. 'Don't you think she should see a doctor?' I asked.

'If we think it's necessary then of course we will consult a doctor,' she said, her usual terseness returning, and clearly resenting my suggestion.

'And you don't think it's necessary now?' I asked as I began returning Paula's toys to the baby bag.

'No. And I'd appreciate it if you didn't discuss it with your friends in the playground,' she said. 'I know you like a chat.'

I was mortified. I stopped what I was doing, straightened and looked at her. 'I wouldn't dream of discussing Laura, but I am very concerned for her.'

'So are we,' she said tartly.

She waited, watching me, while I finished packing away Paula's toys, almost as if she was on guard. Then she led the way to the front door.

'I'll let you know when Laura feels up to having visitors again,' she said as we went out.

'Thank you.' The door closed behind me.

I breathed in the warm spring air, relieved to be out of the crushing, depressive atmosphere in the house but also very worried. It wasn't time to collect Adrian from school yet and I didn't feel like going home, so I put Paula in the stroller and told her we were going to the park. She clasped her hands together in glee. As I walked I went over what I'd seen and heard at Laura's. Was she suffering from postnatal depression, also known as postpartum depression? I didn't know. What were the symptoms? I wasn't sure. My friend with the thyroid problem had confided in me that she'd felt 'low', and another friend had told me she'd felt 'down' after the birth of her first child – a dose of the baby blues, she'd said, and had put it down to tiredness and having to adjust to a new baby. But that was surely very different from what Laura appeared to be going through: constant tears, wanting to sleep all day and talking of suicide. That must be more than the baby blues or a 'bad day'? Thankfully I'd escaped all of this – other than feeling tired, I'd been fine when I had my children. We arrived at the park and I let Paula out of her stroller and then lifted her into one of the toddler swings where I pushed her gently.

If it had been Shelley or someone who had social services' involvement suffering as Laura was, I would probably have telephoned their social worker and discussed my concerns. But Laura didn't have a social worker – there was no reason why she should – and she had her husband and mother-in-law looking after her. From what Laura had said, they'd brought her through a similar episode after she'd had Kim, so I had to assume they knew what they were doing, although I still thought a year was too long to wait if Laura didn't feel significantly better very soon.

I was still thinking of Laura, or rather worrying about her, when twenty minutes later I returned Paula to her stroller and headed towards Adrian's school. It was a sunny day in late May and he had the following week off school for the spring bank holiday. If the weather stayed fine we'd make the most of it in the garden, visiting parks and so on. I arrived in the playground with five minutes to spare and kept a look-out for Geraldine, wondering what, if anything, she'd say to me. But she hurried in just before the Klaxon sounded, collected Kim and walked swiftly out again without looking in my direction. Adrian arrived at my side, excited by the prospect of only one more day of school before a week off, and gave his sister a big kiss, which as usual made her chuckle. Having had plenty of exercise in the park she was happy to stay in the stroller, so our walk home was much quicker than usual. As we passed number 53 I glanced at the house, but there was nothing to be seen. I saw Paula look too and her little face clouded over. She didn't have the vocabulary to express how she was feeling, but she'd seen Laura crying and I knew that it had probably upset her. It had upset me too. 'I'm sure Liam's mummy will be better soon,' I said, reassuring her.

As I made dinner that evening and then played with the children my thoughts returned to Laura, and I wondered what she was doing with her evening. Had the lie down done her good, as Geraldine had said it would? If so, perhaps she was making dinner for her family or playing with Kim or nursing Liam. I hoped so. Although I knew very little about postnatal depression, I instinctively felt that what Laura was suffering from would need more than a lie down, and I doubted that the instructional phrase her mother in-law used of 'Get a grip' would help either. When Adrian and Paula were in bed asleep I decided to consult the fount of much knowledge on motherhood and telephoned my dear mother.

She wasn't surprised to hear from me; we often spoke during the week and always at weekends if we weren't seeing each other. Having asked how the other was and after catching up on our news, I said, 'Mum, do you know anything about postnatal depression?'

'Oh, love,' she said, immediately concerned, 'you're not suffering from that, are you?'

'No. I'm well, but someone I know with a young baby is feeling very low.'

'The poor dear,' Mum said. 'She has my sympathy. I felt like that for a while after having your brother.'

'Did you?' I asked, surprised. 'You've never mentioned it.'

'Well, you don't, do you? I mean, it was a long time ago and we just got on with it back then. Now I think you can get pills if you're really low. I remember feeling very tearful and crying for no good reason, but I put it down to being permanently tired – having a toddler and a baby to look after.'

'Do you remember what it felt like? Apart from crying, did you have any other symptoms?'

'I don't think so. I really can't remember. Tearful and tired summed it up for me. It passed after about three months.'

'And you didn't go to the doctors?'

'Good gracious, no, dear. I wouldn't have bothered the doctor with something like that. They've got better things to do.' My mother was of a similar age to Geraldine and like many of her generation didn't consult the doctor unless it was absolutely essential and couldn't be treated from the pharmacy or by having a rest. 'But I wouldn't have called it depression,' she added. 'Not like some people get depressed. It was more feeling down. I think they call it the baby blues.'

We chatted for a while longer and then I talked to Dad before saying goodnight to them both. Interesting that Mum had never mentioned suffering from the baby blues before, I thought. How many other women had had similar experiences but never mentioned it? Perhaps they were ashamed to admit it at a time when everyone around them was overjoyed by the arrival of a new baby. It seemed a bit of a taboo subject, although as Mum had said there was a big difference between feeling down (the baby blues) and depression.

The following day was Friday and that morning I was delighted to receive a telephone call from Shelley.

'Hello, love,' I said. 'What a nice surprise. How are you?'

'Back to normal and no toothache,' she said.

'Great. And how's Darrel?'

'He's good. He often talks about you, Adrian and Paula.'

'We've been talking about you too,' I said. 'Have your ears been burning?'

'No, why? What have you been saying about me?' She laughed.

'Nice things. Adrian and I have been saying what a beautiful voice you have. We've started humming the lullabies you sang that night. We can't sing well, so we hum them.'

'Aww, that's sweet. I'll think of you then the next time I sing to Darrel. The reason I'm phoning is that I was wondering if you'll be in on Saturday morning. I've bought you a little something to say thank you.'

'You shouldn't have done that,' I said. 'You should keep your money. But of course we're always pleased to see you. Come for some lunch if you like.'

'That would be terrific. Thank you. Darrel will love playing with Adrian again.'

'Shall we say twelve o'clock?"

'Fantastic. See you then.'

* * *

I hadn't long finished talking to Shelley when the telephone rang again. It was a social worker from the children's services department of the local authority. 'Your name is on the whiteboard,' she said. 'I'm looking to place a child on respite for a few days next week and I see you are free.' The whiteboard was on a wall at the far end of the social services' open-plan office and showed the names of foster carers in the area who were free to take a child. When a social worker was looking for a carer, either because they were bringing a child or children into care, or they were looking for a respite placement, they checked on the board to see if a suitable carer was free. If not, they approached one of the independent fostering agencies. It's a basic method, but it works well and many local authorities use it.

'Yes, I am available for respite,' I confirmed.

'Good. The little boy is called Samson. He's six. I need respite care to give his gran a break. She's the main caregiver in the family. It's the half-term holiday next week and she doesn't feel she can cope with Samson for the whole week. She's not in the best of health and struggles as it is.'

From this I learned that Samson was living at home and being brought up mainly by his grandmother, but his situation was being monitored by the social services.

'Yes, OK. Which days do you want?' I asked.

'Wednesday to Friday. You will need to collect him and return him to Gran, as she doesn't drive. I'll put all the details in the post to you.'

'All right, thank you.' And we said goodbye.

I thought three days of the half-term break would work out fine, so that afternoon when I collected Adrian from school I had two pieces of good news to tell him.

'Darrel and his mother are coming for lunch tomorrow,' I said. 'And then on Wednesday we're looking after a six-year-old boy for three days.'

'Nearly the same age as me!' Adrian said, delighted.

I thought he'd be pleased, for while Adrian obviously loved his sister dearly, nothing can beat having a playmate of a similar age. The background information on Samson that I needed was being posted to me, and I was looking forward to a relatively relaxing week out of the school routine with the children playing contentedly. What could possibly go wrong?

CHAPTER EIGHT

A PLAYMATE?

At exactly twelve o'clock the following morning Shelley and Darrel arrived, both smiling broadly, as pleased to see us as we were to see them. Shelley presented me with a beautiful potted plant.

'Thank you so much, love,' I said, kissing her cheek. 'But you really shouldn't have.'

'I wanted to give you something to say thank you, and I noticed you like plants.'

'I do. That's kind of you. It's lovely.'

She also gave me three packets of chocolate buttons for the children to have after lunch. Adrian took Darrel's hand and rushed him through to the living room where he'd already set out his train set for them to play with. Paula toddled after them and Shelley came with me into the kitchen to make some drinks. Toscha was there and Shelley stroked and fussed over her as I set the plant on the windowsill and then poured juice for us all. I carried the tray of drinks into the living room and Shelley and I settled on the sofa. For a few moments neither of us spoke as we watched the children playing, then Shelley lowered her voice and said quietly to me, 'Darrel would love a brother or sister, but that's not going to happen now.'

'Why not?' I asked. 'You're young. You could meet someone and fall in love.'

She smiled reflectively. 'That would be nice, but I won't hold my breath. It would take someone very special who would love Darrel as his own. I've no idea how I would meet him, as I never go out anywhere to meet people.' She gave a small, dismissive laugh. 'Although I am hoping to get some training and a job when Darrel goes to school, so who knows?' She ended with a shrug.

'Exactly,' I said. 'Many relationships start in the workplace. I'm a great believer in chance meetings, if it's meant to be.'

She smiled and took a sip of her drink. 'I do have news, though – good news.'

'Oh yes?'

'You remember I told you I was trying to get Darrel dry at night and you said to give him his last drink earlier in the evening?'

'Yes.'

'Well, it worked. It only took two nights and he's dry now.'

'That's fantastic,' I said. 'Well done.'

'It's a big saving on nappies; they're so expensive. He's pleased he's dry too.'

'Yes, he's a big boy now,' I said, glancing at Darrel, although he was concentrating on playing with the train set.

'I have another piece of good news,' Shelley said, now turning to me with a glint of excitement in her eyes. 'And it's because of you again.'

'Really?' I asked tentatively, wondering what I was being held responsible for.

'You know we were talking about my experiences in foster care and I said the only foster carer I regretted not keeping in touch with was Carol? And you said she'd still be pleased to hear from me even after all this time?' I nodded. 'Well, I gave it some thought and I asked the social worker if she could find Carol's telephone number for me. I explained I was thinking of trying to contact her. She said she'd look into it, but if they did have her number on file she'd have to check with Carol first before she gave it to me. She phoned back a few days later and had spoken to Carol. She's still fostering and said she'd love to hear from me, so I called her yesterday.' Shelley's face lit up and my eyes rounded too.

'Fantastic. Well done.'

'She was over the moon to hear from me,' Shelley continued. 'It was great hearing her voice. It brought back some really good memories of my time with her. She couldn't talk for long as she had to collect a child from contact, but she's invited me over there next Sunday. Her own children will be there. They're grown up, but they want to see me again, so it will be a family reunion. That's what Carol said – "a family reunion" – like she still thinks of me as family. I couldn't believe it.'

'I'm sure she does think of you as family,' I said. 'You were with her for three years. That's a long time.'

Shelley's eyes glistened. 'It feels so good. So a big thank-you. If it wasn't for you I would never have thought of contacting her.' She gave me a big hug.

'I expect Carol will want to keep in touch in the future now you've made contact,' I said.

'I hope so. That would be wonderful. I've never had a family of my own.'

Shelley was a lovely person who, despite being badly let down by her parents and the social-care system, wasn't at all angry or bitter, which said a lot about her.

We continued talking as the children played, then Shelley suddenly turned to me again in earnest, a serious expression on her face. 'Cathy, there's something I would like to ask your advice about if you don't mind.'

'No, of course not. Go ahead. I'll help if I can.'

'It's about my singing. I saw a card on the noticeboard in the library about a local amateur choir. They meet once a week in the evening to practise and then give little concerts in the community hall. I saw them singing at Christmas – they were very good, and since then I've been thinking, well, that maybe I'd like to try and join them.' She stopped and looked at me hesitantly.

'Yes, that sounds good. What's stopping you? A babysitter for Darrel?' I was ready to offer to look after him so she could attend the choir.

'No. My friend would do that. She's offered before. It's more ...' She hesitated again. 'Two things really. I'm not sure if I'm good enough – they may not want me – and I don't know anyone there.'

'Shelley,' I said, looking at her carefully, 'I'm sure you are good enough, but you won't know unless you try. And I fully understand how daunting it can be to walk into a room full of strangers, but if you want it enough you'll do it. Go for it, I say. I think it's a fantastic idea. You love singing and I'm sure they'll be pleased to have you.'

She gave a little shrug. 'I'll think about it,' she said, not wholly convinced.

'Is there a telephone number for you to call or do you just turn up for an audition?'

'Either,' she said.

'If it was me, I'd telephone first and have a chat with the

organizer. Then, if you decide to go for an audition, you'll already know them, so it will be a bit easier.'

'And you think I stand a chance of getting in?'

'Yes. Absolutely.'

'Hmm. I'll think about it,' she said again.

Self-effacing and a little short on confidence, Shelley didn't fully appreciate what a lovely singing voice she had, but I didn't say anything further; it was her decision, and I now had to put the finishing touches to lunch. I left Shelley in charge of the children while I went into the kitchen. Meatless sausages, chicken dippers, quiche and jacket potatoes were already cooking in the oven, and I now warmed some baked beans and set salad and coleslaw on the table. When everything was ready I called them to the table and we served ourselves, with Shelley helping Darrel and me helping Paula. Adrian served himself. There was rather a lot of giggling from the children, as they were excited, but they also ate, so it didn't matter. Once we'd finished I suggested we went into the garden as the weather was good. Toscha, not wanting to be left out, came with us. I took the children's garden toys from the shed and arranged them on the lawn. Paula began pushing the walker up and down while Adrian and Darrel kicked a football. Shelley and I stood watching them for a while and then sat on the bench by the tree where we could see them as we chatted. Toscha quickly settled between us. We talked intermittently as Shelley absently stroked Toscha, and it wasn't long before she was telling me about Carol again, and the time just after she'd left her.

'I don't know why I didn't keep in touch and answer her phone calls,' Shelley said. 'I should have done. I certainly needed her support. I was in a bad place when I first left care and had to go into lodgings, and then when Darrel was born it got even worse. We were living in the bed and breakfast and I had no one. I was isolated and got really low. The room was damp and smelly and I had to share a bathroom with other families, which didn't help. Then I was up at night with Darrel and got tired and depressed. Everything was such an effort, even getting dressed. Sometimes I didn't get dressed and stayed in for days on end. Thankfully my social worker knew what to do.'

'Which was what?' I asked, glancing at her.

'Go to the doctor's. He gave me some tablets. I didn't want to take them at first, because I thought I might get addicted to them, but my social worker told me I should, as the doctor had prescribed them. I'm glad I did. I started to feel better almost straight away and I came off them after six months.'

'What sort of tablets were they?' I asked, interested.

'Anti-depressants. It's what they give you if you have post-natal depression.'

'Is that what you had?'

Shelley nodded. 'The doctor said I should have gone to see him earlier, but I was worried that it might affect my chances of keeping Darrel. The social services were monitoring me then to see if I could cope. I thought if I admitted I was depressed they would think I couldn't and would take Darrel away.'

'Clearly that didn't happen,' I said.

'No. My social worker was great. She said one of her sisters had had postnatal depression, so she knew what to do.'

I nodded and obviously thought of Laura. 'Did you have any other symptoms apart from feeling very low and finding everything an effort? If you don't mind me asking …'

'I cried the whole time. If something didn't go right – even something small, like changing a nappy – I'd burst into tears. I cried for no reason too. I felt a complete failure, worthless, and no good to anyone. I thought others were getting at me and I even started to think that Darrel would be better off without me. It seems awful now, but then I felt overwhelmed and everything seemed pointless. It was like I was in a deep, dark pit with no way of getting out. The doctor also arranged some counselling for me, which helped too. I dread to think what would have happened if I hadn't gone to see the doctor. It was just as well I had a good social worker.'

'Yes, it was,' I said thoughtfully. 'Although you may have gone to the doctors in the end anyway.'

'I'm not so sure.'

I stood and went over to Paula, who'd taken a tumble and was looking as though she might cry. Adrian and Darrel got to her first and helped her up. I brushed her down and she was soon smiling again.

We stayed in the garden for another hour or so, talking and playing with the children, and then we returned indoors for the pudding, which we'd been too full to eat at lunchtime. Apple crumble with custard or ice cream (or both). We all had both, the combination of melting ice cream, warm custard, the sweet, crunchy topping and slightly tart apple was too good to resist, so we all had seconds too.

Shelley and Darrel stayed until nearly six o'clock and then, with a reluctant sigh, Shelley said they had better be going. I offered to take them home in the car, but she insisted they'd be fine on the bus. As she pointed out, it was still daylight, she had fully recovered from the operation and didn't have any heavy luggage, so I was persuaded to let her go on the bus. We all went to the front door to see them off. I told Shelley to stay in touch and that I hoped to see them again before long.

'Yes, I'd like that,' she said. 'We both would.'

'Have a good time at Carol's,' I added. 'And don't forget to phone that choir leader.'

Shelley smiled, but changed the subject. 'I'll think about you this evening when I'm singing to Darrel,' she said.

'We'll think about you too,' I said.

We hugged and kissed goodbye and then stood on the pavement and waved until they were out of sight.

'I'm having a lovely time,' Adrian said as we returned indoors. 'First Darrel, and then on Wednesday that other boy is coming. I'm so lucky.'

'Yes,' I agreed. But lucky wasn't the term I would be using by the end of the week – stretched to the limit was more like it.

The next day, Sunday, the first day of June, we went to my parents. On Monday we were mainly at home and on Tuesday we went to a local adventure park. I find that during the school holidays a combination of days out and time spent playing at home works well for the children. The paperwork for Samson had arrived in Monday's post and I'd read it that evening. Respite information for carers is less detailed than the placement information a carer usually receives when a child is staying for longer. It is a brief résumé of what they need to know. It contained Samson's full name, date of birth, home address, his grandmother's name and telephone number, then lines for additional information. *Medication: none. Special dietary requirements: none. Religion: Catholic.*

Other significant adults: Samson lives with his gran, aunts and uncles, and has some contact with his father but not his mother. There was also space to include any special needs and challenging behaviour, and beside this was typed: *Samson can show challenging behaviour at times* – but with no details. I didn't think much of this, as many of the children I'd fostered had shown some challenging behaviour, and given that Samson was being brought up by his grandmother, whom the social worker had said wasn't in good health and was finding it difficult to cope, I assumed it would be a matter of putting a few boundaries in place and keeping Samson happily occupied.

Adrian was so excited on Wednesday morning, planning all the games he and Samson were going to play, that he could hardly eat his breakfast. I intended to take Adrian and Paula with me to collect Samson rather than ask a friend to babysit. The note from the social worker that had come with the information had said I should collect Samson at ten o'clock. I knew the estate where he lived; it was about a twenty-minute drive away, so we left in good time at 9.30 a.m. The estate was a mixture of private and social housing, and had a complicated and confusing series of criss-cross walkways designed to keep cars out of the central residential area. I found the designated car park for flats 15–27 (Samson lived in flat 17) and opened the back doors of the car, which were child-locked, to let the children out.

I held Paula's hand and with Adrian on the other side of me we began down the path to the communal entrance to the flats. It was a three-storey block identical to others on the estate. It was a warm day and many of the residents had their windows wide open. The sounds of life filtered out, converging and echoing in the central courtyard: a television blaring, a baby crying, children shouting, music, a dog barking, as well as various cooking smells. Adrian gave a little skip of happiness and Paula tried to copy him. As we approached the main entrance the net curtain at the window of the ground-floor flat on our left was suddenly pulled back and a boy with a shaved head and piercing blue eyes yelled, 'Are you the foster carer?'

Adrian stopped dead beside me.

'Yes,' I said.

'Gran, she's here!' the boy yelled at the top of his voice. And the net curtain was flung back into place.

'Is that Samson?' Adrian asked quietly, moving slightly closer.

'I think it might be,' I said.

Someone in their flat must have released the security lock on the main door, for it clicked open. With a child on each side I went in and turned left to number 17. Although the occupants clearly knew we'd arrived no one came to the door, so after a few moments I pressed the bell. Noise immediately erupted from inside. The claws of a very heavy dog pounded down the hall and then scratched furiously at the other side of the door as it barked loudly. Adrian darted behind me and I picked up Paula. There'd been no mention of a dog in the information I'd been sent, and I was not pleased. Social workers often have to insist that a dog is shut away before they enter premises, but it would be awkward for me to make the same request.

'Get down, Bruno!' a male voice now yelled from inside the flat. There was more angry barking and scratching, then a yelp, and the door opened. I took a step back.

A boy in his late teens with a shaved head held the Doberman by its studded neck collar. It strained to be free. 'Stop it!' he shouted, yanking on its collar, then looked at me.

'I've come to collect Samson,' I said.

'Gran!' he yelled over his shoulder. 'The social worker's here.'

'Foster carer,' I corrected.

'Foster carer!' he yelled.

'Shut him away, will ya?' a woman's voice came from down the hall.

The lad tugged hard on the dog's collar and managed to turn it around and drag it down the hall, its claws scratching on what was left of the lino.

'Take no notice of him,' the woman who now appeared said. 'His bark is worse than his bite.'

I assumed she was referring to the dog. 'Is the dog shut in a room now?' I asked.

'He will be,' she said. 'I'm Samson's gran.'

'Hello,' I smiled. 'I'm Cathy, the foster carer.'

'Jason! Is Bruno shut in?' she yelled over her shoulder.

There was no reply, but the silence seemed to suggest that he was and she beckoned us to go in. Still carrying Paula and with Adrian holding tightly onto the back of my jeans, we went in. 'I hope you don't mind me bringing my children,' I said.

'No, not at all. I like kids.' She closed the door. 'Come through.'

We followed Samson's gran slowly down the short hall. She was badly overweight and her heavily veined legs and swollen ankles looked painful, causing her to hobble rather than walk. She used the wall to steady herself. Little wonder

90

she struggled to look after Samson, a high-spirited and energetic six-year-old, I thought.

We went into a cramped and cluttered living room where
she collapsed into an armchair, out of breath from the exer-
tion of coming to the front door. A large, middle-aged man
with a mug of tea balanced on his stomach sat in the other
armchair, staring at the television. Naked to the waist, he had
the name of a football club (presumably the one he supported)
tattooed across his chest. I assumed he was one of Samson's
uncles referred to in the information sheet. He looked up and
nodded in my direction, then returned his attention to the
television. Controlling the television with the remote and
sprawled on the sofa beneath the window was the boy we'd
already seen at the window. 'You've met Samson,' his gran
said, nodding towards him.

'Hello, Samson,' I said brightly. 'How are you?' Adrian
peeped out from behind me.

Samson ignored me and continued pressing the remote to
channel hop.

'Say hello to your foster carer,' his gran said sternly.

'Say hello, boy,' the man repeated gruffly. 'And leave the
bleedin' control alone.'

'Hello,' Samson said, without taking his eyes from the
television.

'Will you leave that thing alone and get your stuff,' his
gran now said to him.

'Give it here,' the man demanded, reaching out for the
remote.

Samson jumped up, tossed the remote into the man's lap
and ran out of the room. At the same time two women in
their early twenties, hair ruffled from sleep and dressed in

pyjama shorts and T-shirts, sauntered in carrying a mug of tea each. They seemed unfazed and indeed uninterested that I, a stranger, was in the room, and with barely a glance in my direction wandered over to the sofa where they sat down and gazed at the television.

'Aren't you gonna offer her a cup of tea then?' Samson's gran said to them.

'It's OK,' I said, smiling. 'I'm fine. We're going as soon as Samson is ready.'

'You know to bring him back at six o'clock sharp on Friday,' Gran said to me.

'Yes.'

'He must be here for six or I'll catch it from his dad. He goes out with his dad every Friday at six o'clock.'

'I'll have him back in plenty of time,' I confirmed.

Samson reappeared with a small backpack. 'Are we going then?' he demanded.

'You got everything, mate?' his gran asked him, from which I assumed Samson had done his own packing.

'Yeah, what do you take me for?' he returned cheekily. No one corrected him, so I guessed that was how he usually spoke to his gran, and possibly to the other adults too.

'Give us a kiss then,' his gran said.

Samson went over and kissed her cheek and then, navigating his way around the clutter on the floor, he continued round the room, giving the two women a kiss on their cheeks and slapping the man on his shoulder. It wasn't an emotional parting; saying goodbye seemed perfunctory, and the adults hadn't taken their gaze from the television screen.

'See you Friday then,' his gran called after him as he shot from the room. 'Be good.'

'Yeah, see ya,' he returned.

I went after him. It appeared we were seeing ourselves out and I called goodbye as we left. I was still carrying Paula, and Adrian was staying close beside me. Samson was already at the door with his hand on the doorknob ready to open it. 'Bye, Bruno!' he yelled at the top of his voice.

From somewhere in the flat the dog barked furiously.

CHAPTER NINE

SAMSON

Poor Adrian, his face was a picture and said it all. This wasn't the playmate he'd envisaged and had been hoping for.

'Where's your car, missus?' Samson demanded as we left the path that led from the flats and approached the designated parking area.

'It's that sliver Ford there,' I said, pointing the fob at my car.

He sneered, unimpressed. 'That ain't much of a car. My last two carers had four-by-fours.'

'Very nice,' I said.

'Give me the key then,' he said, making a grab for the fob. 'I'll unlock it for you.'

'It's OK,' I said. 'Thank you anyway, but I can manage.' I wasn't putting Samson in charge of anything yet until I knew what he was capable of.

'I'll sit in the front then,' he said, yanking the passenger door open.

'No. Children ride in the back,' I said, closing the door.

'I always ride in the front in my uncle's car,' he protested.

'Things are a bit different with me,' I said, opening the rear door. 'The law states that children have to ride in the back of a car with an age-appropriate seat and harness. We don't want to break the law, do we?'

'No. Blimey. We don't,' he said. 'I'll have to tell my uncle. He don't need more trouble with the law.'

I hid my smile. With his streetwise, cheeky manner Samson reminded me of the Artful Dodger in the Dickens classic *Oliver Twist*, but it was already clear to me he was going to be hard work. I adjusted my previous expectations of putting in place 'a few boundaries' and the children all playing happily together, just as Adrian must have been adjusting his. Once I had all three children secured under their seatbelts in the rear of the car I began the drive home. It was a very lively journey. Samson talked non-stop at the top of his voice about anything and everything that came into his head, to the point where I was wondering if he was hyperactive.

'Have you had breakfast today?' I asked over his babble.

'Yeah, of course. I always have breakfast. Our teacher says we must, so Gran makes me. I take it to my room and eat it.'

'What did you have?' I asked, glancing at him in the rear-view mirror.

'Me usual. What I always have. A bowl of dry Chocca cereal and a Mars bar.'

'And to drink?'

'Lemonade. I like lemonade. Lemonade and Coke are me favourites.'

Little wonder he was buzzing, I thought, with all that sugar in his blood. Most parents will agree that food with a very high sugar content can make a child hyperactive. The effect is even more pronounced if eaten on an empty stomach, but once the sugar rush is over the child can easily become irritable and crave more sugar. I didn't say anything, but I could foresee a confrontation looming when he didn't have his sugary cereal and chocolate bar for breakfast. He resumed his chatter: why he didn't like school, the horror films he watched with his (hero) dad, his boring aunts who were only interested in make-up and men, and then what he could see through his window. Adrian was very quiet; he didn't say a word. I could see him in the rear-view mirror looking concerned, and Paula was staring at Samson open-mouthed and in awe, not sure what to make of him. As I pulled onto our driveway Samson was asking Adrian if he had a PlayStation.

'No,' Adrian replied quietly. 'I'm not old enough.'

'Of course you're old enough, boy!' Samson exclaimed. 'Who said you weren't?'

'Me,' I said, saving Adrian the embarrassment.

'Jesus, missus! I had my PlayStation when I was three. It's in me bedroom and I have it on when I like. Anything to keep me quiet.'

Doubtless Samson was repeating what one of the adults in the flat had said, and I appreciated why keeping Samson quiet with the PlayStation was an attractive option. Gran, the main carer, had very limited mobility, so she wouldn't be able to take Samson out and give him the exercise a boy of his age needed. In the small, overcrowded flat, having Samson out of the way and entertaining himself must seem like a blessing. He clearly needed some exercise now to burn off all that excess sugar so that he calmed down.

'It's a lovely day, so you'll be able to play in the garden,' I said as I opened the rear door to let the children out. 'We've got bikes, footballs and plenty of other garden toys and games.'

'But I always watch television in the morning,' Samson said, disgruntled.

'We don't usually have the television on in the day,' I said. 'But you can watch some this evening for a while.'

'What's a while?' he asked, turning to Adrian.

Adrian shrugged.

'About an hour,' I said.

'Fucking 'ell. That ain't much telly, missus.'

Adrian stared at him, dismayed, aware that he'd said a really bad word. 'Samson, we don't swear,' I said as I helped Paula from the car. 'And please call me Cathy.'

'OK,' he said easily.

I locked the car and took hold of Paula's hand, and we all walked up the path to the front door.

'Do you often stay with foster carers?' I asked Samson as I unlocked the door.

'Yeah. It's cos me gran can't cope with me,' he said. 'I don't think the other carers coped with me either, cos I never saw them again.' Out of the mouths of babes, I thought, as I opened the door. He shot in ahead of me and down the hall. By the time I arrived in the living room he was sprawled on the sofa, backpack and shoes still on, with the remote control aimed at the television.

'Samson,' I said, taking the remote from him, 'I said we weren't watching television right now.'

'Ain't fair,' he said, giving the sofa a kick.

'And we take our shoes off in the house.'

'But you said I was going in the garden, and I need me shoes out there, don't I?' he replied cheekily.

I crossed to the patio doors, released the catch and slid one door open. 'Take off your backpack and you can go outside.

See if you can run fifteen laps of the lawn. Do you know what a lap is?'

'Yeah, of course. I ain't silly. I've seen the runners do it on the television.' He grinned, delighted by the challenge, and immediately stood. Slipping off his backpack he threw it on the floor and ran to the door.

'On the count of three then,' I said. 'And no cheating. I'll be watching. A lap is right round the edge of the lawn.'

'Yeah. I'm ready,' he said, adopting a sprinter's starting position.

'One, two, three, go!' I cried.

With a flying leap he was out of the door, running across the patio and then around the edge of the lawn on his first lap. Adrian and Paula joined me on the patio to watch him. Samson's face was set in concentration and his arms worked at his sides as he pounded around the imaginary track. 'That's one lap,' I called as he passed. 'Keep going.' Our garden is rather long and narrow and mostly lawn, so one circuit was about 250 feet (or 76 metres) – a fair challenge for a six-year-old. 'Two laps! Well done!' I called a few moments later as he completed a second circuit. He was smiling broadly and waved as he went past as though on a victory run. 'Good boy.'

Adrian, standing beside me, was still looking anxious. 'Don't worry,' I said, giving him a hug. 'He'll be fine, and I'll keep a close eye on him.'

Although Adrian and Samson were of a similar age, that was where any similarity began and ended. Samson was thickly set, appeared to be physically strong and I guessed liked nothing more than play fighting, given the opportunity. Like many children I'd seen come into care he was self-sufficient from having largely brought himself up and meeting his own needs. He therefore assumed that he was in charge, not only of himself but everyone else, which wasn't healthy for a six-year-old. It wasn't his fault, but I knew that if these three days weren't going to be a foster carer's nightmare I needed to establish that I, the adult, was in charge, not him – in the nicest possible way, of course.

'Three!' I called as Samson sped past, his arms bent and fists working the air beside him. 'Well done.' I continued counting and praising him as he completed each lap until he reached fifteen. 'Excellent!' I said. He ran over to us and flopped onto the patio, exhausted.

'I need a drink,' he gasped, clutching his throat dramatically.

'Of course. Take off your trainers and come inside.'

He kicked off his trainers and I led the way into our kitchen-cum-diner. 'This is where you will sit at the table,' I said, drawing out a chair.

He threw himself into it as though collapsing from exhaustion. 'I'm knackered,' he said.

Adrian silently took his place opposite Samson and I helped Paula onto her booster seat. She was mesmerized by Samson; I think he was the best entertainment she'd had in a long while.

'What would you like to drink?' I asked Samson. 'Water, milk, juice or squash?'

'Ain't you got no fizzy drinks?' he asked, his cheeks flushed from the exercise.

'We only have fizzy drinks on special occasions, like birthdays,' I explained.

'Jesus, this ain't much fun.'

'The blackcurrant squash is nice,' I suggested. 'That's what Adrian has.'

'OK, give me one of those,' he said as though ordering a shot in a bar.

'Would you like something to eat?' I asked him. 'Adrian and Paula usually have a snack mid-morning.'

'A biscuit. Chocolate if you've got them.'

'I think you've had enough sweet things for the time being,' I said. 'Would you like a sandwich, or cheese on biscuits, or some fruit?'

'Yeah. Cheese sandwich and crisps,' he ordered. Then, looking at Adrian, he said, 'It's just like at the other carers' with this "good" food and having to eat at the table.'

I smiled and thought that would at least make my life a little easier. While carers usually try to give the child what is familiar to them and keep to their routines as much as possible, I knew it was highly unlikely that the previous carers would have indulged his high-sugar diet or allowed extreme negative behaviour. We were therefore all coming from the same place, which would help, as Samson would already have some experience of my expectations.

I prepared the snacks and then sat at the table with the children while they ate. Samson didn't have any table manners, but he did have a good appetite and thoroughly enjoyed the sandwich, crisps and squash, talking as he ate. As soon as he'd finished, before he'd swallowed the last mouthful, he leapt from his chair, ran into the living room and switched on the television. Leaving Adrian to keep an eye on Paula, I went after him.

'I did say we weren't watching television in the day,' I said, taking the remote from him.

'So what am I going to do with no telly or PlayStation?' he asked. These had clearly been his life.

'I'm going to show you around the house, and where you will sleep, and then I'll organize a game in the garden.'

I hid the remote control out of sight, collected Adrian and Paula, who were still at the table but had finished eating, and began a tour of the house. Although Samson was slightly calmer now, he still entered each room like a spring uncoiling, dashing in, touching things, firing comments and then running out and into the next room. Paula had taken a shine to him and wanted to hold his hand, which he did for a while. He was gentle with her, so I felt that although he gave the appearance of being ready for a fight with boys his own age or older, he wouldn't harm a toddler. I was more concerned about Adrian.

'Can you kickbox?' Samson asked Adrian on the landing, thrusting his foot in his face.

Adrian flinched and took a step back.

'No. We don't kickbox,' I said.

'My dad's teaching me. Have you got a dad?' he asked Adrian.

'Yes,' Adrian said quietly. 'He's working away.'

'My dad works away too sometimes,' Samson said. 'Gran says it's for Her Majesty's pleasure.' Being detained 'at Her Majesty's pleasure' is a euphemism for being in prison, but I didn't comment. As we entered Samson's bedroom he suddenly turned and bolted out again. 'I'll get me bag!' he yelled, pounding down the stairs. He returned a moment later with his backpack, which he threw onto the bed. Jumping on top of it, he unzipped it, pulled out the contents and stuffed them all in the nearest drawer. 'I know you carers like us kids to unpack so we feel at home,' he said.

It was true, but I usually helped the children unpack. It was sad that he'd had so much experience of being in respite care that he knew the routine. But then again, if having regular respite meant that his gran could cope and Samson could remain living at home, that was preferable to him having to live in care permanently. No one wants to see a family split up; it's the last resort.

Having seen all the rooms upstairs we began downstairs, and Samson asked me what we were going to do now. Before I had a chance to reply he said, 'Are you going to take me on outings like the other carers did?'

'I was thinking of a day out tomorrow,' I said, aware that this would no longer be a surprise.

'Where?' he demanded.

'Well, there are lots of interesting places not too far away.' I began listing them: 'There's the castle ruins, Merrymoor Farm, the zoo, the activity centre ...'

But after each one Samson said, 'Been there! Done it!' as though he was winning some unnamed game.

Five minutes later I'd exhausted the list. He'd visited every place of interest within a fifty-mile radius. Many of the places Adrian and Paula hadn't been to. Samson had had far more outings than an average child. Of course, it was the well-meaning foster carers who'd taken him, but sadly the regularity of the outings meant that they weren't treats any more, but something he had to go along with as part of the package of respite care.

'What would you like to do then?' I asked. We were in the living room. He scratched his stubbled head in thought and then gazed down the garden.

'Do more laps in the garden,' he said, smiling.

'Really? Well, we could,' I said, 'if you don't want to go on an outing.' But then I had an idea. 'Samson, you're obviously good at sports so let's have a mini sports day of our own.'

'Yeah!' he cried, jumping up and down. 'Like at school. I love sports day.'

Well done me, I thought. I took Paula's hand and we all went out into the garden again. Samson and Adrian helped me organize what we needed for our sports day while Paula toddled after them. We began with running events – sprinting, circuits and relay. Then I balanced a garden cane across two stacks of bricks for the high-jump event, raising it after each go until the boys reached their maximum. Using the play sandpit, we held a long-jump event, and then egg and spoon races, using table-tennis balls balanced on dessertspoons. Paula joined in as best she could. For the sack race the boys and I had a dustbin liner each to hop in, and I gave Paula a carrier bag, as she was much shorter. It was fun and I was pleased that Adrian was enjoying it as much as Samson. A few times I had to curtail Samson's enthusiasm when he became too boisterous, and I steered him away from his idea of sharpening a garden cane for a javelin event and throwing bricks for shot put.

I took everyone indoors for lunch at one-thirty and then we continued the sports day in the afternoon. I promised a little prize-giving ceremony on Friday, the last day Samson was with us, which would give me a chance to put together some prizes. By the end of the afternoon everyone was exhausted and I settled the children in front of the television while I made dinner. Samson was worn out and no trouble, and I felt comfortable leaving him sitting on the sofa with Adrian and Paula, although I looked in regularly to check on them. After we'd finished eating I trusted Samson enough to leave him playing a board game with Adrian while I took Paula upstairs to bed.

'Samon?' Paula asked, making a good attempt at pronouncing Samson's name.

'Yes, Samson will be here in the morning,' I said, tucking her in.

I took the boys upstairs to bed at 7.30 p.m., oversaw their washes and teeth cleaning and then, leaving Adrian in his bedroom, I saw Samson into his.

'Can we have another sports day tomorrow?' he asked as he climbed into bed.

'Yes, if that's what you would like to do.'

'Yeah, I do. It was fun. Will you give me a goodnight kiss like I ask me gran to?' he said.

'Of course.' Despite all his bravado, he still liked his good-night kiss and hug.

I tucked him in and reminded him where my room was if he needed me in the night.

'I'm not scared of the dark,' he said, his cheeky little face peering up at me from under the duvet. 'But I have me light on.'

'That's fine,' I said. I adjusted the dimmer switch until the light was how he liked it. 'Good night then, love.'

'Night,' he called as I came out. I drew the door to, but didn't close it completely so that I could hear him if he called out or was out of bed.

I checked on Paula, who was sound asleep, and then I went into Adrian's room and sat with him. I praised him for help-ing me make Samson's day enjoyable and the sports day a success, for I couldn't have done it without his cooperation.

'I guess Samson is OK really,' Adrian said. 'He just tries to be tough.'

Which I thought summed him up quite perceptively.

The following morning Samson was awake and out of bed at 5.30. I quickly threw on my dressing gown and went round the landing to his room. Quietening him down I told him he had to stay in his room and play until I was ready to go downstairs. I never leave young children unattended downstairs.

'That's why you need to get a PlayStation,' he said cheekily. 'To keep me quiet.'

'There are lots of other enjoyable things you can do,' I said. 'Stay there.'

I hurried downstairs and brought up one of the toy boxes containing puzzles and cars, which I placed on his bedroom floor. I told him to play quietly until I was dressed. But 'quietly' wasn't a word Samson was familiar with, and I could hear his brum-brumming as he played with the toy cars from the bathroom, although he did stay in his bedroom. By six o'clock Adrian and Paula were awake too, and I got Paula up as Adrian dressed himself. We were all downstairs having breakfast at seven – unheard of on a day when we didn't have to be up for school. If Samson had been staying with me for longer I would have settled him into a better routine, insisting that if he woke early he amuse himself quietly in his room until seven o'clock when I would come in and tell him it was time to get dressed (using rewards and sanctions to achieve the goal). But because he was only with me for a short while it was impossible to achieve very much, which I'm sure the other respite carers who'd looked after Samson had found too.

Samson was eager to hold another sports day and Adrian was happy to go along with this, but by mid-morning the novelty had clearly worn off and Samson was becoming disruptive and in need of a new activity. I took the children indoors and arranged various board games, then Play-Doh modelling and crayoning, all of which Samson enjoyed, although he couldn't be left to play unattended, even for a short while – he needed constant supervision. By lunchtime, when he was growing fractious again, I realized a change of scenery was required. There wasn't enough time for a full day out, so I suggested that after lunch we went to a fairground that was in the area for the half-term holiday. Although predictably Samson had been to fairgrounds before, he was more than happy to go again and quickly pointed out that I'd have to give him money to spend at the fair. Adrian had only been to a fair once before, so it was a treat for him, and Paula had never been. It was a successful outing and I gave each boy £5 to spend, although I had to keep a close eye on Samson, who darted off as soon as a ride ended.

We had another early start on Friday morning, although Samson was quieter once I'd resettled him with some toys, and then after breakfast we went into the garden again, this time playing fairgrounds. The bikes, tricycle, skateboard and roller skates were the fairground rides, and we had various sideshow stalls: throw three balls in a bucket for a prize, knock the tin can off the wall (using tennis balls), hook the duck and so on, using anything we had. The boys and I were quite inventive. That afternoon, as promised, I arranged a little prize-giving ceremony, where I stood on the patio and presented each child with a few small gifts for the races they'd won. We applauded after each presentation and Paula had a prize for making a good attempt.

Samson had to be home by six o'clock that evening, as he kept reminding me: 'I see me dad at six on Friday and you can't be late.'

I left our house in plenty of time and we arrived at the flats at 5.45. I wanted to give Samson's gran some feedback on how the respite had gone, which was usual practice. The window of Samson's flat was slightly open and as he ran past he banged on the glass and yelled 'Bruno!' at the top of his voice, which set the dog barking manically.

We went in the main entrance, but no one was at the door of Samson's flat, so he banged on the wood and yelled, 'I'm home!' The dog went frantic.

Then a man's voice shouted, 'Shut up, Bruno!'

The barking stopped and the door was opened by the man I'd previously seen in the living room with a mug of tea. 'You're back then,' he said flatly to Samson as he shot in. 'Thanks,' he said to me and closed the door. So I didn't get the chance to give his gran feedback or to say goodbye to Samson, which was a pity.

However, I felt that the three days had gone reasonably well, although looking after Samson had been hard work. I hadn't done any laundry or housework, let alone worked on my dissertation, as my time had been completely taken up with Samson. Had he been staying for longer, or if I had him again on respite, I would start encouraging him to play independently. So often children who spend a lot of time in front of a screen for their entertainment (PlayStation, television, handheld consoles, etc.) never learn how to play creatively and amuse themselves, which is important for social development, problem solving and decision making now and in later life.

That evening after Adrian and Paula were in bed I had a good tidy up and then sat in the living room and enjoyed the peace and tranquillity. There's never a dull moment in fostering, and while I loved the challenge each new child brought I knew I really needed time to complete my dissertation. I decided that if I was asked to do more respite I'd have to be firm and say no for the next month or so. However, as it turned out it wasn't a foster child who occupied me, but someone much closer to home.

CHAPTER TEN

THE DEVIL'S CHILD

School resumed on Monday after the half-term break and the air temperature rose dramatically by ten degrees, as it can do in England, catching everyone unawares and causing the weather reporter to pronounce a heat wave. The sun shone in a cloudless sky and the air was alive with birdsong and the scent of summer flowers. We didn't need to wear our jackets to walk to school that morning.

Adrian was pleased to see his friends again and they ran around in the playground before school began. Parents chatted to each other, catching up on their news and asking each other if they'd had a nice holiday, and sharing what they'd done. Some families had spent the week at home just relaxing, pleased to be out of the school routine, while others had been more energetic, going out most days, and a couple of lucky families had been abroad for the week. As I talked to my friends I looked around for any sign of Laura, hoping she was now feeling well enough to bring Kim to school, but I couldn't see her. Then just before the start of school Geraldine walked into the playground, with Kim beside her pushing the pram. Kim was looking around her, proud to be in charge of her baby brother, while Geraldine kept her gaze straight ahead, her face expressionless. I assumed therefore that Laura still didn't feel up to coming out, or possibly she was just having a lie-in. I'd ask Geraldine how she was if I got the opportunity.

When the Klaxon sounded the children said goodbye to their parents and then lined up ready to go into school. The little groups of parents began dispersing, making their way towards the main gate. I looked over to where Geraldine had been standing. She was now walking briskly towards the exit. She was always one of the first out, slipping out ahead of everyone else, but this time her progress was slowed by the pram. I caught up with her as she waited for her turn to pass through the main gate.

'Good morning,' I said. Paula was holding my hand and toddling beside me.

Geraldine threw me her usual tight smile.

'Baby,' Paula said, pointing to the pram.

'Yes. Baby Liam. How is he doing?' I asked Geraldine. I could just see his little face over the cover, sleeping.

'He's well,' she said.

'And how's Laura?'

'These things take time.'

'She didn't feel up to coming here today then?' I asked.

'No.'

We were now through the main gate and on the pavement outside and it was clear Geraldine didn't want to walk with us.

'Give her my love,' I said.

She nodded stiffly and then, head down, she set off, pushing the pram at a brisk pace.

'Baby Liam,' Paula said again.

'Yes,' I said absently. 'With his grandmother.'

As we passed number 53 Paula and I both glanced at the house, but there was no one to be seen, and we continued our haltingly slow journey home. It didn't matter that it took us ages; it was a beautiful day and Paula was finding plenty to interest her along the way: ants scurrying across pavements, a cat basking on a sun-drenched wall, front gardens with an array of brightly coloured flowers, all of which were wonderfully new and inspiring to the enquiring young mind of a small child. I wished I had Laura's telephone number – I could have phoned her; just a friendly call to see how she was, for I didn't feel I could simply arrive on her doorstep. The last time I'd visited, Geraldine had made it clear that she'd let me know when Laura was up to having visitors again.

Once home, Paula and I went straight into the garden and I played in the sandpit with her. It was nice being able to give her some one-to-one time again, and she enjoyed it. Mid-morning I settled her for a nap and continued my dissertation. I wondered if Samson's social worker would telephone for feedback on Samson's respite, but she didn't. However, at lunchtime Shelley's social worker telephoned to ask if I could foster a four-month-old baby they were bringing into care the next day. Reluctantly I had to say no, and I explained about my degree.

'OK. Good luck with it,' she said. 'I'll make a note on the whiteboard.'

'Thank you.'

That afternoon Geraldine was in the playground again with Liam in the pram, and as usual she stood by herself with her eyes fixed firmly ahead. When the children came out I saw

Kim pushing the pram towards the exit, but they were well ahead of us by the time we left the playground, as Paula wanted to walk. The next day was the same: Geraldine brought Liam to school in the morning and the afternoon. I didn't know what this said about how Laura was feeling, but I had to believe that Geraldine and Laura's husband, Andy, knew what was best for her, as they were close to her and had helped her through a difficult time after the birth of Kim. There's a fine line between being friendly and neighbourly and being intrusive and a nosy parker, so I felt any further enquiry from me about Laura at that time would be unwelcome and probably resented. If Laura had been an old friend it would have been very different, but for now I just had to accept that Geraldine was in charge and knew best.

However, all that changed the following morning.

It was another fine day and we were walking to school. Paula, as usual, was in her stroller with the promise that she could walk back. As we passed number 53 the front door suddenly burst open. Kim ran out and down the path as Geraldine stood in the doorway. 'Gran says can you take me to school today,' Kim said. 'She has to stay with Mum.'

'Yes, of course,' I said. I looked towards the open door, but Geraldine gave a cursory wave and closed it.

'Is your mum all right?' I asked Kim.

'I don't know. She had a bad night. Gran didn't want to leave her alone, and my daddy had to go to work. We've been looking out for you.'

'Is your mum sick?' I asked, worried. I had no idea what a 'bad night' meant in this context.

'Not really,' Kim said, and looked uncomfortable. I knew not to question her further. She was only seven and I didn't want to place her in an awkward position by asking questions that she couldn't or didn't want to answer.

'I gave Liam his bottle this morning,' Kim said proudly, brightening, as she fell into step beside us.

'Well done. That was a big help,' I said.

'I don't like helping to change his nappy, though,' she said, pulling a face.

'Yuk!' Adrian agreed. '*She* still poos in a nappy,' he said, pointing at Paula, and dissolved into laughter. He was at an age when he and his friends found toilet talk hilarious.

'Baby Liam?' Paula asked, leaning out of her stroller for a better look at Kim.

'Hi,' Kim said sweetly. 'Liam's at home.'

She took hold of Paula's hand and we continued down the street with Kim on one side of the stroller and Adrian on the other. Adrian and Kim began talking about school and then a popular children's television programme, while I thought about Laura. Why didn't Geraldine want to leave her alone? It didn't sound good, and I thought maybe this was the excuse I needed to call in on the way home.

Once in the playground I let Paula out of the stroller and she immediately crouched down and began examining the tarmac, poking her finger at a couple of loose chippings. It's incredible what little ones can spot and play with. A mother approached me with a child of a similar age to Kim. I knew her slightly from seeing her in the playground.

'You've brought Kim,' she said. 'Is Laura all right? I'm Fran. Our girls are friends. How is she?'

'I'm not sure,' I said honestly. 'Her mother-in-law asked me to bring Kim to school this morning.'

'I'm worried about her,' Fran confided. 'I've tried phoning

and I've left messages, but she hasn't got back to me.' The two girls took skipping ropes from their bags and began skipping.

'I'm thinking of stopping by her house on the way back this morning,' I said. 'We live in the same street. I'll tell her you were asking after her.'

'Oh yes, please do.' She hesitated. 'I hope I haven't done anything to upset her. We were both relatively new to the area and seemed to hit it off as friends. But I haven't seen or heard from her since she was in the playground that morning weeks ago.'

'I'm sure it's nothing like that,' I said.

Clearly I didn't know how much Laura had confided in Fran, and Geraldine's words about not discussing Laura in the playground rang in my ears – although, of course, we were only concerned for her wellbeing.

'Give her my best wishes,' Fran said. 'And tell her I hope to hear from her soon.'

'I will.'

The Klaxon sounded and I said goodbye to both Adrian and Kim and watched them line up. 'We're going to see baby Liam on the way home,' I told Paula, taking her hand.

'Baby Liam,' she said and chuckled excitedly.

I wasn't excited, I was very apprehensive, partly from having to confront the formidable Geraldine again, but also because I wasn't convinced I was doing the right thing in just dropping by. Perhaps I was turning into the busybody up the road – 'You know, that woman, the foster carer who thinks she knows everything.' But on the other hand I had a gut feeling that I should stop by and try to see Laura, and sometimes I think it's best if we follow our instincts or intuition.

With the promise of visiting baby Liam, Paula walked

faster than usual and didn't stop to examine every little thing that caught her eye. 'Baby Liam,' she said every so often with a smile.

'Yes, I hope we can see him.' For obviously we might not be invited in.

Undaunted, Paula continued at her best toddling pace along the street until we arrived at Laura's house. 'Baby Liam,' she announced, trying to open the gate.

I lifted the latch, opened the gate and we went up the front path. I parked the stroller in the porch and pressed the door-bell. I felt my pulse speed up a notch and my stomach tighten. I had no idea what to expect, and as we waited for the bell to be answered I prepared myself for most eventualities, including the door not being opened or opened and then shut in my face – most eventualities except … Geraldine answering the door in tears.

'Oh. I'm sorry,' I said, embarrassed and completely taken aback. 'I've called at a bad time.'

She looked at me, a tissue pressed to her lips and despair in her eyes. I didn't know what to do. My instinct was to hug and comfort her, but given her previous hostility I didn't think she'd want my comfort, yet I couldn't just walk away.

'Is there anything I can do?' I asked awkwardly. Paula looked at her, also concerned.

Geraldine shook her head and wiped her eyes, but fresh tears formed. Usually so capable, determined, even hard, her vulnerability shocked and deeply saddened me. With a heart-felt sigh she turned from the door and walked down the hall, leaving the front door wide open. I assumed she wanted me to go in, so I helped Paula over the doorstep and then once in the hall I closed the door. The house was quiet – unnaturally quiet considering there was another adult and a baby inside. There was a stale smell of burning as though food had caught fire. Geraldine had disappeared down the hall and into the living room. Still holding Paula's hand, I followed her. Paula had fallen silent, perhaps sensing the atmosphere.

In the living room Geraldine was standing with her back to me, gazing through the glass patio doors. There was no sign of Liam or Laura, but there were a few of his soft toys propped on the sofa and, dropping my hand, Paula went over to them. I crossed the room and stood beside Geraldine. She was staring, unseeing, down the garden.

'Is there anything I can get you?' I asked after a moment. 'A drink of water or a cup of tea?'

She wiped her eyes and shook her head. 'It'll take more than tea to put this lot right, Cathy,' she said.

She'd never used my name before and I sensed a shift in her attitude towards me. 'Do you want to talk about it?' I asked gently, touching her arm.

'It wouldn't do any good,' she said, her eyes filling again.

Then a terrible thought struck me. 'Are Liam and Laura all right? They're not hurt?'

'No. Laura is in bed upstairs and Liam is asleep in his cot in the front room.'

I remained standing beside Geraldine, not sure what to say or do but feeling I should stay. Paula began playing silently with the soft toys as Geraldine and I gazed down the garden, the joy of the summer outside now at odds with the unhappiness inside. Sometimes silence is more empathetic than words, so I stood quietly beside Geraldine, close but not touching. I sensed she wanted to talk, possibly to confide; that was why she'd left the front door open for us to come in. With her guard down she was less hostile to me, but she was finding it difficult, almost impossible, to know where to begin. I'd seen this before in children I'd fostered who were trying to disclose and tell me about something dreadful that had happened and which they'd kept a secret for a long time. They needed to tell but were fearful of the consequences, so I did now what I did then and waited until they found the strength to start.

After some minutes Geraldine took a deep breath and, still looking straight ahead, said faintly, 'We moved Liam's cot downstairs last week. Andy and I are taking it in turns to sleep on the sofa in the front room so we can keep an eye on him. It's no longer safe for him to be upstairs with his mother.'

An icy chill ran down my spine. 'Why not?' I asked gently.

'Because Laura thinks he's the devil's child. My little grandson, the work of the devil! I ask you, Cathy, it would be laughable if she didn't believe it.' Her face crumpled and she wiped away fresh tears.

I'd heard many terrible disclosures in the past from abused children and I knew it was important that I hid my shock and remained outwardly calm and in control to give them the strength they needed to continue.

'Shall we sit down?' I suggested.

She nodded, and we crossed to the sofa, where I moved Paula to one end to make room for us. 'Good girl,' I said quietly to her, for she was looking worried.

Geraldine sat upright on the sofa and stared straight ahead. 'It's worse this time,' she said. 'Far worse than when Laura had Kim. She seems to be losing touch with reality, and she's started threatening me.'

'Laura is threatening you?' I asked, shocked.

'Yes. She doesn't want me here. She resents me, but she

can't manage on her own, and Andy has to work. She rarely sleeps. She's up most of the night and often doesn't know where she is. She's started having weird waking dreams, like she's hallucinating. She wanders around. Last night I smelled burning and found her in the kitchen, making toast. It was two o'clock in the morning and she kept saying she didn't like the toast I made, as I didn't toast it enough. So she kept putting the same slice of toast back into the toaster until eventually it caught fire. I threw it in the sink and she became aggressive. I had to fetch Andy to put her back to bed. I try not to wake him, but she could have burned the house down.' She took a deep breath and wiped her nose. 'I'm sorry.'

'Don't be. It's all right,' I said, touching her arm.

'She's started doing other irrational things and talking a lot of nonsense,' Geraldine continued, keeping her eyes down. 'Liam has a birthmark on his back. It's not very big, but Laura read somewhere that in ancient times they thought birthmarks were put there by the devil, so the child belongs to the devil and does his work. It's ridiculous, obviously, but she seems to believe it. She's wary of him and I'm frightened she could do him harm. You won't tell anyone, will you?' she said, suddenly turning to me.

'No, of course not, but Laura does need help. More than you and Andy can give her. What did the doctor say?'

'She won't go. She hasn't been. Now she's got worse she doesn't think there is anything wrong with her. When she was just depressed she agreed to tell the doctor, but now she refuses to believe there is anything the matter with her. She says we're ganging up on her and making it up.'

'She was going to talk to the doctor at her six-week postnatal check-up. Did that not happen?'

'I don't think so. I took her to the appointment, but she wouldn't let me in when she saw the doctor. I can't force her to tell a doctor. And to be honest I'm worried that the same thing could happen to her as to her mother. She spent over six months in a psychiatric hospital following the birth of Laura.'

'Oh, I see,' I said. 'Laura mentioned her mother had suffered from postnatal depression, but I didn't realize it was that severe.'

'We don't talk about it. Laura's parents didn't have any more children after Laura,' Geraldine said. 'She and Andy weren't going to have another one after Kim. But then it happened and we all hoped for the best. I read somewhere that because a woman has been depressed after having one baby it doesn't mean it will happen again. But it has. And it's getting worse.' Geraldine shrugged with despair. 'I thought we'd be able to cope and that I could help them through like I did last time. I've only done what I thought was right, Cathy, but it seems I've made things worse – far worse.' Her face creased and, holding her head in her hands, she wept openly.

Now I had no hesitation in putting my arm around her shoulders and comforting her. Gone was the stern-faced, domineering mother-in-law who was firmly in charge and knew best no matter what, and in her place was a frail, broken woman, overwhelmed by the crisis unfolding in her family and not knowing what to do.

I lightly rubbed her back and also took hold of Paula's hand, for she was looking at Geraldine as though she, too, might cry. 'It's all right, love,' I said gently to her.

'I'm sorry,' Geraldine said, raising her head. 'I'm upsetting everyone.'

'There's no need to be sorry,' I said. 'You have a right to be upset. You've been carrying a huge burden.'

She wiped her eyes. 'Thank you for taking Kim to school this morning. Was she all right?'

'Yes. She met up with a friend. I stayed until it was time for them to go in.'

'I couldn't leave Laura alone this morning. She was in such a state. And Andy had to go to work.'

'I'm happy to help any time,' I said. 'I can bring Kim home from school this afternoon if you wish. But I think Laura needs to see a doctor. If she won't go to the surgery then perhaps you could arrange a home visit.'

Geraldine shrugged despondently and reached for another tissue. 'I don't know. I'd have to explain to the receptionist what was so urgent.'

'The surgery staff are bound by confidentiality,' I said. 'Or, if you don't want to talk to the receptionist, you could make an appointment to see the doctor yourself.'

'That won't be necessary,' a voice suddenly said.

Geraldine and I started as Laura came into the room, barefoot and in her dressing gown.

'Oh, you're up,' Geraldine said, shocked and immediately standing.

'Yes. Is that allowed?' Laura asked caustically. 'I'll shower and dress later.'

'How are you?' I asked, feeling I had to say something.

'Very well, thank you. So there's absolutely no need for me to see a doctor.'

And my first impression was that Laura did indeed look well and completely normal.

CHAPTER ELEVEN

TRYING TO HURT HIM

'I'm gasping for a coffee. Would you like one?' Laura asked me, lightly running her hand through her hair.

'Yes, please, if you're making one.'

'I'll do it,' Geraldine said. 'And I'll check on Liam.'

With her cloak of efficiency firmly back in place, Geraldine walked swiftly from the room. Laura sighed and sank into one of the armchairs. 'She won't let me do a thing, it's so frustrating. And she fusses over Liam constantly. She's even got him sleeping downstairs with her now.'

'I think she's just trying to help,' I said awkwardly.

We heard Geraldine go into the front room to check on Liam and then into the kitchen.

'Fran sends her best wishes,' I said. 'She said to phone her when you have a chance.'

'Yes, I must phone her. I keep meaning to. But you know how the time flies when you have a baby. The days just seem to disappear. I'll put it at the top of my to-do list,' she added with a smile.

I smiled too and we were silent for some moments, both gazing at Paula who was playing with one of Liam's soft toys. It was difficult to know what to say. I didn't want to make things worse by saying the wrong thing, but I was amazed at how well she looked – not at all what I'd expected after what Geraldine had just told me. Her cheeks had colour and there was no sign of her previous anxiety or depression. She seemed relaxed and, apart from being irritated by Geraldine, happy.

'It's a lovely day outside,' I said, glancing towards the garden.

'Yes. I was thinking I might collect Kim this afternoon and take Liam, if *she* lets me.'

'Good idea,' I said, ignoring her jibe at Geraldine. I felt uncomfortable; I'd just been sympathizing with Geraldine and now I was being asked to take Laura's side against her. Yet Laura's resentment at having her mother-in-law make her decisions was understandable, as she appeared rational and capable of making her own decisions.

'See how you feel later,' I suggested. 'I can bring Kim home if it helps.'

'You can help me by removing the mother-in-law from hell from my house,' Laura said with a sigh, unable to resist another dig. 'She's outstayed her welcome. Do you know, I'm not even allowed to make myself tea and toast when I feel like it? I fancied some last night. Then the next minute she's in the kitchen saying I'm going to burn the house down. Just because I overcooked the toast! I mean, Cathy, tell me who hasn't burned toast? Then she wonders why I snap at her. I get hungry breastfeeding.'

'Yes, I did too,' I said. 'It's important to eat and drink regularly when breastfeeding.'

'She likes to give him a bottle of formula at night,' she said, and glanced at the wall clock. 'He'll be awake soon for his ten o'clock feed. You don't mind if I bring him in here to feed him, do you?'

'No, of course not.'

'*She* does,' Laura said, again lambasting her mother-in-law. 'She doesn't think it's proper to breastfeed in front of others, especially at the meal table. She told me she fed all of hers in the privacy of her bedroom. Well, good for her, I say. Times have changed. I'll see if he is awake.'

Laura stood and began towards the living-room door as Geraldine came in carrying a tray of coffee and biscuits.

'Where are you going?' she asked Laura.

'To see if Liam's awake for his feed,' Laura replied with attitude. 'Is that OK?'

I felt embarrassed. Keeping her eyes down, Geraldine hurriedly set the tray on the occasional table and went down the hall after Laura. I heard their hushed voices coming from the front room in what sounded like a sharp exchange, and then a few moments later Laura returned carrying Liam in her arms. She raised her eyes in exasperation, which I pretended not to see, and she returned to her armchair.

'Baby,' Paula said, pointing.

'Yes. He's going to have his breakfast,' I explained.

'The second one today,' Laura said with a smile, putting him to her breast.

I watched Paula's face. It was a picture. As Laura fed Liam I sipped my coffee and we talked. Paula took a few steps closer to her for a better look. Laura didn't mind. I saw the love that was in Laura's eyes as she gazed at her son suckling contentedly. It was impossible to imagine what Geraldine had told me. Far from being wary of him as the devil's child, Laura held him close, protectively. I'm sure she would have died for him rather than let any harm come to him, as most mothers would. Her tenderness and compassion were obvious, but why would Geraldine have made all that up?

When Liam finished suckling on one side Laura gently turned him round to finish feeding on the other side, all the time smiling down at him, full of love and kindness. Once he'd finished she winded him and then drank her now-lukewarm coffee. We continued talking, about babies, the school and fostering, which so many people are interested in and ask questions about, then I said I should be going, as I had things to do.

'Thanks for stopping by,' Laura said. 'Can you see yourself out?' Liam was fast asleep in her arms.

'Yes, of course. Take care, and I hope to see you in the playground this afternoon.'

'Yes.' Paula clambered down from the sofa and we quietly left the room so we wouldn't wake Liam. As we approached the front door Geraldine suddenly appeared from the front room. I had the feeling she'd been waiting there for me to leave.

'If I'm not in the playground this afternoon, can you bring Kim home, please?' she said quietly.

'Yes, but Laura seems fine now,' I said. 'She's talking about collecting Kim herself, and taking Liam.'

'We'll see about that,' Geraldine said stiffly, all vulnerability gone. 'She may seem fine now, but her moods can change very quickly. It will ease my mind to know that you will collect Kim if I'm not there.'

'Yes, of course,' I said. Although it seemed she'd already ruled out any possibility of Laura collecting Kim.

'Thank you,' Geraldine said flatly as she opened the front door.

I helped Paula out and over the step and the door closed behind us.

With Paula holding one hand, I pushed the stroller with the other and we walked slowly down the garden path and then along the street towards home. I was perplexed, worried and bemused by what had taken place and began to wonder if Geraldine was the one with issues, for I'd seen no evidence of the paranoia she'd described in Laura. Indeed, Laura had acted perfectly rationally, had talked in positive terms and seemed well balanced and the picture of health. True, she resented her mother-in-law big time, but who could blame her if she was trying to control and dominate her? But then again, why would anyone in their right mind make up such dreadful stories about their daughter-in-law? I didn't know who or what to believe.

Once I'd settled Paula for her nap I took out my books, but I didn't get very far with my research or writing. My thoughts kept returning to number 53 and the awful atmosphere that must pervade there, especially when Laura and her mother-in-law were there alone. Did they try to talk civilly to each other, or did they continuously argue or avoid each other by occupying different rooms? What a dreadful atmosphere for Kim to come home to, though perhaps they made an effort when she was there. I wondered what Andy, Laura's husband and Geraldine's son, made of it all. He must have felt as though he was caught between a rock and a hard place, with his mother and wife feuding. Surely he would take the necessary action, either by ensuring that Laura saw a doctor, if what Geraldine had said was true, or if it wasn't then sending his mother home? Laura had needed help when she'd been depressed, but if Geraldine was now trying to create that need then it really fell to Andy to sort out the mess, difficult though it may be.

I was half expecting to see Laura in the playground that afternoon, as she'd seemed confident that she would be collecting Kim, but she didn't arrive. Then, as the Klaxon sounded for the end of school, I realized that Geraldine wasn't in the playground either. I moved closer to the door where the children would come out and watched carefully for Kim. Adrian's class was out first and then Kim's. When she emerged I went over to her.

'Your gran asked me to collect you,' I said.

'Is Mum all right?' Kim asked, immediately concerned.

'Yes. I saw her and your brother this morning,' I said with a cheery smile. It was all I could say, as clearly I didn't know what had happened in the interim.

On the walk back home Kim baby-talked to Paula, which I guessed she did to her brother. It was sweet and Paula loved the attention. Then Kim told us about her class's project on the Vikings. Their teacher had asked them all to take in as many cardboard boxes as they could the next day, as they were going to make a big model of a Viking boat, big enough for all the class to sit in and row.

'That sounds great,' I said. 'How exciting.' Children's learning is so much fun now.

'I'll have to go to the shop if we haven't got any boxes big enough,' Kim said thoughtfully.

'Do you still go shopping for your mum sometimes?' I asked.

'Not really. Gran's there now.'

I would have liked to hear Kim's views on what was going on at home, but it wasn't appropriate for me to question her. We continued towards her house with Adrian joining in the talk about Viking boat building and Paula trying her best to say 'Vi-King', making it sound like a person.

I intended to walk Kim right up to her front door, but Geraldine must have been watching out for us, for as we stopped at her garden gate the front door opened and Geraldine appeared. Kim said goodbye to us and ran up the path. Geraldine gave a perfunctory wave of thanks and as soon as Kim was inside she closed the door, so I had no idea how Laura was.

We continued home and the evening passed as most school nights do, with the children playing while I made dinner, followed by Adrian's homework, some television and then the children's bath and bedtime routines. But Laura wasn't far from my thoughts, and I wondered how their evening was progressing. That night, as Adrian and I hummed Brahms's 'Lullaby', my thoughts turned to Shelley and Darrel. I hoped she'd let me know how her visit to her old foster carer, Carol, had gone, and whether she'd plucked up the courage to audition for the choir. But even if I never heard from her again I would still remember them both, as I was sure Adrian would.

I was in bed by ten-thirty and asleep before eleven, but then I was jolted wide awake by the telephone ringing. I grabbed the handset from my bedside cabinet with my heart thumping loudly and my mouth going dry, convinced a tragedy had befallen a loved one. It was the only reason I could think of for someone calling at this time, and with my husband, John, working abroad, the chances of it being bad news seemed dramatically increased.

'Yes? Hello?' I said, my voice shaking.

'Cathy? Is that you?'

'Laura?'

'Yes, you sound different. Hope you don't mind, but I thought I'd phone you for a chat.'

I looked at my bedside clock; it was 11.40. I heaved myself up the pillow and tried to calm my racing heart.

'You don't mind me calling, do you?' Laura asked.

'No. It's just rather late. I was asleep.'

'I'm sorry. I didn't realize the time. Shall I call you back another time?'

There didn't seem much point now that I was awake. 'It's OK. Are you all right?'

'Yes, I'm fine. It was nice of you to drop by today. I enjoyed your visit. I haven't seen many people recently because I felt so down, but now I'm better I'll catch up. I've just finished talking to Fran. We were on the phone for ages.' She gave a small laugh.

'That's good,' I said. I hoped Fran was a night owl.

'I told her I'd be in the playground tomorrow.'

'Great, although I thought I might see you there today.'

'I intended to go, but then I nodded off on the sofa and Geraldine didn't like to wake me or just slip out. You know how she fusses. Thanks for bringing Kim home.'

'You're welcome. Did she find some cardboard boxes for her class's Viking project?'

Laura laughed. 'Yes, lots. We had loads in the loft from when we moved. Andy went up there and got them down when he came home from work. I won't go in the loft – there are spiders up there and I hate spiders.'

'Yes, so do I.'

Our conversation continued – a perfectly normal chat between friends, if it hadn't been so late. Laura did most of the talking, and I saw the clock ticking off the minutes to midnight. Then, at 12.15 a.m., I said, 'I'm going to have to go now, Laura, and get some sleep. Why don't you come to me tomorrow for a coffee after you've taken Kim to school?'

'Yes, that would be lovely, thank you. I'll let you sleep now. Sorry to have woken you. See you tomorrow.'

We said goodbye and I hung up. Yes, a perfectly normal conversation apart from the timing. No one with young children telephones a friend just for a chat in the middle of the night, but I assumed it was as Laura had said – that she'd lost track of time while talking to Fran. Thankfully the phone ringing hadn't woken Adrian or Paula, but it took me a while to get back off to sleep.

As Laura was planning to take Kim to school the following morning I kept a lookout for her as we walked down our street. Parents with children who attended the local school left home more or less at the same time, so we often saw others walking the same route. That morning the children in Kim's class were all carrying cardboard boxes, but there was no sign of Kim with her mother, either ahead of or behind us. They weren't in the playground either, but Fran was and she came towards me with a cardboard box under each arm. Her daughter was carrying another two boxes. 'Did Laura telephone you late last night?' Fran asked me.

'Yes.'

'Oh dear. I am sorry. She told me she was planning on phoning you when we'd finished and I tried to persuade her not to. It was so late.'

'Don't worry. It was nice to hear from her, although it was late.'

'It must have been. We were about to get into bed when she phoned me and we were talking for ages. My hubby wasn't amused, although I explained I hadn't heard from her in a long while. Laura said she'd been depressed but was all right now. I invited her for coffee this morning.'

'So did I,' I said, smiling, and again looking around for any sign of Laura. 'I wonder where she is.' There were others arriving with cardboard boxes of all sizes. Some of the children were carrying them on their backs like tortoise shells. It was comical.

'She might have slept in,' Fran said, also glancing around. 'Laura told me she can't sleep at night, and then sleeps in late or nods off during the day. Oh look, there's her mother-in-law with Kim and the baby. So Laura hasn't come. I'll go over and see how she is.'

I turned as Fran went over and saw Geraldine with Kim pushing the pram. She was carrying a couple of cardboard boxes and had another one balanced on the pram. Geraldine was straight-faced as usual and, avoiding eye contact, kept her gaze ahead. I saw Fran say something to Geraldine and she responded with a curt nod and what looked like a very short reply. Fran then went over to speak to another mother, so I guessed she hadn't learned much. The Klaxon sounded and I kissed Adrian goodbye. I saw Geraldine with the pram, speeding towards the exit, but I didn't try to catch up. Fran looked at me and shrugged. 'Not sure,' she said as we left the playground. Then we went our separate ways.

I didn't knock at number 53 on the way home. There was no reason to, and to do so would have crossed the line between good neighbourliness and intrusiveness. But of course I speculated on what exactly was going on.

Laura didn't come for coffee, and I wasn't surprised. Something told me that if she wasn't up to taking Kim to school then she wouldn't be coming to me. Maybe she'd gone to Fran's instead, but I doubted it.

Laura wasn't in the playground that afternoon either, and it was only after the children had come out of the building that I realized with a stab of horror that Geraldine wasn't there either. Kim was waiting with her teacher as they were told to do if a parent or carer didn't arrive to collect them. Grabbing Paula's hand, and with Adrian in tow, I shot over to them.

'I'm so sorry,' I said to her teacher. 'I'm taking Kim home.'

'No problem,' she said, and Kim came with me.

But there *was* a problem. I knew then that I needed to clarify the arrangement I had with Geraldine for collecting Kim. I would ask her to telephone me when she wanted me to collect her. If you do something every day it becomes part of your routine, or if you're asked to do something specifically it's at the forefront of your mind. But this loose, *ad hoc* arrangement where I was expected to collect Kim if Geraldine (or Laura) wasn't in the playground could easily lead to me forgetting Kim, as I'd just shown. Fortunately no harm had been done on this occasion.

I didn't get the chance to speak to Geraldine when I saw Kim home that afternoon, as she opened and closed the front door just long enough to let Kim in. I decided I would either catch her in the playground the following morning or, if not, I'd knock on their door on the way home when I just had Paula with me. I would tell Geraldine that I was more than happy to take Kim to school and bring her home, but that I'd appreciate it if she could telephone me before I left to let me know. It seemed a reasonable request.

That night I'd just got into bed when the telephone rang. It was 10.45 – earlier than the previous night's call, so I wasn't asleep, but it was still late for a chat. I knew straight away there was something wrong.

'Cathy,' Laura said in a whisper. 'I need your help. Can you come? Geraldine is downstairs with Liam and she's trying to hurt him.'

CHAPTER TWELVE

VERY SERIOUS

'I can't tell Andy because he's on his mother's side,' Laura whispered. 'But you're my friend. You understand, don't you? You must come here and help me.'

As a foster carer I'd faced many unusual and difficult situations, sometimes having to make a snap decision on whether someone was telling the truth, but nothing had prepared me for this, in either my fostering experience or my personal life.

'Why do you think Geraldine is trying to harm Liam?' I asked, my thoughts whizzing and my senses on full alert.

'Why?' asked Laura, raising her voice above a whisper. 'I don't know. But she's barricaded herself in the front room with Liam and won't let me in.'

'But how do you know she's harming him?' I asked.

'I can hear him crying. And she won't let me in to see him. I'm in the hall outside the front room. I'm going to wait here until she comes out and then I'll rush in. Do you think I should phone the police?'

If what Laura thought was true, the short answer was yes. If a child is in immediate danger then the police needed to be called as an emergency, but I wasn't convinced Liam was in danger. 'Where's Andy?' I asked.

'Upstairs. Settling Kim,' Laura said. 'All the shouting and screaming has woken her. I'm sorry I've upset her, but I have to protect my baby.'

'Is Liam crying now?' I asked. For Laura had said she was outside the front room but I couldn't hear him crying.

There was a pause when I guessed she was listening out for him, then she screamed: 'No! Oh my god! I can't hear him. He's dead!'

I heard the phone clunk as she either dropped or threw it down, but the line was still open. I heard her shouting and banging frantically on what I assumed was the front-room door. 'Let me in, you evil witch! What have you done to my son?' Then there was nothing to be heard but her hysterical screaming.

I sat on the edge of my bed, rigid with fear. I wondered if I should call the police, but then I heard a man's voice, presumably Andy's, take control.

'That's enough, Laura,' he said firmly. 'Liam is fine. I'm taking you back to bed now.'

The shouting, screaming and banging on the door suddenly stopped and was replaced by the sound of Laura whimpering like a wounded animal. It was heartbreaking to hear, but she must have allowed Andy to take her upstairs and see her to bed, for the whimpering faded into the distance and then there was silence. I kept the phone pressed to my ear, my knuckles white from gripping it so tightly. It must have been ten minutes before I heard another sound – Andy's voice close by, asking, 'Mum, are you and Liam all right? You can come out now. Laura's calmer. I've put her to bed.'

I heard the door to the front room open and then Geraldine's trembling, desperate voice. 'Oh, son, what are we going to do? This can't go on.'

There was no reply, but Andy must have spotted that the telephone was out of its cradle, for I heard him say, 'Who was Laura talking to, Mum? Do you know?'

Geraldine replied 'No.'

There was a small noise as the phone was picked up and then Andy's voice came on the line. 'Hello. Is there anyone there?' he asked tentatively.

I was very tempted to just hang up.

'My name is Cathy,' I said. 'I'm a friend of Laura's. I live further up the street.'

'Jesus!' he exclaimed. Then to Geraldine, 'It's a friend of Laura's – Cathy?'

I couldn't hear what she said, but a moment later Andy came back on the line, his voice tight and controlling. 'I don't know what Laura has told you, but whatever it was just forget it, please. She's very upset tonight and not herself.'

That was the biggest understatement I'd heard in a long while, I thought, but I knew from what I'd just overheard that I couldn't stand impotently by any longer.

'I'm sorry, I can't just forget it,' I said. 'I'm assuming that your mother wasn't harming Liam as Laura said, in which case Laura needs help.'

'I'm aware of that,' he said defensively. 'That's why my mother has moved in with us.'

'I think Laura needs more help than you and your mother can give her,' I said as gently as I could.

There was silence, and then I heard him sigh resignedly. 'I know. You're right. She attacked my mother tonight because she thought she was harming Liam. Mum had to shut herself in the front room. It's a nightmare. I'll take the morning off work tomorrow and make sure she sees a doctor.'

'I think that's for the best. If you need help taking Kim to school or collecting her, or someone to look after Liam, let me know. I'm a registered foster carer and I have two children of my own. My son and your daughter go to the same school.'

'Thank you. Do we have your telephone number?' he asked more conciliatorily.

'Laura does. Shall I give it to you too?'

'Yes, please. Let me get a pen.' Then, 'Thanks, go ahead.'

I gave him my telephone number.

'Thank you,' he said, all trace of resentment now gone. 'I'm sorry you've had to hear all this and be drawn into it.' So I guessed he didn't know of my previous involvement.

'Take care,' I said. 'Give Laura my best wishes. And phone if you need me.'

'I will.'

We said goodnight and I replaced the receiver. My heart was racing and I felt queasy from shock, but at least I'd said what I had to. I got back into bed, but I knew I couldn't sleep. I sat upright, propped up on my pillow, and by the small light coming from the street lamp I stared across the bedroom as my thoughts somersaulted. I took some relief from the fact that Andy was now going to make sure Laura saw a doctor the following day. I sincerely hoped he meant it and would keep his word. Cleary he and his mother had been complicit in trying to deal with Laura's illness – for that was how I now saw it – and had kept it to themselves long after they should have sought professional help. Andy said that Laura had attacked Geraldine, which was bad enough, but if she'd been holding the baby at the time the outcome could have been much, much worse. There was also Geraldine's concern that Laura could intentionally harm Liam, which was the reason she was sleeping with him downstairs and didn't leave him alone with her. I knew the symptoms of postnatal depression included feeling low and experiencing mood swings, anxiety and irritability, but did they include wanting to harm others? I didn't think so.

It was after midnight by the time I fell asleep, and then I was wide awake again at five o'clock, thinking and worrying about Laura and her family. Perhaps it was because of the nature of fostering that I was getting involved, although I doubted that many would have walked away.

I didn't receive a telephone call that morning to take Kim to school, so I continued our routine as normal. Geraldine arrived in the playground with Kim just before the Klaxon sounded. I assumed Andy was with Laura and Liam. She threw me a cursory glance, but that was all. She then rushed off as soon as Kim had gone into school. But from that brief glimpse I'd had of her I could see she was tired and tense, and seemed to have aged in the last week. Little wonder, I thought, with all that she had to cope with. She may not have been the warmest person and clearly thought she knew best, but without doubt she was acting in what she believed was her family's best interests.

That afternoon after lunch I put Paula in the stroller and took her to our local library, or 'lie-rabry' as Paula called it. I had some books I wanted to return, but I also wanted to see if they had any books on postnatal depression. I felt I needed to know more: what the symptoms were and the treatment. Inside the library I let Paula out of her stroller and then parked it in the foyer with the other strollers. She held my hand as I began browsing the shelves, trying to work out where the books I wanted were. The Dewey classification system libraries use in England for arranging books on shelves has always flummoxed me, but eventually I found two books in the social sciences section that looked hopeful. I carried them over to the area for young children and sat on one of the bean bags, while Paula toddled around looking at the brightly coloured and enticing early-years books displayed on the low-level stands.

The first book I opened was too theoretical for what I wanted, with lots of references to postgraduate research. The second was more user-friendly, and it wasn't long before I'd found what I wanted: a list of the symptoms of postnatal depression, also known as postpartum depression. I was surprised by the length of the list, but as the author (a doctor) pointed out, the majority of women only experienced a few of the symptoms. Apart from the ones I already knew about – feeling very sad, crying easily, lethargy, inability to cope, anxiety and low self-esteem – others included feelings of hopelessness and despair, suicidal thoughts, guilt, insomnia, flashbacks, fixating on bad things that have happened in the past, worrying excessively about the baby, panic attacks, problems interacting with others and strange thoughts. The author said that if a new mother experienced three or more of these symptoms or they were particularly acute then she should seek medical help, as it was likely she was suffering from postnatal depression.

The author distinguished between the 'baby blues' and postnatal depression. The baby blues were far less severe, with mothers feeling low and tired for a few weeks after the birth but then recovering, usually of their own accord. The treatment for postnatal depression was usually a course of anti-depressants and sometimes counselling or therapy.

Reassuringly, with treatment, recovery was usually quick, although the longer the condition was left untreated the longer it took, which wasn't such good news if this was what Laura had. Yet while the symptoms listed had included strange thoughts, there was no mention of what Laura was now experiencing – believing the baby had the mark of the devil and that her mother-in-law was harming him, or being physically aggressive.

Then I turned the page and began to read the next section, headed 'Postpartum Psychosis', and I had a cold, sinking feeling. Although postpartum or postnatal psychosis is a relatively rare condition, many of the symptoms fitted Laura: strange beliefs, delusions, paranoia, suspiciousness, hallucinations, as well as some of those also found in postnatal depression, such as insomnia, anxiety and despair. The onus again lay on seeking medical help early, and treatment usually included anti-psychotic drugs, therapy and sometimes admission to hospital if the patient was critical. I read that a woman's chances of developing the condition were increased if her mother had suffered from it after giving birth, or the woman had developed it after a previous birth. Both of which applied to Laura. The author wrote that if there was a history of postpartum psychosis then the woman should be carefully monitored and supported throughout her pregnancy and after the birth. If she was, the outcome was very good, with the majority of women not developing the condition. But of course Laura hadn't been monitored, because her doctor hadn't been told of the problems she'd experienced after the birth of Kim. I guessed her doctor hadn't been told that her mother had spent time in a psychiatric hospital after having Laura either. I realized then that in keeping it to themselves and trying to deal with it in the family, Geraldine and Andy had inadvertently stopped Laura from receiving the help she desperately needed and had probably worsened her condition.

I continued reading until Paula had tired of amusing herself. I returned the books to the shelves and helped her pick some storybooks to check out and take home. I could have checked out the book I'd been reading, but I felt I'd read enough about postnatal depression and psychosis. And while I knew it was dangerous for people without medical training to diagnose (and I would never have voiced my thoughts to anyone, especially Laura and her family), as I left the library and began the walk home, deep in thought, I was almost certain that Laura was suffering from postnatal psychosis, and it was very serious indeed.

When I returned home I wasn't wholly surprised, therefore, to hear Andy's message on the answerphone. 'Cathy, it's Andy, Laura's husband. We're all at the hospital.' His voice was tight and tense. 'I may need to ask you to collect Kim from school today. I'll phone you in about an hour when I know for certain. Thank you.' It was timed half an hour previously. I didn't know if they'd been to the doctor's first or had gone straight to the hospital. An anxious thirty minutes followed, and then fifteen minutes before I had to leave to collect Adrian the phone rang again.

'Cathy, it's Andy. Did you get my message?'

'Yes. How is Laura?'

'Not good. They've sedated her.' His voice caught. 'She's been admitted to St Mary's [our local hospital] for the time being, but they're trying to find a place in a hospital with a mother-and-baby unit so she can keep Liam with her. I don't know how long this is going to take and I can't leave Mum here to deal with this alone. Can I ask you to collect Kim from school, please, and then take her back to your house for a couple of hours? I'll be with you as soon as I can. Is that possible?'

'Yes, of course. I'll give Kim dinner. She can stay the night if necessary. Don't worry.'

'Thank you. Please tell her that her mum is being well looked after and I'll see her soon. The poor kid has been through so much.' His voice broke.

'I'll explain and reassure her,' I said. 'Try not to worry.'

'It's a nightmare.'

'But Laura is getting the help she needs now,' I said, trying to reassure him.

'Yes, I hope so.' We said a quick goodbye and I replaced the receiver.

Five minutes later I locked the front door and left for school in plenty of time. When Kim came out of school I was waiting for her and explained what her father had said. Her face clouded at the thought of her mother being in hospital, but then she brightened a little when I reassured her that her mother was being well looked after and she could play with Adrian and Paula, and have ice cream for pudding. Although Andy and Geraldine would have done their best to protect Kim from all the upset of Laura's illness, as Andy said she had been through a lot, for what affects one member of a family obviously impacts on the rest – adults and children.

Once home, I made a cold drink and a small snack for us all, which we had in the garden, and then I took the toys out of the shed. I stayed in the garden playing with the children until it was time for me to go indoors and make dinner. I asked Adrian and Kim to keep an eye on Paula, although I could see them through the kitchen window as I worked. Kim popped in once to ask if her daddy had phoned yet and I told her I'd let her know as soon as he did. Once the meal was ready I brought the children indoors. Quiche, new potatoes and sweetcorn, followed by tinned fruit and the promised ice cream, with a choice of chocolate or strawberry topping. Adrian had both.

'Yuck,' Kim laughed as Adrian stirred the deep red and brown sauces together into the melting ice cream.

'Yummy,' he retaliated, smacking his lips.

Paula looked on bemused, not really sure what was funny but laughing anyway.

After dinner storm clouds closed in and we just had time to put the toys in the shed before the first drops of rain splattered large on the patio. A minute later it was pouring down and the sky had darkened so much that I had to switch on the lights. I suggested we could play a game of cards or a board game, but Adrian and Kim wanted to watch a Walt Disney film and chose one from our collection. I'd already mentioned to Kim that there was a chance she might be staying the night but that her daddy would telephone and let us know for certain. As the time ticked by her staying the night seemed increasingly likely, but then just before seven o'clock Andy telephoned.

'I'm just about to leave the hospital. I'll be with you in half an hour.'

'OK, I'll tell Kim. Do you know which house I live at?' I thought to ask.

'No, sorry, I'm not thinking straight.'

I gave him my house number.

'Thanks. Tell Kim I'll see her soon.'

I returned the phone to its cradle and told Kim what her father had said, and she met the news with a mixture of relief and disappointment, for most children like a sleepover. Also, I think being away from the very difficult and upsetting atmosphere that must have prevailed at home in recent months had given her some light relief.

'You can come and stay overnight another time,' I said.

'Yes, when Mummy is better,' she said, and returned to watching the rest of the film.

It was really Paula's bedtime now, and I knew it would be too late if I left putting her to bed until after Andy had collected Kim, so I told Paula it was time for bed and to say goodnight. She wasn't pleased. 'No!' she said, screwing up her face, wanting to stay with Adrian and Kim. But she was tired – she'd had a busy day with going to the library as well – and I knew that, like most children, she'd become fractious if she grew overtired.

'Say goodnight,' I said a little more firmly. Taking her hand, I led her first to Adrian and then Kim, who both said goodnight and kissed her.

'Night,' she said, giving in to a yawn.

We went upstairs and she yawned again as I washed and changed her ready for bed, then she fell asleep almost immediately. I'd just returned downstairs when the doorbell rang. It was Andy.

'Cathy?' he asked, for we hadn't actually met.

'Yes, come in.'

'What a day,' he sighed, stepping in. He looked drawn and tired and was wearing a suit, so I guessed he'd originally planned to go to work after he'd taken Laura to the doctor, but clearly that hadn't happened.

Kim heard his voice and rushed into the hall. 'Daddy, Daddy!' she cried and ran into his arms. 'Where's Mummy?'

'She's at the hospital,' Andy said. 'Having a sleep now. The doctors and nurses are looking after her, so don't you worry.' He hugged her hard.

'Where's Liam?' she asked.

'With your gran. She's taken him home. I need to talk to Cathy and then we'll go home too.'

Clearly Andy wanted to talk away from the children. 'Kim, you finish watching the film with Adrian while I speak to your daddy,' I said. I led the way down the hall and into the living room where Andy said hello to Adrian. Kim returned to sit beside Adrian on the sofa.

'Would you like a tea or coffee?' I now asked Andy, showing him through to the kitchen-cum-diner.

'Coffee, please.'

He sat, or rather collapsed, into one of the chairs at the table, while I went into the kitchen and filled the kettle.

'What a day,' he said again with a heartfelt sigh, running his fingers through his hair. 'Thanks for looking after Kim. I might need your help again tomorrow if that's all right.'

'Saturday? Yes. I haven't any plans.'

He sat back in the chair and stretched out his legs as though forcing himself to relax. 'There's been so much going on,' he said. 'I'll try to explain, although from what Mum has told me I think you know some of it.'

'I know Laura hasn't been well,' I said, glancing at him.

He nodded. 'But we didn't realize how ill she was. We should never have let it go on for so long, I know that now. We should have got help sooner instead of letting it get to crisis point. Mum and I were up most of last night with Laura and I telephoned the doctor first thing this morning. He agreed to see Laura as an emergency, but then she wouldn't leave Liam with Mum, so we all went. She was still acting odd in the surgery, saying ridiculous things and shouting and crying. When the doctor saw her he said she needed to see a psychiatrist and to go straight to hospital. We had to wait ages there and Laura got more and more confused and agitated. She was convinced everyone was out to get her, and we couldn't calm her. She began screaming and then locked herself in the toilets with Liam. They had to use the emergency key to unlock the door and get her out. I wanted Mum to take Liam home, but Laura clung to him and started shouting that Mum was trying to steal her baby. Then the psychiatrist came. He examined her and has made an initial diagnosis. I'm sure you won't have heard of it – I hadn't. It's called post-partum psychosis.'

I set the two cups of coffee on the table and sat opposite Andy.

'It's very serious then?'

'Yes, very.'

CHAPTER THIRTEEN

WORRY

'The psychiatrist wanted to know Laura's medical history,' Andy continued, resting his elbows on the table for support. 'I was honest and told him she'd suffered from depression after the birth of Kim. He questioned me as to why she hadn't received medical help back then, and why we'd left it so long before going to the doctor's now. He was very concerned and seemed to blame me. I guess I am to blame. I just let Mum get on with it. She helped Laura after she'd had Kim, so I assumed it would be OK now.' He sighed. 'He asked about Laura's mother too, and I told him she'd once had a mental breakdown many years ago – after having Laura. I didn't realize its significance until today. It wasn't something we ever talked about.' He sighed again and paused to drink his coffee.

He was a tall man with broad shoulders that were now hunched forward under the burden of worry. I could see the likeness to his mother, and I thought he was probably used to being in control too, but he now looked a broken man.

'It seems that a lot of this could have been avoided if we'd been honest with the doctor from the start,' he said, returning his cup to the saucer, 'instead of trying to hide it and deal with it ourselves. I should have been more involved and insisted Laura saw the doctor earlier, rather than going off to work each day and leaving Mum to deal with it.' He sighed again and ran his hand absently through his hair, beating himself up over what should have been.

'So Laura is staying in St Mary's for now?' I asked.

'Just for tonight. She's in the psychiatric wing, but they're going to try to move her tomorrow. St Mary's doesn't have the facilities for a baby to stay, that's why Mum and I had to bring Liam home. Laura fed him before we left. We'll go back first thing in the morning. He's used to having formula sometimes, so that shouldn't be too much of a problem.'

'And Laura didn't mind you bringing Liam home without her?' I asked, mindful that Andy had said she wouldn't be separated from him.

'She was asleep by the time we left, sedated. We didn't have a choice. He couldn't stay there.'

I nodded and drank some of my coffee.

'The psychiatrist explained that a few hospitals have specialist mother-and-baby units for women suffering from this type of condition,' Andy continued. 'But the admission has to be planned. You can't just turn up. He's making a referral today, so hopefully she can go tomorrow. It's an hour's drive away, but he's assured us that it's the best place for Laura to receive the specialist help she needs. As I say, it would probably never have reached this point if we'd got Laura help earlier. She could have stayed at home with medication and therapy.' He drained his coffee and stared past me, deep in thought.

'They'll soon have her better,' I offered. 'Tell me how I can help.'

He returned his gaze to me. 'Yes. Mum and I will go to St Mary's with Liam tomorrow, as soon as we've fed and changed him. We've been told not to get there before nine o'clock and to take a bag of clothes and essentials for Liam and whatever Laura needs. I'll have to make a list. We don't know what time she'll be transferred and I don't want Kim there hanging around all day. Also I don't want her seeing her mum if she's still very disturbed. It's frightening. So could you look after Kim from about eight-thirty tomorrow morning? I know it's asking a lot.'

'Of course. No problem.'

'Thank you. Assuming Laura is calmer, I'll take Kim to visit her on Sunday at the mother-and-baby unit. Kim is going to miss Liam and her mum, but there's no other way round it.'

'She's a sensible girl,' I said. 'She'll understand once you've explained to her why her mother is there, and that you'll be taking her to see her regularly. Do you know how long Laura will be kept in?'

He shook his head. 'We should know more in a few days when a full assessment has been made. Which reminds me, I need to phone Laura's mother as soon as I go home to tell her what's happened.'

'She doesn't know?'

'No. She lives out of the area and works full-time. She saw Liam when he was a few days old but hasn't seen him since. Laura has spoken to her on the phone, but I don't think she's told her how bad she's been feeling. And recently we've been stopping her from phoning when she was distraught and saying ridiculous things.' He sighed again. 'Thanks, Cathy. I'd best be off now.' He drained the last of his coffee and stood.

We went into the living room where the film had finished and Adrian was proudly showing Kim his toy car transporter complete with cars. She was looking suitably impressed.

'Come on, love, time to go home,' Andy said to her.

She stood and went over to her father and, tucking her arm through his, rested her head against him. Adrian came with us to the front door to see them out. The evening had grown dark early as fresh storm clouds rolled in. 'See you tomorrow,' I said. 'Take care.'

We watched them go down the path and then I closed the front door as the first clap of thunder sounded in the distance.

That night Adrian and I had to hum Brahms's 'Lullaby' a little louder over the noise of the storm, and I thought of Laura, alone in her hospital bed, and prayed she would get better very quickly.

I was up and dressed the following morning earlier than usual for the weekend and ready for Kim's arrival. The storm had passed in the night and the sky was clear, promising a fine day. Adrian and Paula were up too but still in their pyjamas when Andy arrived with Kim. Geraldine stayed with Liam in the car, parked outside, but looked in my direction with an almost friendly nod. I smiled.

'I won't come in,' Andy said. 'Kim understands that we need to get to the hospital as soon as possible. She's brought some of her favourite toys and books.'

'That's great,' I said, smiling at Kim. She came in with a small rucksack on her back, looking very sad. I touched her shoulder reassuringly.

'She didn't want any breakfast,' Andy said.

'Don't worry. I'll fix her something when she's ready.'

'I've no idea what time we'll be back, but I'll phone you with an update as soon as I know something.'

'OK. I might take them to the park later if the weather holds, so leave a message on the answerphone if I'm out.'

'Will do. Bye then, love,' he said to Kim. 'Give me a kiss.'

He bent down and Kim wrapped her arms tightly around his neck and smothered his face in kisses. He kissed her cheek and then gently unwrapped her arms from his neck and straightened. 'Be good for Cathy,' he said.

'See you later,' I said, taking Kim's hand. I could see she was close to tears.

I didn't prolong their goodbye but closed the door as soon as he'd returned down the path to his car.

'It's lovely to have you with us for the day,' I said positively to Kim with a cheerful smile. 'Are you going to show us some of your toys? Then I'll make you something to eat. We haven't had our breakfast yet.'

Kim gave a small, brave nod and slipped the rucksack from her shoulder, but then I saw her bottom lip tremble and her tears began to fall. 'I want my mummy,' she sobbed.

'Oh, love,' I said, putting my arm around her. 'Don't cry. The doctors and nurses are looking after your mummy. There's no need to worry.' But seeing a child upset is heartbreaking, and I felt my own eyes fill. Adrian and Paula were looking sad too.

'Let's go and have a seat in the living room,' I said, and I took the three of them through. I sat Kim on the sofa beside me. Adrian and Paula stood a little in front of us, looking at her.

'I know I have to be brave for my daddy,' Kim said through her tears. 'But I can't.' I swallowed hard as Adrian's eyes misted and Paula rubbed her eyes.

'You two find something to do until Kim is better,' I said to them. I didn't think watching her was doing them or Kim any good. They sat on the floor by the toy box.

'Why can't Mummy and Liam come home?' Kim asked with a sob. 'I miss Mummy.'

'Of course you do, love.' I was sure her father would have explained the situation, but clearly Kim needed more reassurance. 'Your mummy isn't well at present,' I said gently, taking her hand in mine. 'She's staying in hospital so the doctors can make her better.'

'What's wrong with Mummy? Daddy said she was ill, but that you couldn't see she was ill because it was inside. Not like if you get a rash or have a cold. You can see those.'

'That's right,' I said. 'Mummy has an illness that has made her very unhappy. Perhaps you've seen her crying and staying in bed?'

Kim nodded. 'And she said some horrible things to Daddy, Gran and me. Daddy said that was because she was unwell.'

'Yes, that's right. So Mummy is staying in hospital while the doctors make her better. They'll give her some medicine and then when she comes home she'll be your old mummy again.' Adrian glanced over and I threw him a reassuring smile.

'Is it Liam's fault Mummy is ill?' Kim suddenly asked, wiping her eyes on her hand. I passed her a tissue. I guessed she'd either made this connection from something she'd overheard, or her father had tried to explain her mother's illness, which was very difficult for a child to understand.

'No, it's not Liam's fault,' I said. 'When a woman has a baby lots of changes happen inside her body. They are caused by hormones, and sometimes some women have a bad reaction to all the hormones and changes. It's no one's fault. It's just something that happens, and once the doctors know they can put it right.'

'Like when I eat strawberries, I come up in a rash?' Kim asked, brightening a little.

I smiled. 'Yes, it is a bit like that. You had a reaction to eating strawberries.'

'Mummy says I mustn't eat strawberries, but Gran forgot and gave me some. I don't think Mummy should have any more babies if it makes her ill.'

'Well, if your mummy does have another baby the doctors will know what to do next time to stop her from being ill,' I said. 'It's nothing for you to worry about. Your daddy and gran are making sure your mummy is well looked after and has all the help she needs.'

'I heard Daddy and Gran talking last night,' Kim said, her brow furrowing. 'They thought I was asleep. I think they were arguing, because Daddy's voice sounded angry. He told Gran she should have told him sooner about the things Mummy was saying and doing. You know, the angry and frightening things she said sometimes. But I don't want Daddy telling off Gran. I don't like it.'

'Your daddy was very worried last night, and tired,' I said. 'Sometimes when people are worried and tired they can say things they don't really mean, and they are sorry afterwards. Your daddy and gran are friends this morning, aren't they?' She nodded. 'So don't worry. Is there anything else you want to ask me?'

'I hope Mummy and Liam can come home soon.'

'I think it will take a while,' I said. 'The doctors will want to make sure your mummy is completely better, but your daddy is hoping to take you to see her and Liam tomorrow.'

She nodded and managed a small smile. 'I know. He told me that.'

'Good girl.' I took a fresh tissue and wiped away the last of her tears. 'Are you ready for some breakfast now? I'm going to make a cooked breakfast.'

'I'm not really hungry,' she said.

'What about some cereal or toast or a piece of fruit?' She shook her head. 'I think you need something.'

'Can I have a banana, please?' she said quietly.

'Of course. And perhaps you'll have something else when it's ready. Now, you could show Adrian and Paula the toys and books you've brought with you while I make breakfast.'

Kim picked up her rucksack and opened it as Adrian and Paula moved closer for a better look. I left the three of them sitting in a circle on the floor as Kim proudly showed them a new book and a game of Guess Who? In the kitchen it wasn't long before Toscha was purring around my legs as the enticing smell of bacon rose from the grill. I cooked extra in case Kim changed her mind and wanted some, and I also slipped a rasher into Toscha's bowl. I scrambled eggs, lightly fried some sliced tomatoes and popped some bread in the toaster. Once it was all ready I called everyone to the table and told Kim there was extra if she wanted some, but she just had a banana and a drink of milk. She was quiet at the table but did say that her daddy liked a cooked breakfast at the weekend too when he had time to eat it.

After breakfast the children played first in the house and then in the garden. I took out drinks and a small snack of cheese and biscuits mid-morning, and Kim had some. She asked a couple of times during the morning if her daddy had telephoned and I said I thought it was too soon, but that we could hear the telephone ring from the garden. Although Kim hadn't eaten much breakfast, she ate a reasonable lunch of cheese pasta and salad, and after lunch I suggested we go to our local park. Kim knew the park from living in the same street; her parents took her there. It was about a fifteen-minute walk. Just before we left – at a little before two o'clock – Andy telephoned.

'The paperwork for the transfer has only just been completed,' he said. 'So we'll be leaving St Mary's shortly to go to the mother-and-baby unit. I'll phone you once Laura is settled and before we leave to come home. Can I speak to Kim, please?'

'Yes, of course.'

I passed the handset to her and she listened carefully while her daddy spoke. He must have told her something about her mother, for she asked, 'Can I speak to her?' She was silent again and then replied, 'Tell Mummy and Liam I love them.' She then said goodbye, replaced the handset in its cradle and looked at me with a small smile. 'Mummy told Daddy to tell me she loves me loads. And I'm definitely going to see her tomorrow.'

'That's fantastic,' I said. I guessed Laura was less distraught now or Andy wouldn't have confirmed the visit.

Our trip to the park was a success. Adrian and Kim played on all the apparatus while I took Paula into the adjacent toddler section, which had smaller swings, a low seesaw and rocking horses. I bought us all a drink, and ice creams for the children, from the park café, and it was about four o'clock when we started for home. The children were pleasantly tired from playing in the park and, once home, collapsed on the sofa. I let them watch some television while I fed Toscha and made our dinner. I didn't know what time Andy and Geraldine would be returning to collect Kim, so I was carrying on my day as usual.

It was a little after six o'clock and we'd just finished eating when Andy telephoned again. 'Laura is settled in the unit,' he said. 'It's a nice place. We'll be leaving soon. We should be with you at about seven o'clock. I won't speak to Kim now, but tell her we're on our way and Mummy sends her love.'

'I will,' I said. Andy sounded far less stressed.

I told Kim what her father had said and she looked at the clock. 'That's about an hour,' I said.

She returned to the game she was playing with Adrian and I took Paula up for her bath and bed. It was a while before Paula settled, but Andy was later than he'd thought and didn't arrive until 7.30 p.m. By that time I was downstairs again in the living room, watching Adrian and Kim playing another game of Guess Who? Kim came with me to answer the front door, eager to see her father again. Geraldine was with him.

'Come in,' I welcomed.

Kim fell into her father's arms. 'I've missed you,' she said.

'I've missed you too,' he said, scooping her up and kissing her cheek.

'I've missed you more,' Kim said, covering his cheek in kisses.

Geraldine looked on, slightly disapproving of this open display of affection. I thought she may have been brought up differently, where the expression of feelings and emotions wasn't encouraged.

'Can I finish my game of Guess Who?' Kim asked her father as he set her down.

'Yes, as long as it doesn't take too long.'

'Would you like a tea or a coffee?' I asked as we went down the hall to the living room.

'No, I'm fine, thanks, Cathy,' Andy said. 'What about you, Mum?'

'No, thank you,' she said stiffly. Perhaps she wanted to go straight home.

Geraldine and Andy sat on the sofa and I took an easy chair as Kim returned to finish the game. She and Adrian were perched on stools either side of the coffee table. From where I was sitting I could see the game from both sides. Kim was clearly winning, but I didn't say anything.

'So the transfer to the mother-and-baby unit went all right then?' I asked Andy and Geraldine.

'Yes,' Andy said. 'It's a lovely place, set in the grounds of a teaching hospital. There are only six bedrooms and each one is like a small studio flat, with a bed, cot, baby-changing facilities, shelves, carpet and curtains. There's a call button in each room if the woman needs help and they are supported and monitored day and night. They share a kitchen, bathroom and laundry room. And there's a communal lounge with a television. The staff are very friendly and there's always at least two nurses on duty. The doctor and psychiatrist are on call and they see the patients regularly. It's not home, obviously, but much better than the hospital, and of course Laura can have Liam with her. She was so pleased to see him this morning.'

'I bet she was,' I said.

'We had a short meeting with the doctor before we left. I'll see him and other members of the care team next week for an update after the assessment. They encourage family to be involved, so we can visit any afternoon and evening. But I have to work and they understand that. We'll spend all tomorrow afternoon there, but Mum doesn't drive, so next week we'll have to go as soon as I'm home from work.'

Kim looked up at her father. Although she'd been concentrating on the game, I knew she'd been taking in every word. 'Am I going to visit Mummy in the evening as well?' she asked, concerned.

'Yes, of course, love,' Andy said. 'That's as important as me seeing her.'

'It's going to be a lot of driving for you, going every night after work,' Geraldine said to him.

Andy shrugged. 'It can't be helped, Mum. I'll leave work early. They'll understand. The average stay in the unit is about two months, so hopefully Laura won't be in for long, although women can stay for up to twelve months if necessary.'

Kim was looking serious again. 'Twelve months is a year, Daddy,' she said.

'Yes, but Mummy will be better before then,' he said.

Reassured, Kim returned her attention to the game.

'The staff are very supportive,' he said to me. 'They're specialists and know how to deal with odd or distressing behaviour. Mum and I feel far more positive now than we did yesterday. Laura's a bit drowsy from the medication, but the doctor explained that it would be adjusted and then reduced as she recovers.'

I nodded. 'Are you sure you wouldn't like a tea or coffee?' I offered.

'No, thank you, we must be going,' Geraldine said.

'Once Kim has finished her game, Mum,' Andy replied firmly. I saw Geraldine's lips tighten.

'When you see Laura tomorrow please give her my love,' I said. 'I've bought her a few chocolates.' I passed him the box I'd bought on the way back from the park.

'Thank you, that's kind of you,' Andy said, and Geraldine nodded stiffly.

'Do you want me to tell Fran what's happened?' I asked. 'She's a close friend of Laura's and she's been worried about her.'

Geraldine looked pointedly at Andy, cautioning him that she shouldn't be told, but Andy said, 'Yes, Laura's mentioned Fran, and I've met her a couple of times. Please explain, and tell her Laura will phone her when she feels up to it.'

'I will,' I said. 'And if Laura would like a visit from me, do let me know.'

'I will. Although I'm hoping she won't be in for long.'

Geraldine was sitting upright with a sanctimonious, disapproving look on her face, but gone were the days when mental-health problems went unacknowledged and the sufferer was shut away. Of course Fran, as Laura's friend, would want to know how she was, and doubtless she'd want to visit her too, just as I did.

'Winner!' Kim cried, revealing the last tile on the game.

'Well done,' I said. 'Well played, both of you.'

Geraldine immediately stood, eager to be off, and told Kim to quickly help pack away the game.

'It's all right,' I said. 'I'll do it later.'

Andy and Kim also stood and I saw them out. It was nearly eight-thirty and time for Adrian to go to bed. Adrian is a sensitive child, but like many boys he often hides his feelings. It wasn't until I was lying on his bed beside him and we were having our little chat last thing at night that he confessed something that had been worrying him. Even then, he didn't come straight to the point.

'Is it only mummies with very young babies who have what Kim's mummy has?' he asked.

'Yes,' I said.

'So you wouldn't have to go into hospital? Paula's too old.'

'No. It wouldn't happen to me now.'

'Are you sure?' he asked. 'Because Daddy is working away and there wouldn't be anyone here to look after us like Kim's daddy is doing.'

'Adrian,' I said, hugging him, 'stop worrying. If I had to go into hospital for any reason, your daddy would come straight home. And what about your nana and grandpa? Have you forgotten them? They'd look after you if I wasn't well, wouldn't they?'

'Oh yes, silly me,' he said with an embarrassed smile.

'I'm glad you told me what was on your mind,' I said, holding him close.

But I was reminded how easily a young child could worry and fret, even if they felt secure and well loved.

CHAPTER FOURTEEN

GINA

On Sunday we went to my parents' house for the day. We tend to take it in turns – they come to us and then we go to them. They're the archetypal loving grandparents who dote on their grandchildren and spoil them with their time and affection. They also welcome into their home and hearts any child or children I am fostering. As was usual for a Sunday, Mum cooked a full roast for dinner, followed by her delicious homemade apple pie with melt-in-your-mouth pastry, served with lashings of warm custard. We ate ourselves to a standstill. The weather wasn't so good, but we managed a short walk after dinner and then spent the rest of the afternoon playing games indoors. My parents have endless enthusiasm and patience for even the most trivial and repetitive of children's games, whether it is pushing a line of toy cars around and around the living-room floor, creating domino runs and watching them fall, or role-playing superheroes – Batman and Robin, and so forth.

We left around six o'clock after a sandwich tea and returned home in plenty of time for John's phone call from America. He spoke to Adrian first, then Paula and me. His contract had eight weeks to run and then he would be home, hopefully for good. Five minutes after we'd finished speaking to him the phone rang again. 'We're popular tonight,' I said to Adrian as I picked up the handset in the living room. It was Shelley.

'Hi, love, great to hear from you,' I said. 'How are you both?'

'Fantastic. Couldn't be better.' She sounded really upbeat. 'I thought you'd like to know how my visit to Carol's went.'

'Yes, indeed. I have been wondering.'

'It was perfect. Carol is lovely, just like I remember her. She was so pleased to see me, and so were her family. They were all there when we arrived and they kissed and hugged Darrel and me as we went in like we were family. I said I was sorry that I hadn't kept in touch, but they were OK about that. They said they'd often thought about me and wondered how I was doing. I was really touched. Carol is still fostering and she's looking after a really stroppy teenager at present, Chantelle. She was there and she had a right face on her. She's fourteen and reminded me of how I was at her age. I told her she needed to lighten up and appreciate all Carol was doing for her. Carol was nearly in tears when I said that.'

I knew exactly how Carol must have felt.

'Chantelle said she wanted a baby like me, so when Carol was out of the room I gave her a good talking to. I told her that although I love Darrel loads I wish I'd waited to have him until I had a career and flat of my own. I don't know if she was listening, but I had to say something. I know how she feels – that having a baby will make you feel loved – but it's not the answer, and I told her how difficult it was bringing up a child alone.'

'That was sensible,' I said.

'Maybe she was listening, I don't know. Carol's own kids are all grown up and her eldest daughter was there with her fiancé. They're both teachers and they're getting married next year. She said I could go to her wedding, as long as I kept in touch. Which of course I will do.' Shelley chuckled. 'I feel like I've got a family. I've never had a family of my own. Carol even said I could go there next Christmas. I know it's a long way off – seven months – but I'm already looking forward to it. I told her Darrel and I had spent Christmas alone last year and she was sad and said that would never happen again. I'm going to start buying one present a week for Christmas. I can afford that and I want to give them all a little something.'

'That's very kind of you,' I said. 'Although I'm sure Carol won't expect it.'

'No, she was over the moon with the box of chocolates I gave her. Thank goodness I got back in touch. Thanks to you.'

'Thanks to you,' I said, 'for making that phone call. Well done.'

'I've made another important phone call too,' Shelley said, bubbling with excitement. 'To the lady who runs the choir.'

'Excellent. Tell me what happened.'

'I'm going for the first time next week. It took me a while to pluck up the courage to phone, but Jenny, the choir mistress, sounded really nice. It's not an audition; you just have to go each week and be able to sing. Jenny said they could do with some more young voices in the choir, as some of their members are getting on a bit.' She laughed. 'It's Tuesday. I'm nervous, but I will go. I've promised myself I will.'

'Good. I'm sure they'll be really pleased to have you, Shelley. You've got a beautiful voice. Are you all right for a sitter for Darrel?'

'Yes. My friend is going to stay with him. It's only from seven o'clock till nine, so I won't be too long. I'm nervous, but I'm also looking forward to singing with others. Do you and Adrian still sing the lullabies?'

'I wouldn't call it singing,' I said with a laugh. 'But we do our best. We always think of you and Darrel when we hum Brahms's "Lullaby".'

'That's nice. We think of you too. Darrel is here beside me. Can he speak to Adrian? He's learning to use the phone.'

'Yes of course.'

I passed the handset to Adrian.

'Hello,' Adrian said.

There was a long pause before Darrel said hello, and thereafter the conversation was rather one-sided, with Adrian, that much older and more confident in using the telephone, doing most of the talking. After a few minutes they said goodbye. Not wanting to be left out, Paula asked to 'speak' to Darrel too, so Shelley put him on again. There was silence. 'Say hello to Darrel,' I encouraged.

'Hello,' she said in a small voice.

'Hello,' Darrel replied.

Satisfied that she'd spoken on the phone, she returned the handset to me and I finished talking to Shelley and wished her good luck for Tuesday.

'Thanks,' she said. 'I'll keep in touch.'

And I was sure she meant it.

I wasn't expecting to hear any more from Andy until Laura felt well enough to have friends visit her, when I hoped Andy or Geraldine would remember to tell me. Neither was I expecting Geraldine to go out of her way to give me updates on Laura's progress, although it would have been nice. When she brought Kim to school on Monday morning she managed a nod in my direction, while Kim smiled and waved at us. Once the children had gone into school Geraldine, as usual, walked swiftly out of the playground ahead of everyone else, while I stayed behind to talk to Fran. I asked her if Laura had telephoned her again and when she said no I explained that at the weekend Laura and Liam had been admitted to a mother-and-baby unit, where Laura was being treated for acute post-natal depression, and that Andy would let us know how she was getting on.

'Oh, the poor dear,' Fran said, immediately concerned. 'I'll visit her as soon as I can.'

I explained that the unit was some distance away and Andy was going to let us know when Laura felt up to having friends visit.

'OK. I'll give him a ring later and see how she is,' Fran said. 'And if there is anything I can do to help. I'll ask him for the address so I can send some flowers and a get-well card.' Which was a really nice thought. 'I hope she's better very soon.'

'Yes,' I agreed. 'Andy said she was being well looked after.'

Talking about Laura wasn't playground gossip as Geraldine had suggested; friends are naturally concerned when someone is unwell and rally together in an emergency. I thought how pleased Laura would be to know her friends were thinking about her and to receive a get-well card and flowers from Fran.

* * *

I had it in my mind that if Geraldine hadn't told me by the end of the week how Laura was doing then I would summon my courage and ask her. Approaching Geraldine felt a little like going to see the bank manager or headmistress. I wasn't expecting Andy to telephone me with an update – he'd be far too busy going to work, dashing home and then driving backwards and forwards to visit Laura each evening. However, that Monday afternoon, as I walked down our street to collect Adrian from school and we neared number 53, a woman I hadn't seen before came out. Early fifties, I guessed, with fair, shoulder-length wavy hair, she was wearing a pretty floral summer dress with a pale blue cardigan. She continued someway ahead of us to the bottom of the road. I didn't know who she was and I didn't give it much thought until I saw her again in the playground. Perhaps she was another friend of Laura's – a parent with a child at the school – although I couldn't remember seeing her here before. But then when Kim came out of school she rushed to her and greeted her with a big hug.

'That's Kim's other gran,' Adrian told me.

'Oh, I see. Laura's mother. That's nice. I expect she's come to help.'

'Kim told me at playtime she might be coming,' Adrian said. 'She was well excited. She likes this gran more than the other one.'

As I looked over I could see how at ease Kim was with Laura's mother. They were holding hands now, both of them smiling and chatting as they crossed the playground towards the main gate. There was a relaxed lightness in Kim's step that I hadn't seen on her recent walks to and from school when she'd been rushed in and out of the playground by

Geraldine. Kim was looking at us as we waited for our turn to go through the gates, proud to be with her gran, then she whispered something to her. She turned and looked at me.

'Hello,' I said with a smile. 'I'm Cathy, a friend of Laura's.'

'Hi, so pleased to meet you,' she said. 'Kim's just told me who you are. You live in the same street, don't you?'

'Yes, that's right.'

'I'm Gina, Laura's mother. Andy mentioned that Kim had spent Saturday with you. Thanks for helping out.'

'You're welcome. How is Laura?'

'Comfortable, as they say,' Gina said. 'I haven't seen her yet. I'm going this evening. I phoned her earlier. She sounded a bit groggy, but that would be the tablets.' I nodded. 'Not sure why no one thought to tell me about all this sooner, but at least I'm here now, and I'll be staying for as long as necessary. I've sent Geraldine home for a rest,' she added with a smile.

We paused at the kerb and then all crossed the road together. Paula began agitating to be let out of the stroller. 'I usually let her walk from here,' I explained to Gina, stopping the stroller. 'It takes us a while, so do go on ahead if you want to.'

'It's OK. There's no rush. Andy won't be home until five and I've got dinner ready.' She smiled at Paula as I let her out, and then we continued walking up the street with Kim and Adrian slightly in front.

'You foster, don't you?' Gina asked me.

'Yes, although I haven't got a child at present.'

'Andy mentioned it when he telephoned me on Saturday evening. He said Kim had stayed with you a couple of times and you were a foster carer. It's a nice thing to do, but it must be difficult to say goodbye.'

'Yes, I'm afraid that's the downside of fostering,' I said. 'Although some of the children keep in touch.'

'Good, must be nice to hear how they are doing.'

'Yes,' I agreed. 'It is.'

I'd taken an immediate liking to Gina. She came across as warm and open, with a bubbly personality that reached out to others, and she was very easy to talk to. I could see the family likeness between her, Laura and Kim, and of course she was a very different character to Geraldine, who had a far more serious demeanour and kept her distance.

'Do you know Geraldine well?' Gina asked as we walked.

'Not really. I've only known her since Laura has been unwell.'

'I have to bite my tongue sometimes,' Gina confessed. 'But I was hurt that no one contacted me sooner, when Laura started to slide. I work, but you take time off when there's a family emergency, don't you? When I told my boss my daughter and baby grandson were in hospital he said I could take as much time off as I needed. I caught the train down this morning and I'll stay until Laura is well on the way to recovery. But I feel guilty that I didn't spot the signs sooner. I should have done, having been through something similar myself. Anyway, she's in the best place now.'

'Yes, she is,' I said. 'They'll soon have her right, I'm sure. Please give her my love when you see her this evening. And let me know if there is anything I can do.'

'Thanks, Cathy. I'll tell you tomorrow how she's getting on.'

* * *

The following morning Gina was already in the playground with Kim when I arrived with Adrian and Paula, and as soon as they saw us they came straight over, both of them smiling.

'I saw my mummy and brother last night,' Kim told Adrian happily, and they began talking between themselves.

'Laura was so pleased to see us,' Gina said. 'It made me cry. She wanted lots and lots of hugs and held my hand like a little child for nearly all the time we were there. She seemed to want me rather than Andy, but I think he understood. She's obviously got a long way to go yet, but Andy could see an improvement already. She gets confused sometimes and we had to explain why she and Liam were in the unit, as she wanted to come home. She said some other things, too, that showed she wasn't completely with it. After we'd left, Andy and I explained to Kim that it was part of Mummy's illness, and that it would go once she got better.'

I glanced at Kim. 'Yes, it must be difficult for her to understand.'

Gina nodded. 'Unfortunately, Laura's had to stop breast-feeding, because of the medication getting through to the baby. It's a pity, but it can't be helped. She's on quite a strong dose at present. And she tires easily – I think that's from the tablets too – so we didn't stay too late. We'll see her again this evening and every evening. But how things have changed since I was in hospital! No long psychiatric wards now. Her room is lovely, bright and airy, and she's encouraged to mix with the other mums. They have individual therapy, group therapy and occupational therapy, so there's a lot going on. They're expected to look after their babies too, although the nurses help when necessary. Andy and I have to go to a team meeting there on Thursday afternoon, so Andy is going to take time off work.'

'Let me know if you want me to collect Kim from school,' I offered.

'Thanks, Cathy, but Andy has already said he's going to ask his mother. It's important she's still involved.'

'Yes, indeed,' I said.

'I told Laura you sent your love, and she said to thank you for the chocolates. She's worrying about Fran. She wants me to tell her that she's really sorry she hasn't been in touch and she'll phone as soon as she can. Do you know who Fran is?'

I looked around the filling playground and spotted her talking to another mother. 'Over there,' I said, pointing.

'Thanks. I'll catch her now if you don't mind. Then I'm going into school to see Kim's teacher. Andy and I think she should know what's going on in case Kim is upset in school.'

'Yes, good idea.' I knew from fostering that the school liked to be informed if there was a crisis in the family so they could help support the child in school.

'I'll see you later then,' Gina said. And, taking Kim's hand, she went over to speak to Fran.

Thereafter Gina made a point of seeing me every day to tell me how Laura was doing, either on the way to school, in the playground or walking home from school. We didn't just talk about Laura, but lots of other things as well. Gina liked a chat and was very easy to get on with. We had a laugh too. She obviously didn't know anyone in the area apart from her family and she said she was pleased to have my company. At home that week I continued with my dissertation whenever I had the chance, and made the most of fine days by playing outside with Paula and taking her to the park. It was early July now and like many summers in the UK the weather was changeable, with a beautiful, warm sunny day that seemed like it could go on forever followed by a drop in temperature and thick cloud cover that saw us reaching for our jackets and umbrellas.

On Thursday afternoon Geraldine collected Kim from school, as Andy and Gina were at the meeting at the unit. She gave me a perfunctory glance as she rushed in and out of the playground. Then on Friday morning Gina was in the playground again and she told me that the meeting the previous day with the mental-healthcare team had been very useful. They'd gone over Laura's healthcare plan and had answered their questions. Some of the team would continue to support Laura once she was discharged from the unit and went home.

'It was a lot of rushing around for Andy,' Gina admitted. 'After the meeting we came back, he gobbled down his dinner, which Geraldine had ready, and then she went with him and Kim to see Laura while I cleared up. He was exhausted when he got back. It's a pity neither Geraldine nor I drive. It'll be less of a rush at the weekend when we're all going.'

That afternoon when Kim came out of school she was carrying a giant get-well card for her mother, which the class had made and all signed. It was a lovely thought and I could see how proud Kim was. Not only would Laura appreciate it, but it would also give Kim a boost to know she had the best wishes of her class. Although Kim appeared to be coping, she must have been missing her mother and Liam dreadfully. We all walked home together, with Kim and Adrian carrying the card between them.

Adrian, Paula and I had a relaxing weekend with a trip to the park on Saturday and games at home on Sunday. Sometimes it's nice to just chill out at weekends, otherwise they can become as hectic as weekdays with shopping, outings and visiting family. The long summer holidays were in three weeks' time, but I hadn't booked for us to go away as John wouldn't be home until the end of the school holidays, so I was planning on days out instead, including a day trip to the coast. On Monday Gina and Kim came out of their house just as we passed on the way to school, so we all walked together. Having spent a large part of the weekend with her mother and Liam, Kim was full of it.

'My brother is growing bigger,' she told us. 'And he's awake more now. I gave him his bottle and I helped one of the other mothers too. Her baby has a trainer cup and Liam will have one when he's older. Then my daddy helped Mummy cook a meal in the kitchen there and we all had dinner together at the table. When Mummy feels better we can go out.'

'Fantastic,' I said. 'You had a great weekend by the sound of it.' Then to Gina I said, 'So everything's going well?'

'Absolutely. I've started to see an improvement in Laura.'

That afternoon as I passed number 53 the front door opened again and Gina came out, but I could see straight away that she was worried and had probably been looking out for me. Her usual smiling face was tense. 'Are you all right?' I asked as she opened the gate to join me.

'Not really. I need to ask you something. You might know, as you deal with the social services.'

'I'll help if I can,' I said.

She fell into step beside me. 'You remember I told you that there was a social worker at that meeting last Thursday?'

'Yes.'

'Well, she telephoned me this afternoon. She says she has to visit us – to do a home visit.'

I nodded. 'That would be standard procedure,' I said.

'That's what she said, but I didn't like her tone. She told me Andy had to be there, and when I said I didn't think that would be possible, as he had to work, she got on her high horse. She said she had to see us all to write her report and that it was important we made the time. She also said she would have to look around the house during her visit. When I asked her why, she said it was part of the assessment, as she needed to be certain it was a safe environment for when Liam returned. I went ballistic. How dare she! Of course it's a safe environment. Who does she think she is?'

'Gina, it's standard practice,' I said. 'Don't worry. She just phrased it badly.'

'Do you think so?' Gina asked, turning to me. 'It's worried me. It was like she was suggesting he might not be safe with us. So you think I should let her snoop around the house then?'

'Yes. Show her around and then she'll be able to write in her report that all is well. The social services have to be ultra-careful where children are concerned. I know it feels like an invasion of your privacy. When I'm fostering the child's social worker always looks at the child's bedroom at every visit, and then at my annual review the whole house is checked.'

'You're good to put up with all that,' Gina said. 'I'm sure I wouldn't. I'll tell Andy what you said. If he can't get time off work I'll ask Geraldine to come round. We'll present a united front.'

While I liked Gina, I could see she was feisty – not necessarily what was required when the social worker visited. I hesitated and chose my words carefully. 'Gina, my advice would be to cooperate fully. Remember, the social worker is just doing her job. Answer her questions, show her around and I'm sure all will be fine.'

CHAPTER FIFTEEN

EVERLEY

It is sometimes said that social workers are 'damned if they do and damned if they don't', meaning that they'll be criticized whatever course of action they take. I knew that the social worker was following procedure to ensure that Liam and Kim were safe at home. I also knew that it was in everyone's interest to cooperate. So often when the social services are involved a 'them and us' situation develops, with the family on one side, feeling threatened and going on the defensive, and the social worker, who in this instance may not have been sufficiently diplomatic, on the other. I hoped that once Gina had calmed down she would feel less hostile.

On Tuesday morning as we all walked to school together Gina told me that Andy had managed to book the following afternoon off work so he could be present when the social worker visited at one o'clock. Gina said they'd also asked Geraldine to be present. 'She's helped a lot,' Gina said. 'So it's important she's there. We want the social worker to see that we're all working together.' Which was a sensible approach. I also thought that having Andy and Geraldine present, who were more reserved in temperament, would be a calming influence on Gina, so there would be less chance of her going 'ballistic', as she'd put it, at the social worker as she had done on the telephone. She was still quite indignant that the visit had to happen at all.

On Wednesday morning as we walked to school I wished Gina luck and told her again not to worry, that it was procedure and everything would be fine. That afternoon I had one eye on the clock as I made lunch for Paula and me and one o'clock approached – the time the social worker was due to arrive at number 53. Then I spent a fair bit of the afternoon wondering how the visit was going in between doing some housework and playing with Paula. I was expecting to see Gina in the playground that afternoon, but it was Andy who strode in to collect Kim. Dressed in a suit, with his tie loosened, he saw me and came straight over.

'So you're meeting Kim today,' I said with a smile. 'She will be pleased.' I knew how delighted children were when fathers who were usually at work suddenly came to meet them.

'Yes,' he said absently, frowning. 'It'll give Mum and Gina a chance to recover. We had the social worker visit this afternoon. She's only just left.'

'How did it go?' I asked.

He rubbed his forehead. 'Not too good, to be honest. It feels as though we're being investigated – some of the questions she asked. Mum was in tears at one point.'

'Why?' I asked, shocked.

'Mum believes it's her fault all this has happened, although I keep telling her it's not. The social worker asked a lot of questions around why we hadn't sought medical help for Laura sooner. We tried to explain that we thought Laura would get better like she had last time, after having Kim, but the social worker said her symptoms were less severe then, and even so her recovery had taken almost a year. She said she had concerns that if Liam and Laura came home and Laura needed help we would "cover it up again". That was the term she used. Mum took it personally. Granted, she didn't want people to know, but she thought she was doing what was best. And the way the social worker was talking it sounded as though Laura and Liam might not come home – well, not in the short term at least. She has to complete an assessment first.'

'An assessment is normal practice,' I offered, trying to reassure Andy, for although he was calm he was clearly very worried.

'That's what the social worker said,' Andy replied, digging his hands into his pockets. 'She asked who would be the main caregiver when Laura and Liam came home, as Gina would have to return home to go to work. Mum said she would be, so the social worker questioned her again about seeking appropriate help for Laura if it was needed. She implied that as Mum had hidden the seriousness of Laura's condition before, even from me, she couldn't be trusted to get help if Laura needed it in the future. That made Mum cry.'

'Poor Geraldine. It sounds as though it wasn't put very well at all.'

'The social worker did apologize. She said she hadn't meant to upset Mum, but she had to be certain Laura would receive appropriate help and support from professionals in the future if it was necessary.' I nodded. 'Then she started talking about concerns around Liam. She said that Laura's medical condition had included hallucinating about the baby and this had placed him at risk. I told her Liam hadn't ever been at risk as Mum had slept downstairs with him when things got really bad. I don't think that helped. She wrote it down, and then she asked about the impact Laura's illness was having on Kim, and we said Kim had been protected as much as possible.'

'Yes, that's very true,' I said.

'But as she pointed out, Kim must have seen at least some of what was going on, living in the same house. She then started talking about bonding. She said some mothers with severe postnatal depression or psychosis fail to bond properly with their children, especially if treatment is delayed. Mum was close to tears again, blaming herself, but I said Laura and Kim were very close, and she wrote that down. Then she said she wanted to see Kim this afternoon, but I said we had to do a quick turn-around to go and see Laura and Liam. So she's going to see her on Friday after school. It seems she's going to be talking to the school too.'

'That's usual,' I said. 'And the school will confirm what you've said – that Kim is a happy and well-adjusted child.'

'I guess,' Andy said, no less worried. 'But the social worker said they might consider applying to the court for a supervision order, which would include Kim. If they got it, we would be monitored by the social services for up to two years. Gina had a right go at her then and said she'd be better off leaving us alone and spending her time working with families who were abusing their children instead.'

'It sounds as though the social worker has put it all very badly,' I said, my reassurance now sounding less effective.

Andy sighed. 'I asked her how long she thought it would be until Laura and Liam could come home and she said she didn't know. It would be a decision made by the mental healthcare team – of which she is a part. Gina was fuming by then and said that if it went on too long she'd bring Laura and Liam home anyway. The social worker said that although Laura was in hospital voluntarily, if she tried to discharge herself and Liam before she was considered well, the social services could apply for an order under the Mental Health Act to keep Laura in hospital and even take Liam into care. Mum was in tears again.' He stopped.

The Klaxon had sounded while he'd been talking and now the children were streaming out. 'Here comes Kim,' he said. 'Mum or Gina will tell you what I've forgotten.' He set his face to a smile, ready to greet Kim, and she ran into his arms. 'You won't mind if we dash off,' he said. 'We're going straight over to see Laura.'

'No, of course not, you go on ahead,' I said. 'Give my love to Laura and try not to worry.'

He nodded stiffly, a little like his mother did, but I could see the pain behind his eyes. His family was under threat and he was very worried. So was I, from what he'd said. After I'd hugged Adrian we began home, and I thought of what Andy had said and how different his family's experience in dealing with the social services had been compared to Shelley's when she'd been suffering from postnatal depression. From what she'd told me her social worker had been highly sensitive, non-threatening and very supportive in getting her the help she needed. I knew Shelley's condition had been less serious than Laura's, but even so I felt that Laura's social worker had been heavy-handed. Families are very fragile at times of crisis and can easily misinterpret what they're being told, seeing a threat where there is none intended. Social workers don't always realize the power they hold, and as a result can unintentionally scare the family, causing a lot of unnecessary worry.

Having said that, what Laura's social worker had told them was true. By not seeking medical help for Laura sooner Andy and Geraldine had unwittingly placed Liam in danger, and of course the social worker had to be certain that if Laura and Liam came home it couldn't happen again. The word *if* haunted me, as I was sure it did Andy, Gina and Geraldine. Here was a loving family who now faced the possibility of having their children taken into care and their mother sectioned under the Mental Health Act. If only they'd sought help sooner, I was sure none of this would have happened.

The following morning Gina was still seething, although she didn't say anything until the children were in school. 'Did you know the social services hold meetings about families without any family member being there?' she asked, her eyes blazing.

'Yes.'

'It's shocking. How do you know that what they're saying isn't a pack of lies? It shouldn't be allowed.'

'There does need to be more transparency in the system,' I agreed.

'Andy's going to get some legal advice. Meetings about us that we're not invited to! And now that bloody social worker – excuse my language – says she has to talk to Kim without us being there. We've tried to protect her as much as possible. How dare she?'

'It's normal practice, Gina,' I said tentatively. 'All the children in the family are usually seen by the social worker. When I'm fostering the child's social worker always spends time alone with the child in case they want to say something they might not feel comfortable saying in front of the carer.'

'But those are foster children who've been abused!' Gina said indignantly. 'Not one of your own who's loved and cared for.'

'As part of my annual review Adrian is asked what he thinks about fostering, without me being in the room,' I said. 'Paula will be asked, too, when she's old enough.'

'Little wonder they're short of foster carers!' Gina snapped.

'Did she look around the house?' I asked, on a lighter note.

'No. She didn't have time. She's going to do that on Friday, after she's seen Kim.'

'And how was Laura when you saw her last night?'

'All right,' Gina said, calming down. 'Obviously we didn't tell her what the social worker had said, and we hid how worried we are. She asked when you and Fran could visit, so she must be feeling a bit better. I said I wasn't sure, as you had the kids and your husband works away. It's an hour in the car. Visiting is any time after one.'

'Could I take Paula?' I asked.

'I don't see why not.'

'Adrian has been invited to a friend's for tea tomorrow,' I said. 'I wonder if I could visit her then. I don't have to be back to collect Adrian until six o'clock.'

'Give the unit a ring and check it's OK,' Gina said. 'Come into the house and I'll write down their details for you. I'll make us a coffee as well.'

'Thank you.'

We'd arrived outside number 53 and I explained to Paula that although we were going into baby Liam's house he wouldn't be there.

'Bay-bee Lee-am, Bay-bee Lee-am,' she said, a little disappointed.

Indoors, Gina showed us through to the living room and produced some toys for Paula to play with and then went into the kitchen to make coffee. It was strange being in Laura's home without her and Liam. I thought how difficult it must be for Kim when she came home from school not to have her mother or brother here. She was being taken to visit them each evening, but it wasn't the same as having your mum at home. The framed family photographs on the walls that had been there on my previous visits now seemed to underline that the family was separated. There were some smaller photographs of Laura cradling Liam propped on the mantel-piece, taken, I guessed, when Liam was a few days old – lovely pictures, but another stark reminder that they weren't here. Through the patio windows I could see the garden, which had been Laura's domain when she'd been well but was now starting to look unkempt. I guessed none of them had the time or inclination to tend it as Laura had done.

Gina told me a bit about Everley, the specialist mother-and-baby unit, as we talked and drank our coffee and Paula played. When I'd finished my coffee I said I needed to go as I had things to do. She wrote down the contact details of Everley and also the telephone number of their house, which I hadn't been given before. I think Gina would have liked me to stay longer, as she admitted she worried more when she was alone in the house and often walked into the High Street just to get out. I appreciated what she meant. With Laura and Liam not there the house felt like a mausoleum, with the images of loved ones displayed but no longer present.

At home I telephoned Everley and explained to the lady who answered that I was a friend of Laura's and would like to visit her the following afternoon, but that I would have to bring my fifteen-month-old daughter with me. She said that should be fine, but she'd need to check with Laura first. She took my name, address and telephone number and said that if I didn't hear anything further from her to assume it was all right to go. That afternoon in the playground I told Fran I was going to visit Laura the following day and I asked if she'd like to come, but it was too short notice for her to arrange childcare for her daughter after school, so she said she'd visit another day and to send Laura her best wishes.

No one from Everley called back, so by Friday morning I assumed my visit was going ahead. I saw the mother of the friend Adrian was going to have tea with in the playground and confirmed I would collect him from her house at six o'clock. On the way home I stopped off at our local super-market to buy a bunch of flowers for Laura. I didn't put Paula down for her nap that morning in the hope that she would sleep in the car. An hour's journey can be tedious for a young child and I needed to concentrate on driving and finding my way there. I made us an early lunch and explained to Paula that we were going in the car to see Liam, and she clasped her hands together in delight. 'Bay-bee Lee-am, Bay-bee Lee-am.' Then she 'helped' me pack a bag of things she would need, including a change of nappy, her trainer cup, a small snack and some of her toys. Just after twelve-thirty we set off with my notes on the route and the flowers on the passenger seat beside me. I tuned the radio to a station playing soft classical music, guaranteed to send most children off to sleep, and five minutes later Paula's eyes had closed. She didn't wake until I pulled into the car park at the front of Everley.

It had been an easy journey. I'd known my way to the neighbouring town and from there the hospital, in the grounds of which Everley stood, had been clearly signposted. It was a two-storey 1950s brick building, which I guessed had originally served a different purpose. Now modernized, it was surrounded by a small fenced landscaped garden.

'We're here,' I said to Paula as she blinked and rubbed her eyes, still heavy with sleep.

'Bay-bee Lee-am,' she said, puzzled and peering out of her side window.

'Yes, we've come to see baby Liam but in a different home.'

I went round and opened her car door, undid the safety harness and helped her to clamber out. I'd put the stroller in the car but we didn't need it, as the main door was only a short walk away. With the bag looped over my shoulder, the flowers in one hand and holding Paula's hand with the other, we went to the wooden gate where I slid the bolt. A short, paved path led to the security-locked main door and I pressed the buzzer. No one answered, so I pressed it again, and then a female voice came through: 'Yes, can I help you?'

'I telephoned yesterday, Cathy Glass. I've come to see Laura –'

'Come in. I'll open the door.'

The security lock released and we went in. A nurse in a uniform of a white top and navy trousers greeted us. 'Could you sign the visitor's book, please? Laura is in the lounge, down that corridor on the left.'

'Thank you.' I could smell food, so I guessed someone was cooking their lunch.

With Paula toddling beside me we went down the corridor and I knocked on the door marked LOUNGE before opening it. Laura was sitting on the sofa with Liam in a bouncing cradle at her feet. She was alone and immediately stood and came over, smiling. 'Hello, Cathy. Thanks for coming.' She kissed my cheek and hugged me.

'You're looking very well. A few flowers,' I said, passing her the bunch. 'They match your blouse.'

She laughed, for the deep cerise of some of the flowers in the bouquet was the same shade as her top. 'Thank you so much. I'll put them in my room later.'

'This is a lovely place,' I said, glancing round. The lounge was spacious, bright and airy, and furnished with two sofas, bean bags, scatter cushions, bookshelves and a television and sound system, which stood on a cabinet. The gaily patterned curtains matched the cushions on the sofas.

'It's OK,' she said with a shrug. 'But it's not home. The other residents are in their rooms. I can show you my room later if you want.'

'Yes, I'd like that.'

Paula had toddled over to where Liam sat in his bouncing cradle and was kneeling beside him, peering at him intently. He looked a bit startled.

'Nice and gently,' I said to her, going over.

'Would you like a drink?' Laura asked. 'And I'll find a vase for the flowers.'

'Yes, please, if you're making one.'

'I need a drink. The tablets make me thirsty. Tea or coffee?'

'I don't mind. Whatever you're making.' I tensed and could have kicked myself as my thoughts flashed back to a similar scene at Laura's home when I'd given the same reply.

Then, unable to cope with making a choice between tea or coffee, Laura had gone to pieces.

But it was different now. 'Tea then,' she said easily. 'Can you watch Liam while I'm in the kitchen?'

'Yes, of course. Could Paula have some water as well, please?' I took the trainer cup from my bag and handed it to her.

I joined Paula on the floor beside Liam where we made some weird and wonderful coochie-cooing noises. He was a gorgeous baby, round-faced with big blue eyes. He grinned and gurgled contentedly, oblivious to the rocky start he'd had in life. At his age he wouldn't be missing home as Laura was; as long as he was warm, well fed and cared for he didn't mind where he was.

Laura returned with two mugs of tea and Paula's cup of water on a tray, which she placed on one of the small occasional tables. 'I've put the flowers in a vase,' she said. 'I'll take them up to my room later. Thanks again. Everyone is being so kind to me.'

I smiled. 'You're welcome.'

Paula drank some of her water and then squatted down beside Liam again as I sat next to Laura on the sofa. 'You don't take sugar, do you?' she said, passing me one of the mugs of tea.

'No. That's perfect, thanks.'

There was then an awkward silence as we both sipped our tea and occupied our gazes by watching the children.

'Liam's grown since the last time I saw him,' I said.

'Yes. He's doing well. They're very pleased with him here.'

There was another silence and then I commented on the weather and what a lovely view there was through the lounge window. Laura agreed. She didn't attempt to initiate conversation and if I'm honest it was a bit difficult, as I didn't know which subjects were safe and what I should avoid, which was silly really, I suppose. So I asked about Liam – if he slept well and so on, and I told Laura that Fran sent her best wishes and was hoping to visit soon. 'That's nice of her,' she said.

I mentioned that Adrian, Paula and I often walked to and from school with her mum (Gina) and Kim, and that Kim always told us what she'd been doing the evening before when she visited. 'It sounds as though she's a big help here,' I said as I finished the last of my tea.

'Yes. Kim's made friends with the other mothers. They all like her.'

I then said again how comfortable the lounge was, how easy the journey here had been and a bit about Kim and Adrian's school.

'The schools break up soon,' Laura said. 'I've told my doctor I want to be out of here and home in time for the summer holidays.'

I nodded. I didn't know how realistic this was – the end of term was only two weeks away. Laura seemed well enough in many respects; there was no sign of the gnawing anxiety and debilitating depression that had plagued her before coming here, yet there was still something. Her conversation was slow and faltering, and she'd lost spontaneity, which I guessed could be another side effect of the medication – slowing her thought processes as it calmed them. She seemed to be aware of this; a couple of times when she was trying to think of a word and it just wouldn't come she said, 'Sorry, my brain's stopped functioning.' She gave a small laugh.

'Mine stopped a while back too,' I said, and she smiled.

Presently Liam grew bored with being in the bouncing cradle and having Paula amuse him and he began to grizzle. Laura picked him up and soothed him. 'There, there,' she said, gently rocking him. He immediately stopped crying.

'Would you like to see my room now?' she offered. 'I usually put Liam in his cot for a sleep about now. But we need to return the cups to the kitchen first. House rules.'

I clipped the lid on Paula's trainer cup and put it in my bag and then, with Paula toddling beside me, I carried out the tray with the mugs as Laura carried Liam.

'Just leave it in there,' Laura said, nodding to a door marked KITCHEN. 'I'll wash them up later.'

I went in. There was no one else in the kitchen and I left the tray by the sink, with some other mugs waiting to be washed.

Laura's room was up one flight of stairs and, like the lounge, it was bright and well furnished. A single bed and a cot in white wood stood against one wall, with a matching white wooden chest of drawers and chair against the other. Laura's and Liam's clothes and personal belongings were dotted around the room, so it looked quite cosy. 'Have a seat while I change him,' Laura said, moving a baby shawl from the armchair.

I sat in the chair and Paula stood beside Laura watching, intrigued, as she laid Liam on a changing mat on the bed and saw to his nappy. 'He's going to have a little sleep now,' Laura told Paula when he was clean and dressed again. Laura carefully laid him in his cot and drew up the side. Paula peered through the wooden slats and Liam chuckled and waved his arms towards her. He didn't look like he was going to sleep to me. Laura perched on the bed and there was silence. 'It's a nice room,' I said. 'Do you sleep well?'

'Much better now, thank you,' she said. 'I still get anxious sometimes, especially that something might happen to him in the night – you know, a cot death. But some of the other mothers worry about that too.'

'I used to when they were little,' I admitted. 'Sometimes a baby's breathing is so shallow you can't see it. I used to give Adrian and Paula a little poke to make sure they were still breathing.'

Laura smiled. 'One woman here used to force herself to stay awake all night, she was so worried something would happen to her daughter – not only a cot death, but also other stuff, like she could hurt herself or be taken away. She's getting better now.'

Laura fell silent again and I had the feeling she was tiring, physically and mentally, more so than Liam, who was still chuckling and waving his arms at Paula. We'd been here for nearly an hour and an half and I thought we should probably leave soon. 'We'll go shortly,' I said. 'I expect you could do with a rest before your family visit tonight.'

'Yes, I sometimes have a lie down while he has a sleep,' she admitted. 'I do get tired. It's a side effect of the tablets. They're going to start to reduce the dose soon, so it should improve.'

'That's good,' I said. 'You look very well.'

'Thanks. I hope to be discharged soon.'

I told Paula we were going and to say goodbye to Liam. She blew him a kiss through the bars of the cot. Laura asked if we could see ourselves out, as she couldn't leave Liam in his cot unattended. We kissed goodbye and she stood at the door to her room and watched us go, and then called, 'Bye!' and gave a little wave as we turned into the stairwell.

'Bye. Take care, and see you soon,' I returned.

'Bye,' Paula called, and I heard Laura's door shut behind us.

Downstairs I signed out of the visitor's book. It was 3.05. School would be ending soon and Adrian would be getting excited about going to his friend's home to play and have tea. Gina would be on her way to school to collect Kim, and once home their social worker was coming to speak to Kim. Laura hadn't mentioned her visit, so I assumed they hadn't wanted to worry her with it. The social worker's visit was procedure, but it was important that the family cooperated and Gina kept her cool.

CHAPTER SIXTEEN

HOME AGAIN

Gina had given me Laura's home telephone number and I felt I now had a reason to use it. Having spent Friday afternoon and evening wondering/worrying how the social worker's visit had gone, I decided on Saturday morning that it was acceptable for me to telephone and ask without it seeming intrusive or like I was interfering. I think friends often have to make a judgement on whether to say nothing and wait for news or to step forward. I left it until ten o'clock to telephone – a reasonable time for a family to be up at the weekend. Andy answered.

'It's Cathy,' I said. 'I hope I haven't disturbed you but I was wondering how the social worker's visit went yesterday.'

'That's very thoughtful of you,' he said. 'It went well. We'd worried unnecessarily. She only talked to Kim for about fifteen minutes. Kim told us later that she'd asked about her mum and how she felt with her living away. Then she looked around the house. That was it, really. She was in and out in under an hour.'

'Good. I'm pleased.'

'So were we. And thanks for visiting Laura yesterday. She really appreciated it.'

'It was great to see her,' I said. 'She's looking well.'

'Yes. She's much improved. The healthcare team are meeting next week to decide if she is ready to come home. Fingers crossed. She'll still have to take tablets and attend therapy, but at least she'll be home.'

'That's fantastic,' I said. 'I'll look forward to seeing her again soon then. I won't keep you. I'm sure you've got lots to do, but do let me know if I can help out at all.'

'Thanks, Cathy. Have a good weekend.'

'And you.'

Great news, I thought. It was all very positive. The social worker's visit had gone well and Laura would hopefully be discharged soon. I was so pleased I'd telephoned. I could stop worrying and enjoy the weekend, and it was a busy weekend. An old friend of mine, now a single parent, came with her children on Saturday afternoon and stayed for tea, and then my parents came for lunch on Sunday. The weather was fine for the whole weekend and appeared settled, which boded well for the approaching school holidays. On Monday when I saw Gina in the playground she said she thought that Laura would be home by the end of term; they were just waiting for confirmation from the healthcare team. I could see how pleased she and Kim were.

That week the school staged an end-of-term production, an annual event where all the children dressed up and played a part. This year the production was a story about a journey into space, and the school hall was packed with the children's families and friends, who'd come to watch. Andy had taken the morning off work and he, Gina and Geraldine were seated a couple of rows behind us. Paula and my parents were with me. The children had been practising their lines for weeks and despite last-minute nerves their performances were amazing. I'm sure I wasn't the only parent in the audience to be misty-eyed as they watched their child stand proudly on the stage and deliver their well-rehearsed lines. At the end, all the children came on stage to take their final bow and the audience rose to give them a standing ovation, clapping, cheering and whistling. Then the head teacher said a few words about how well they'd done, thanked us all for coming and wished us a good summer holiday. Before we left the hall I introduced my parents to Kim's family, and then we went our separate ways. Andy was going to work, Gina and Geraldine to their respective homes, and Mum and Dad were coming back with Paula and me for some lunch before driving home.

The following Wednesday, with two days to go before the end of term, Adrian was beside himself with excitement at the thought of six whole weeks off school. Kim was excitedly looking forward to her mother's homecoming, although they were still waiting to hear when exactly this would be. I hoped it had definitely been decided that Laura *was* coming home or Kim would be bitterly disappointed. I knew from fostering how tempting it is to give a child who is continually asking when they can live with their mummy again the good news they crave, but I'd learned to be very cautious. I didn't ever tell a child I was fostering any news about seeing their family or going home until it was a hundred per cent certain and had been confirmed to me by their social worker, even if all the signs were positive. Perhaps it was because the arrangements for Laura's return home were vague that I had a sense of foreboding. Unfortunately my fears were confirmed later that morning when I answered the telephone to hear Gina upset and angry.

'Cathy, that bloody social worker has stopped Laura from coming home! Laura's just telephoned me. She's distraught. I've phoned Andy and he's going to Everley now to try to speak to the doctor. Laura was so upset she couldn't tell me properly what they'd said. Wait until I see that witch of a social worker. She'll get a piece of my mind. God knows what we're going to tell Kim. She'll be devastated.'

What could I say? *You should have waited until after the meeting and a definite date had been confirmed for Laura's home-coming before telling Kim?* But that wasn't going to help; the damage had been done.

'Gina, I am sorry,' I said. 'I suppose the social worker felt Laura wasn't ready to be discharged yet.'

'That's what Laura seemed to be saying, but the nurse thought she was ready to go home.' I couldn't comment. I had no idea what had taken place in the team meeting, but I did know that the social worker wouldn't have delayed Laura's discharge without a good reason.

'Gina, wait and see what Andy says when he's seen the doctor. It may be easier to explain to Kim when you have the reason for the delay. Have they given Laura a date when she will be going home?'

'I don't know. I don't think so. Laura was too upset to tell me.'

'I'd wait to see what Andy has to say. I know it's very disap-pointing, but Laura will be home at some point. It's just been delayed.'

'Because of that social worker!' Gina fumed. 'I'll have to tell Geraldine. I think I'll walk round to her place now rather than phone. I could do with some fresh air and we've been getting on better lately. Having to deal with all of this has brought us together.'

So that was one positive to come out of it, I thought.

That afternoon as I waited for Adrian to come out of school Andy arrived in the playground to collect Kim. Dressed in smart-casual clothes rather than his office suit, I guessed he'd gone home after seeing the doctor instead of returning to work. He saw me and came straight over.

'Gina told you what happened?' he asked.

'Yes. Did you manage to speak to the doctor?'

'No. But I did see the nurse in charge. She was at the team meeting too. Laura and I spoke to her. She's very reassuring and understanding. It seems that the main reason Laura's discharge has been delayed is because of issues with the transfer of her care. Although her social worker will be the same when she leaves Everley, the community mental health team will take over and be responsible for her once home. Because it's the start of the school summer holidays a lot of people are on leave and the community care team is running with a skeleton staff, so realistically there wouldn't be anyone available to support Laura and give her help if she needs it.'

'I see,' I said.

'I asked if the delay had anything to do with us not seeking help sooner, but the nurse said it hadn't and that Laura wasn't the only one to have their discharge delayed. Laura had blamed the social worker because she'd been the one to raise it at the meeting. They're going to review the situation in two weeks, so hopefully she'll be coming home then.'

'Well, that's good news then,' I said positively. 'Laura hasn't had a setback.'

'No, that's right. But the bad news is that after Gina telephoned you this morning she phoned the social worker and had a right go at her.'

'Oh dear,' I said.

'To be honest, I'm not overly keen on that social worker. She's not like the staff at Everley. But it's no good Gina sounding off at her; she's only doing her job. Gina has a very short fuse when it comes to social workers. I think it's because of the way she was treated when she was admitted to a psychiatric hospital after having Laura. Gina doesn't talk much about it, but I know she had a bad time and holds her former social worker responsible. She once said she felt like she'd been locked up and the key thrown away. But times have changed, and Gina agrees that the care Laura is receiving is second to none. I've told Gina to phone the social worker now and apologize. It won't do us any good to make an enemy of her. If she's not in her office she can leave a message on her answerphone.'

I nodded. Andy seemed very positive and in control, and also optimistic after being reassured by the nurse in charge. The children came out. Kim rushed into her father's arms and smothered him in kisses, while Adrian greeted me with a typical boy's reserve: a 'Hi, Mum,' accompanied by a cheeky smile.

We began towards the exit. I thought that Andy might want to go ahead and talk to Kim in private, so I held back, but he waited for us to catch up and we began walking home together.

'I've seen Mummy and her doctor today,' he said easily to Kim. 'They've decided it would be best for Mummy to wait a few more weeks before she comes home.'

Kim frowned. 'Why? That's not fair. You said she'd be home soon, so did Mum.'

'I know, and we were wrong to tell you that. It's what we were hoping would happen, but it wasn't definite.' He then explained about the transfer of care to the community, using age-appropriate words so that Kim could understand, and finished by saying there was going to be another meeting in two weeks' time.

'So Mummy will be home in two weeks?' Kim asked fervently.

'We hope so, but we'll tell you when it's definite – as soon as we know. Now, Nanny Geraldine and Gina are both at home waiting for us. We're not going to have dinner before we see Mummy tonight because we're all going out for a meal.'

'With Liam and Mummy too?' Kim asked excitedly.

'Yes.'

'Yippee!' she cried. Hanging onto her father's arm, she skipped for joy.

'You remember that restaurant we keep passing when we visit Mummy?' Andy continued. 'The one with the children's play area?' Kim nodded. 'We're all going there for dinner. You, me, Mummy, Liam, Nanny Gina and Nanny Geraldine.'

'Yes! I'm so happy!' Kim cried, delighted. 'All my family together again.'

I smiled. 'Well done, Andy,' I said quietly. 'Nicely handled.'

'Thanks, Cathy.'

* * *

School broke up early on Friday and the atmosphere in the playground was electric as the children rushed out, overjoyed at the prospect of six weeks of freedom ahead of them. Adrian, like most of the other children, was clutching carrier bags full of his completed school exercise books and art and craft work, including some models, which he was allowed to bring home. I looped the bags we couldn't carry over the handles of the stroller. Parents and children were now calling their goodbyes to friends and wishing them a happy holiday. Gina and Kim left the playground ahead of us as I continued to say goodbye to my friends and also arrange some play dates for Adrian. I'd already told Gina that if she and Kim wanted to pop in to see us during the holidays they'd be very welcome, and she'd said they'd be in touch. Not knowing exactly when Laura and Liam were returning home, they hadn't made plans to go away, but Andy was taking time off work so they could have some days out together. Gina had also told me that once Laura was home she would need to think about returning to her house and to work. Her boss was being understanding, but she was having to take unpaid leave, so it couldn't go on indefinitely, although she said that in the future she'd be seeing a lot more of Laura and her family at weekends than she had done in the past.

Adrian chatted excitedly on the way home about the fun things they'd done at school for their last day: games organized by the teachers rather than lessons, and a film shown on a big screen in the assembly hall, followed by party food. Once home, he immediately changed out of his school uniform and with great satisfaction deposited it ceremoniously into the laundry basket, declaring that it wouldn't be needed again for six weeks! Then he proudly showed Paula and me some of his schoolwork before going into the garden to play. While I made dinner, John, aware that it was the last day of term and Adrian would be excited, telephoned to wish us a happy holiday and confirmed he would be home at the end of August.

'Why not sooner?' Adrian bemoaned.

'Because my work needs me here,' John replied.

'Tell your work I need you more,' Adrian said, which must have touched John's heart as much as it did mine.

We were late rising on Saturday morning and had a leisurely cooked breakfast, then Shelley telephoned. To begin with all I could hear was her sweet voice running up and down the musical scales, pitch perfect, before she burst into laughter. 'The choir always starts with a warm-up,' she said. 'I do them at home too.'

I laughed. 'So the choir is going well?'

'Perfect. I'm so pleased I joined. It's great fun and everyone is really nice. I was a bit anxious about leaving Darrel to begin with, but he knows my friend well and he was fine after I'd gone.'

'That's good.'

'Cathy, the reason I'm phoning is that in September we're starting rehearsals for our Christmas concert and I want you all to come. There'll be two performances, one in the afternoon and one in the evening, so you could bring the kids to the afternoon one. I don't have the date yet. I'll let you know as soon as I do. I'm going to ask Carol as well. You will come, won't you?'

'Yes. As soon as you have the details, tell me and I'll put it in the diary.'

'Thanks. It will be my best Christmas ever!'

It was half a year until Christmas, but I'd found before that many young people from deprived backgrounds who'd never experienced the joys of Christmas as children look forward to the occasion immensely, wanting to create the magic they'd missed out on as children.

Shelley and I chatted for a while longer and then we made an arrangement for her and Darrel to come for lunch the following week.

The children and I quickly relaxed into the holiday routine; they got up later and often had breakfast in their pyjamas before they washed and dressed. I continued rising at my usual time, which allowed me to put the finishing touches to my dissertation so I didn't have to work on it during the day and could play with them. With a combination of days out and time spent at home, the first week of the school holiday quickly disappeared. Shelley and Darrel came for lunch the following Tuesday and after lunch we went to the local park. She reminded me again about the Christmas concert, and she also talked about the choir, specifically about a lad in the choir who was a couple of years older than her. Did I detect a sparkle in her eyes and a quickness to her breath every time she mentioned his name? I didn't embarrass her by asking. Shelley also mentioned that with Darrel starting school in September she was hoping to find a job, preferably part-time to fit in with school hours, and she'd signed up for a return-to-work programme at the employment centre, which was all very positive.

On Wednesday two significant events occurred, both of which gave me much relief. I finished my dissertation and sent it off. And Laura came home. Having not seen or heard from Gina since school broke up, I didn't know exactly when she was coming home, so it was a lovely surprise when I picked up the telephone to hear Laura say, 'Hi, Cathy, I thought you'd like to know that I'm home.'

'Wonderful! I am pleased. Great to have you back.'

'Thanks. It's great to be back. I was discharged yesterday. Mum's going home on Friday, so I was wondering if you and the children could come over tomorrow to say goodbye. We'll have some cake and coffee.'

'I'd love to, thank you. What time?'

'Shall we say after lunch – about two o'clock?'

'That's fine with me. I'll look forward to it.'

'See you then.'

We said goodbye and I hung up.

Should I have asked Laura how she was feeling? I would have done had she been suffering from a physical illness – how is your leg/stomach/arm/back? Are you feeling better? But that awkwardness that can surround mental illness had got in the way. It was silly of me really, because Laura had been very open with me when she'd been ill, but now I felt that maybe she would want to forget it, put the past behind her and move on, and would be embarrassed if I mentioned it. I'd play it by ear the following day and ask her how she was feeling if it seemed appropriate and she wanted to talk about it.

When I told the children that Laura and Liam were home and we were going to see them the next day they were pleased.

'Kim will be so happy to have her mummy back,' Adrian said.

'Baby Liam home!' Paula cried, delighted.

* * *

Having now finished my dissertation there was no reason why I shouldn't put my name on the whiteboard again to foster, so I telephoned the social services and said I was available. They must have written my name on the board straight away, for no more than thirty minutes later Samson's social worker telephoned and asked if I could look after him for respite the following week, from Monday morning to Wednesday evening. I said I could. Sometimes a carer only looks after a child once on respite, or it can become a regular arrangement to give the main caregiver, in this case Samson's grandmother, a break.

'Thanks, Cathy,' she said. 'I'm afraid Samson's behaviour hasn't improved since the last time you saw him. His gran is really struggling now he's off school for the holidays. We arranged a play scheme for him to go to, but he got excluded in the first week – for knocking another child unconscious, although he said it was an accident. I hope you can cope.'

So do I, I thought.

CHAPTER SEVENTEEN

PROGRESS

The following day I bought a bunch of flowers to give to Laura as a welcome-home gift.

'Thank you so much,' she said, smiling and kissing my cheek as we went in. 'My house is starting to look like a florist. Lovely to see you all again. Hi, Adrian, Paula.'

Kim was standing in the hall just behind her mother and smiling broadly. Gina appeared too. 'Hi, gang!' she called. 'Come on in. I'll put those flowers in water, they're beautiful. You see to Cathy and I'll put the kettle on.'

Laura smiled, passed the flowers to her mother and we followed her down the hall into the living room. Liam was sitting contentedly in his bouncing cradle, wide awake and playing with the mobile attached to the cradle, tapping the brightly coloured toys so that they rattled and spun. Paula went straight over to him and, kneeling down, said cutely, 'Baby Liam home.' Which made us smile.

Kim and Adrian stood by, looking slightly awkward. 'Can Adrian and I play in the garden?' Kim asked her mother.

'Yes, of course, love. We'll bring out some drinks and cakes shortly.'

They shot out of the patio doors, eager to be outside. 'Everyone has been so kind,' Laura now said to me, waving to the flowers and cards arranged around the room. The giant get-well card from school was propped by the hearth, and four smaller get-well cards stood on the mantelpiece between two vases of flowers. Another larger arrangement of flowers was in one corner of the room on a small occasional table. 'Those are from Andy, Kim and Liam,' she said. 'And those on the mantelpiece are from Mum and Geraldine.'

'Beautiful,' I said. 'You can never have too many flowers. Your garden's looking good too.'

'Thanks.' We both looked towards the garden. 'Andy cut the grass at the weekend ready for my homecoming, and Mum's been weeding. I was out there this morning too. I'll soon have it back to normal.'

'It looks really nice,' I said.

Gina appeared briefly at the door of the living room carrying my flowers in a vase. 'Shall I put these in the front room?' she asked Laura. 'We haven't any in there.'

'Yes please, Mum. Do you want any help in the kitchen?'

'No, you chat with Cathy.'

'Shall we sit in the garden?' Laura asked me.

'Yes, I love being outside.'

'Me too.' Laura went over to Liam and Paula. 'Let's take Liam in the garden, shall we?' she said to Paula. Paula nodded shyly, and then came over and held my hand.

We went out onto the decking. A white wrought-iron garden table with four matching chairs stood under a sun umbrella.

'This is perfect,' I said.

Laura smiled. 'We're using it a lot this year. Making the most of every day of sunshine.' Vibrant, happy, at ease with herself and others, I could see a huge improvement in Laura even in the few weeks since I'd visited at Everley.

She placed Liam's cradle in the shade of the sun umbrella and Paula squatted down beside him. Laura and I sat on the two chairs facing the garden so we could keep an eye on Kim and Adrian, who'd begun a game of children's croquet.

'It's a beautiful day,' Laura said, taking in a deep breath of fresh summer air. 'Just right. Warm, but with a slight breeze. I'm learning to appreciate the present rather than worry about the future or the past.'

'You look very well,' I said, feeling comfortable saying this, given her last comment.

'I'm getting there,' she said, gazing down the garden. 'They told me at Everley that it would take time and I shouldn't rush myself. But I can see the light at the end of the tunnel now. It's difficult to describe what it's like if you haven't been there. A bit like swimming up through layers of murky water, slowly reaching the surface. I take it a day at a time. I have some blips, but I'm getting there.'

'I suppose that's true for many illnesses,' I said.

'Yes, but with PND (postnatal depression) acknowledging you are ill in the first place is the first big step and part of the recovery process. I now realize that pretending nothing was wrong was the worst thing we could have done. Andy and Geraldine realize that too. It helps so much to have it out in the open so I can talk about how I'm feeling. I know I can ask for help if I need to, instead of trying to be Supermum.' I looked at Laura and nodded. 'The support group and the therapist at Everley have helped me enormously,' she said. 'And the tablets. I'm on a lower dose now, but I'll keep taking them for a few more months. The doctor reassured me that eventually I won't need them and I'll be my old self – maybe even better!' She laughed and then leaned slightly over the side of her chair, closer to Paula. 'You know you don't have to keep Liam amused,' she said to her kindly. 'You can play with your brother and Kim if you like.' But I could see that Paula was enjoying herself, tapping the mobiles and making Liam chuckle.

'She's fine,' I said.

'That's OK then.' Laura straightened and took another deep breath and gazed down the garden. Clearly she was happy to talk and share her experiences, and I felt comfortable listening. 'Andy's been so good,' she said. 'Really supportive. Some of the women in the group said that their partners and family weren't, and gave them the impression that they just had to get over it and it was all in their heads. Which it is, in a way,' she added with a small laugh. 'But dismissing how rough you feel only makes it worse. It can drive you mad. When I think back to that terrifying place I go cold. I don't ever want to be back there again. It was dreadful.'

'You won't,' I said. 'You will continue to go from strength to strength.'

'I hope so.'

Gina appeared carrying a tray containing a white bone-china teapot, matching milk jug, side plates, cups and saucers, a jug of lemonade and children's plastic beakers, which she set on the table.

'I'll fetch the cakes,' Laura said, standing. She went into the kitchen and returned with two plates of the most delicious-looking homemade cakes: a jam-and-cream-filled sponge and a selection of iced and decorated cupcakes.

'Someone's been busy,' I said. 'They look gorgeous.'

'It's Mum,' Laura said, smiling at her mother.

'I used to love baking when Laura was at home,' Gina said. 'It's nice to have a reason to do it again.'

Kim and Adrian had spotted the arrival of the cake and now ran up the garden. Laura gave them a plate each and they helped themselves to a cupcake and she poured the lemonade. Paula chose a cupcake and I put it on a plate for her and then helped her sit on the doorstep where Adrian and Kim were comfortably perched with their plates on their laps and the beakers of lemonade beside them. At four months old Liam wasn't ready for cake and lemonade yet, but he seemed very interested in what everyone else was eating. Laura poured the tea and I chose a slice of sponge cake.

'Hmm, delicious,' I said as I took the first bite.

'I'm glad you like it,' Gina said. 'I've made you one to take home, to say thank you for all you've done.'

'That's very kind of you.' I was really touched. 'It's so light. It melts in your mouth.'

'The secret is in the whisking,' Gina said. 'The more you whisk the lighter the sponge. I'll let you have the recipe, if you like.'

We continued talking as we ate the cake and sipped our tea. It was a perfect English summer scene – ideal weather with tea and cake on the decking. When the children had finished the three of them went down the garden to play, while Laura, Gina and I drank a second cup of tea and chatted. Gina said she was sorry to be leaving, but she had to get back to work. She said how much she'd enjoyed taking Kim to and from school and being part of the family, but she knew Andy and Laura needed time alone now to get back to normal family life. 'They know where I am if I'm needed,' she said. 'And of course I'll be visiting at weekends.'

We stayed for nearly two hours, during which time Laura gave Liam his bottle and Paula held him for a while – seated on the lawn with Laura and me on either side of her to stop Liam rolling off. When it was time to leave, Gina presented me with the sponge cake in an airtight container, which I said I'd return, and a copy of the recipe. Then they all saw us off at the door, Laura with Liam in her arms. I'd already told Laura I hoped she and the children would visit us in the summer holidays, and she said she'd phone me. It was sad saying goodbye to Gina. Although I hadn't known her for very long, we'd shared quite a journey together through Laura's illness and recovery, and I liked her feisty manner. She was someone I would have continued a friendship with had she lived closer, but fostering had shown me that sadly life is full of goodbyes. 'I hope to see you again one time when you visit Laura,' I said. 'Take care.'

'You too, Cathy.' We kissed and hugged goodbye.

I took Adrian and Paula swimming on Saturday and then on Sunday we met my parents at a well-known beauty spot where we had a picnic lunch. Monday loomed and with it Samson. I'd be lying if I said I didn't have reservations about him staying, especially after his social worker's comment about his behaviour having not improved (read: deteriorated). While his previous stay had gone reasonably well, it had been very hard work. I'd had to keep him occupied the whole time and have eyes in the back of my head to ensure he wasn't getting up to mischief. I wasn't the only one with misgivings.

'Can't we have Darrel to stay instead?' Adrian asked when I told him Samson was coming.

'Fostering doesn't work like that, love,' I said. 'We look after children who need a home. Darrel is fine with his mother and I'm sure we'll see them again. But Samson's grandma needs a rest from looking after him.'

'I'm not surprised!' Adrian said, already developing a dry sense of humour.

'I hope that dog isn't there,' Adrian said anxiously the following morning as we clambered into the car to go and collect Samson.

'Don't worry,' I reassured him. 'I'll make sure Bruno is shut away before we go into the flat. I don't want to be eaten any more than you do.' He managed a small smile.

Paula, that much younger, appeared unperturbed by Samson's visit, but of course at her age she was largely unaware of the problems associated with his visit, or of how much effort and constant supervision it took to keep everyone safe while he was with us.

As it turned out Bruno didn't pose a threat, because we didn't have to go into Samson's flat. As we walked up the path to the main entrance of the flats, Paula holding my hand and Adrian snuggled in close behind me using me as a shield, the net curtain at the open downstairs window of Samson's flat was suddenly and roughly yanked aside. Samson's cheeky face grinned at us. 'They're here!' he yelled at the top of his voice over his shoulder. Then, pushing the window as wide open as it would go, he put one leg over and began to clamber out. His backpack got caught on the hinge of the window and he was stuck half in and half out. 'Someone help me!' he yelled dramatically. 'I can't get out!' Adrian and Paula laughed and I smiled. He did look comical.

'Hi, Samson,' I said, going over. 'How are you?'

'I'm bleedin' stuck,' he said, pulling against the straps and trying to free himself.

'All right. Hold still and I'll get you unstuck.' I unhooked the strap from the hinge and he jumped clear. Bruno barked loudly from somewhere inside the flat and Adrian looked concerned.

'Bye, Bruno!' Samson yelled at the top of his voice. 'Shut your face up!' He went over to Adrian. 'Hello, mate, how are you?' he asked, clapping him on the back.

'I'm all right,' Adrian said, putting on a brave face.

'Where's your gran?' I asked Samson. 'We need to say goodbye to her.' I could hardly just go without letting her know; surely she'd wonder where Samson was?

'She's in there,' he said, referring to the lounge he'd just clambered out of.

I returned to the window and pulled aside the net curtain. I could see her sitting on the sofa in her dressing gown with her legs stretched out in front of her, a plate of toast on her lap and a mug of tea in her hand. She was watching television.

'We're going now,' I said. 'I'll bring Samson back at six o'clock on Wednesday.'

'Thanks, dear,' she said, without taking her eyes from the television. And that was it.

'How have you been?' I asked Samson as we began towards my car.

'Better since school finished,' he said, grinning. 'No hassle from the teachers and no work!' Adrian grinned too.

'So what have you been doing in the holidays?' I asked him, making conversation.

'I dunno.' He shrugged. 'Watching telly, PlayStation, I guess. And getting on Gran's nerves.' I laughed. You couldn't help but like him, he was such a character.

'So what would you like to do while you're with us?' I asked him as I unlocked the car and opened the rear door. 'Any suggestions?'

'Sports day,' he said, climbing in. 'Like we did before. I've been practising since I knew I was coming to you, so no one can beat me. I was good then, but I'm even better now. And I've got some prizes for all of us in me bag.'

'Have you?' I asked, surprised and touched. 'That's very kind of you.'

'They're me toys I don't want, so we can have 'em as prizes. I know you gave us some before, but we need lots and lots.'

'OK. That's nice. We'll use them as prizes, but then you must take them home with you afterwards,' I said. 'They are yours.' I helped Paula into her car seat as the boys fastened their safety belts.

'Nah. You can keep 'em,' Samson said. 'I don't want 'em. Me dad gave 'em to me, so I ain't bothered.' Which I thought was strange. Usually gifts from an absent parent are valued and treasured.

I fastened Paula in her car seat, checked the boys' belts, and then closed the rear door.

'So we can have a sports day today,' I said, getting in. 'What would you like to do tomorrow?'

'Go to the cinema,' Samson said without hesitation, clearly having planned it. 'Gran can't take me cos her legs are bad.

She can't bend them to fit in the seat. And me dad's girlfriend says it's too expensive to take me to the cinema.'

'I'll check to see what is showing,' I said. 'There's sure to be plenty of children's films, as it's the summer holidays.'

'I want to see the new *Death of the Avenger* film,' Samson said. 'But I don't suppose you'll take me to that. It's full of blood and guts.'

'No. It's an adult film and not one I'd want to see anyway. It's horrific.'

'I watch them at home,' he said, which I didn't doubt. And then parents wonder why their child is then being aggressive or having nightmares! I knew enough about this series of films to know they contained shocking scenes of violence and certainly weren't suitable for children. But of course it's the parents who have to censor what is shown in the home, and not all parents appreciate the effect these films can have on young minds.

Samson accepted that he wouldn't be watching that type of film with me, either at the cinema or at home, but was now telling Adrian (and Paula) about some of the scenes in the previous films – blood spurting from the necks of severed heads and eyeballs popping out – so I told him we'd talk about something else.

'Like what?' he asked, giving the back of the passenger seat a couple of good kicks, which I ignored.

'You can tell us what else you have been doing since we last saw you,' I said.

'Nothing,' he said. Then turning to Adrian, 'Why? What have you been doing?'

Adrian looked a little uncomfortable, but then began telling Samson about some of the outings and activities he'd enjoyed, including the end-of-term production at school, day trips and the recent birthday parties he'd been to.

'Cor, I wish I got invited to birthday parties,' Samson said enviously. 'I've never been to one. No one asks me.' I felt sorry for him, although I could appreciate why his unruly behaviour might limit his social calendar. 'What do you do at parties?' he now asked Adrian. It was sad he didn't know. Adrian explained about the football party, and also parties at his friends' homes that he'd been to with games and prizes and a party tea.

'I know, missus!' Samson exploded, giving the seat back another kick.

'Cathy,' I corrected. 'Yes?'

'Instead of having another sports day, we'll have a party! We'll give the prizes I've brought to the winners of the games.'

I glanced at him in the interior mirror. 'If that's what you'd like to do, fine, but there will just be the four of us.'

'That's OK,' he said. 'Can you make jelly and ice cream, like Adrian said?'

'I should think so.'

'Good on you!' He was so excited that a volley of kicks now hit the back of the seat, sending dust motes into the air.

'Samson, don't kick the seat, please,' I said.

'Sorry, missus – I mean, Cathy. I won't do it again. I know I have to behave myself with you.'

'Excellent.'

CHAPTER EIGHTEEN

CHILD ABUSE

It's very sad, I think, that while many children enjoy regular birthday parties – going to them and holding them – other children do not. It doesn't take much to give a child a little birthday party, an experience they'll enjoy and remember to mark their special day. You don't need an expensive professional entertainer, an elaborate dressing-up theme or a costly outing; just a few balloons, a sandwich tea and lots of enthusiasm from the organizer. I was determined that we'd make Samson's party as authentic as possible, given the short notice and the fact that there'd just be the four of us and it wasn't his birthday.

Once home, I sent Samson and Adrian into the garden to run some laps, as Samson was now higher than ever at the thought of his party. While the boys ran off some energy I took Paula with me into the kitchen where I quickly made some jellies and put them in the fridge to set. I knew I had ice cream in the freezer. We'd have to pretend with the birthday cake, but I could put together a party tea with some sandwiches, crisps and biscuits. I called the boys in and made us all a drink and a snack, then with the children still seated at the table I produced some sheets of coloured card and crayons and showed them how to make party invitations, which I explained to Samson was the first step in having a party – inviting people to come. As it was going to be Samson's birthday party, I said he would need to give Adrian, Paula and myself an invitation each. 'Yeah, I've seen the kids at school give them out,' he said cheerfully, and my heart went out to him.

This activity kept everyone occupied for half an hour – I helped Paula make hers. I then gathered together the invitations and told Samson what he needed to write in each card and how to spell our names. To begin with he didn't understand why he shouldn't give himself an invitation, so I explained that as it was his party he would know the details – the date, time and place. This wasn't obvious to him, as he'd never had a party before. Once the invites were written, he carefully slid them into the envelopes, printed our names on the outside and ceremoniously gave them out. We opened them with excited exclamations of 'Wow!' and said we'd love to go to his party, which was at two o'clock that afternoon.

I then set up a board game at the table to keep Samson amused while I found a spare birthday card, which, out of sight of Samson, Adrian and I wrote in. I helped Paula write her name. I hung 'Happy Birthday' banners in the living room, which was to act as Samson's house where the party would take place. Adrian helped me blow up balloons and I pinned a couple of them to the door of the living room to show where the party was being held. We then wrapped up some small gifts – I always had a few spare. After lunch I sent Samson for another run in the garden (he was getting hyper again) while I prepared some party food. At one-thirty he began counting off the minutes until two o'clock when he bellowed at the top of his voice: 'It's time for me party!' He ran into the living room, slamming the door to 'his house' behind him so hard in his excitement that the building shook. Holding a present each, Adrian, Paula and I knocked on the door.

'Who is it?' he yelled from the other side.

'Cathy, Adrian and Paula,' I replied.

'What do you want?' he demanded.

Adrian laughed, for of course this wasn't how you greeted guests coming to your party, but Samson wasn't to know – he'd never done it before.

'We've come to your birthday party,' I said through the door. 'We're all very excited. Can we come in?'

'I'll think about it,' Samson said, which made Adrian laugh even more. Samson then asked, 'Have you brought me a present?'

'Yes,' I said as Adrian giggled.

'OK. You can come in then.' The door quickly opened and he relieved us of our gifts. 'Cor, proper presents!' he said, taking them to the sofa to unwrap them. 'These aren't the ones I brought.'

'Happy Birthday,' Adrian and I said as Samson began tearing off the wrapping paper.

His face was a picture. 'Cor, thanks,' he said, after opening each gift. He had a Batman jigsaw puzzle from Adrian, a word-search book from me and a small, boxed car from Paula, who was looking rather bemused by what was going on. After the door had slammed Toscha had fled to the bottom of the garden and taken refuge on top of the shed. Samson opened the card and I helped him read what we'd written:

To Samson,
Have a lovely party.
Best wishes from Cathy, Adrian and Paula.

'We usually stand our cards on the mantelpiece,' I said to Samson. He handed me the card and I put it in pride of place in the centre.

'Now can we play games and win prizes?' he asked.

'Yes,' I said.

I'd already thought of some games that would work with just the few of us – musical chairs, hunt the thimble, pass the orange, musical statues and sleeping lions. I had some little prizes ready (from my emergency store), but Samson wanted to use the ones he'd brought with him when Adrian, Paula or I won a game. I was therefore able to express genuine surprise when I opened my prize to find a toy ambulance with three wheels missing and half a stale biscuit in the rear. Adrian had a pick-up truck for a prize and Paula a small toy horse. Indeed, many of the prizes we opened were from a toy farm-yard set, including a dog-chewed farmer, bales of hay with teeth marks and a scarecrow with a leg missing. We thanked Samson – it was thoughtful of him, although I'd have to make sure he took his toys home with him. As a foster carer I knew difficult situations could arise if parents discovered their child's possessions were missing, even if the child had given them away. But for now his prizes were part of our play and we were as delighted with ours as Samson was with his – which he would be keeping.

Tea was a success, especially the jelly and ice cream, and cake. I still had over half the cake Gina had given to me, so I decorated it with six candles and set it on the table with the round side facing Samson. He knew it had a piece missing, but it didn't matter. It was the fun of the experience that counted. We sang 'Happy Birthday', he blew out his candles and we all cheered. Samson enjoyed blowing out the candles so much that I had to relight them three times. I helped him cut the cake into four slices. I asked him if he'd had a birthday celebration when he had been six, but he shrugged and changed the subject, so I guessed he hadn't.

'What happens now?' he asked as he crammed the last mouthful of cake into his mouth.

'Well, at the end of a party the host usually sees the guests out and thanks them for coming.'

'Can we have some more games?' he asked, not wanting the party to end.

'All parties have to end some time,' I said. 'And then you have the happy memories to look back on.' We'd been playing at parties for over three hours. 'One more game of sleeping lions and then you can say goodbye to your guests.'

It actually turned into three games of sleeping lions and another of hunt the thimble before Samson announced it was time for us to go. Grabbing Adrian's arm, he began pulling him roughly towards the living-room door.

'No, Samson,' I said, intervening. 'You don't treat your guests like that. You have to be gentle and see them out nicely or they won't want to come again.'

Fortunately Adrian saw the funny side of it and was laughing rather than looking worried. In fact, I'd noticed that Adrian had generally seemed more relaxed around Samson during the afternoon, I think possibly because he'd seen Samson's vulnerable, childlike side when he'd been so involved in enjoying his party.

'You just walk to the door with them,' I said to Samson. 'Thank them for their present and say goodbye.'

Which he now did. Having let Adrian out of the living room, I kept hold of Paula's hand while he saw us out. 'Thank you for my party,' he said.

'You're welcome,' I said. 'Thank you for asking us.'

It hadn't taken much, but I could see it had meant a lot to Samson, and doubtless he would have some happy memories of playing parties that afternoon. Later, I left the boys doing a word-search puzzle while I took Paula up for her bath and bed. Once she was settled, I brought the boys up and then discovered that Samson, having done his own packing, had very little in his backpack apart from the prizes he'd brought with him and his wash bag. I found some pyjamas that fitted him in my spares and a change of clothes for the following day. All foster carers keep spare clothes of different sizes for both sexes for emergency use. As the boys had done a lot of running around and were quite sweaty I thought they should both have a bath, so I settled Samson in his room where he continued the word search while Adrian had his bath. Then Adrian went to his room while I ran Samson's bath. Although Samson had good self-care skills, I made sure the water was the right temperature, then I waited by the bathroom door to check he climbed in safely. As he did I saw a large, angry bruise on his right buttock. My immediate thought was that it must have happened today while he'd been playing. He was so boisterous in his play he often literally threw himself into a game, landing on his knees or bottom. Foster carers have to log any accidents that happen to a child they are looking after and make a note of even minor injuries. I would also need to tell his grand-mother what had happened when I returned him.

'That's a big bruise,' I said as he sat in the water. 'Do you know how you did it?'

'Where?' he asked, examining his arms and legs. Like many boys his age they were dotted with small, fading bruises from tumbles during play.

'No, the one on your bottom,' I said.

He turned to try and see but it was out of view. 'Dunno,' he said, disinterested, and began splashing water on himself.

'Do you remember when you could have done it?' I asked. 'Did you sit down very heavily in the garden, or on the patio?'

He shrugged. 'Dunno.'

'OK. Wash yourself. I'll wait here.'

I stood on the landing by the bathroom door to give him some privacy while he washed himself. I knew he wouldn't be long; most boys his age don't linger in the bath or shower. I didn't think playing musical chairs could have given him the bruise – we'd used cushions – and I couldn't imagine that sitting heavily on the carpeted floor could have caused it either. I therefore assumed it must have happened in the garden or possibly before he'd come to me. I'd still have to make a note of it and mention it to his gran.

Samson had a predictably quick bath and clambered out. Drying his front, he stood with his back to the mirror and then craned his neck round to look over his shoulder to see the bruise.

'Oh, that,' he said nonchalantly. 'Me dad's girlfriend did that. She's always whacking me.'

'Is she?' I said. 'That doesn't sound right. With what?'

'Whatever she has,' he said matter-of-factly. 'The broom handle did that. It blimmin' hurt.' He continued towel-drying himself.

'I'm sure it did hurt,' I said. 'She shouldn't be hitting you.'

'I shouldn't have been naughty,' he replied.

'It was still wrong of her to hit you,' I said. While the law in England at present allows a parent to give a child a small slap or tap on the hand when chastising them, hitting the child so it leaves a mark is illegal. It's also child abuse and cruel. Foster carers, childminders, teachers and other childcare workers are not allowed to smack a child, and personally I have never slapped my own children. I use sanctions – the loss of a privilege – and firm talking to curb negative behaviour.

'When did it happen?' I asked Samson as he began pulling on his pyjamas.

'Friday,' he said. 'When I saw me dad. I don't like her, but he lives in her flat so I'm supposed to show her respect.'

Pity she hadn't shown Samson some respect, I thought. 'Does your dad know she hits you?'

'Yeah, of course, he's there,' Samson said, as though it was a daft question.

'Have you told your gran?' I asked.

'Nah. I'd get into more trouble if she found out I'd been rude. Although she doesn't beat me.'

'It's very wrong to hit people,' I said. 'And no one should hit a child. How often does it happen?' I wondered if it was a one-off and she'd lost her temper, although that wouldn't justify it. The severity of the bruise suggested she'd really lashed out and lost control.

'Every time I see her,' Samson said. 'I hate her and she hates me. Do I have to brush my teeth again? I did 'em this morning.'

'Yes please, you should brush your teeth every night and morning.' He gave a groan but picked up his toothbrush and toothpaste from where I'd left them ready on the basin. 'What's your dad's girlfriend's name?' I asked.

'Tanzy,' he said, squirting a very generous measure of paste onto his toothbrush.

'I'll need to tell your social worker so she can stop it happening.'

'That's OK with me,' he said. 'I don't want to see me dad any more when she's there.'

I waited while he brushed his teeth and then I saw him into bed. I tucked him in, dimmed the light, as he liked it, and then gave him a kiss and hug as his gran did.

'What are we seeing at the cinema tomorrow?' he asked as he snuggled down.

'There's a cartoon film showing about dinosaurs,' I said.

'Do they fight each other and eat people?' he asked, his eyes widening in anticipation.

'I wouldn't be surprised,' I said, although I hoped the film wouldn't be frightening, as Paula would be with us. I'd chosen a film with a Universal rating that was suitable for all ages of children and with a subject matter that would appeal to Samson and Adrian. 'Night then, love,' I said, smiling at him.

'Night,' he said, and then looked at me thoughtfully as though he had something to say.

'Yes?' I asked.

'While you're telling me social worker about Tanzy hitting me with a broom you'd better tell her about the other stuff too. Like when I stay there and she shuts me out of her flat. And locks me in the bathroom when her and Dad go to the pub. Gran never does that. And the time she really lost it and tried to strangle me. Me dad stopped her. Just as well or I'd be bleedin' dead.'

I looked at him carefully. 'She did all those things?' I asked, appalled and trying to hide my shock.

'Yeah.'

'That's very wrong,' I said. 'I will tell your social worker and I expect she'll want to talk to you about what happened. She'll want the details, so it's important you tell her, all right?' It was best if I left further questioning to his social worker who, having worked with the family for some time, knew the case well.

Samson nodded. 'It is wrong of her to do these things, isn't it?'

'Yes. Very wrong.'

'I told me dad she shouldn't be treating me like that, but he said if I made trouble she'd chuck him out and he'd have nowhere to live.'

'He's an adult,' I said. 'He can look after himself. He'll find somewhere else to live if necessary. Where he lives isn't your problem. And as your father he should be protecting you and keeping you safe. Not letting you get hurt.'

'I wish me mum had stayed,' Samson said thoughtfully. 'But I guess that's life.' With a shrug he turned over, ready for sleep.

I touched his shoulder. 'Night then, love. Sleep tight, and see you tomorrow.'

'Night,' his voice came from under the duvet. 'Thanks for me party.'

'You're welcome, love.'

Sad and worried, I came out, closing the door behind me. I believed what Samson had told me about his father's girl-friend. His matter-of-fact resignation to being punished and his childlike description convinced me it was true, but it would be for the social services to investigate. I'd telephone his social worker first thing in the morning. The poor kid, I thought, and I wondered how much of his bad behaviour resulted from the abuse he was suffering. He must be angry, and in children anger often comes out in challenging behaviour.

I went into Adrian's room, spent some time lying with him, then said goodnight and checked on Paula. She was sound asleep. Downstairs, I wrote notes on what Samson had told me and then I finished washing the dishes and tidying up from the party, although I left Samson's birthday card on the mantelpiece. With my dissertation finished I didn't feel guilty watching some television, then after the ten o'clock news I let Toscha out for a run and went up to bed. I didn't sleep. As soon as I started to drift off my thoughts went to Samson and what he'd suffered, and would still be suffering if something wasn't done. I appreciated how much patience it took to look after him, even for a short while, but there was no justification for hitting him or locking him in or out of the flat. My anger rose, not just towards the girlfriend, but also towards Samson's father, who'd put his own needs first and failed to protect his son. By standing by and doing nothing he'd been an accomplice in the abuse and was as much to blame as his girlfriend.

It was after midnight before I finally fell asleep and then the following morning Samson was wide awake at six o'clock. I settled him in his bedroom with some toys while I showered and dressed. After breakfast, and as soon as the social services' offices opened at nine o'clock, I told Samson and Adrian that I needed them to look after Paula while I made an important telephone call. Samson rose to the responsibility and held

Paula's hand, which was sweet. I left the three of them seated on the floor in the living room playing with a selection of games, while I went into the hall to make the call. I could hear them from there. I think Samson knew what the call was about, but there was no need for me to tell Adrian; he was used to me making and receiving important calls in connection with fostering.

Samson's social worker was at her desk and she went very quiet as I described the bruise and what Samson had said. Then she gave a heartfelt sigh, which seemed to say, 'Not more suffering … When will it end?'

'We've had concerns about the level of care Samson has been receiving for some time,' she said. 'But this is new. I'll need to speak to him. I can't make it today or tomorrow. My diary is full. I'll see him on Thursday morning when he's home. Does he know you're telling me?'

'Yes. I told him I'd tell you.'

'Good. Reassure him he's done the right thing in telling you and I'll see him on Thursday. I think I'll need to set up supervised contact at the family centre for Friday so he can still see his father, but I'll explain that to him on Thursday. How is he?'

'Not too bad. He wasn't upset when he told me. He seemed to think he deserved being treated like that because he was naughty.'

'The poor kid. And how is his behaviour generally with you?'

'Very manageable.'

'So if we do need to bring him into care, you could foster him, rather than just do respite?'

'Yes.'

'Thank you, Cathy.'

We said goodbye and I put the phone down and returned to the living room. Just in time! Samson was pretending Paula was Superwoman and had stood her on the coffee table and was now telling her to leap off.

'That's not looking after her,' I said to both boys as I lifted her off.

'Sorry, Mum,' Adrian said guiltily. Samson glared at me.

'Can't have any fun here,' he grumbled. And from then on the day went downhill. Perhaps it was because he knew that what he'd told me would have repercussions, or maybe he was just testing me, I didn't know, but he spent the entire morning trying to wind me up, teasing Adrian and Paula, and unable to settle to anything for more than five minutes. Eventually, although I didn't like doing it, I said that unless his behaviour improved we wouldn't be going to the cinema, and he settled down – until we were in the cinema. Then, with limited sanctions available in the cinema to curb his behaviour, he made the most of it by throwing popcorn, kicking the back of the seat in front, jumping up and down, whooping, shouting, giving a running commentary on the film at the top of his voice and generally making a spectacle of himself. Those around us kept turning and shushing him. Adrian looked embarrassed (as I was) and even told him to sit down and be quiet. Some of Samson's behaviour was natural exuberance – excitability – but most of it wasn't. He was testing the boundaries to the limit. The word 'manageable' I'd used earlier to describe his behaviour to his social worker came back to haunt me and I wondered what on earth I'd done by offering to foster him more permanently.

'Samson,' I eventually hissed in his ear. 'You have to settle down, now. Do you understand me? You're spoiling it for others.'

'Don't care,' he said rudely.

'Well, I do, so sit still, stop kicking the seat and shouting or we'll have to leave, and you'll miss the rest of the film.' Indeed, I didn't know why a member of staff hadn't asked us to leave already. Perhaps no one had reported us yet.

'You wouldn't do that,' he challenged me. 'You paid for the tickets. It would be a waste if we didn't see the film.'

'Try me,' I said, meeting his gaze.

He did, and kicked the seat in front so hard that the boy sitting in it jolted forward. 'I'm so sorry,' I said to his mother, who'd turned round and glared at me, annoyed. Then to Samson I said, 'Right, that's it. You've been warned. We're going now.' I picked up my handbag from the floor and moved to the edge of the seat.

He looked shocked. 'Not really?' he asked incredulously.

'Yes. I've warned you so many times.' I turned to Paula, ready to help her off her seat.

At that point Samson finally realized that I meant what I said. 'All right, I'll be good,' he said in a loud whisper.

'No. You've had your chances. It's not fair on the others here.' I made another move to go.

'I promise,' he pleaded. 'Really, I won't do it again.' I looked at him and hesitated. 'Pleeeeze,' he said.

'This will be your very last chance,' I said. 'One more naughty thing and we go home.'

'Will you be quiet?' the woman in front said, turning again.

'Sorry,' I said. Although a bit of patience from her wouldn't have gone amiss – she could see I was dealing with a difficult situation.

Samson sat back in his seat and I tried to relax back in mine. My heart was racing and I felt completely stressed. I held Paula's hand in the dark and waited for Samson's next outburst, when we would leave straight away. But it didn't come. He sat back as good as gold for the rest of the film, and eventually I relaxed too. Samson had tested the boundaries, tested me to the limit and had finally accepted my guidelines for good behaviour – in this situation at least. I knew that if I brought him to the cinema again he'd remember how to behave and it would be that little bit easier.

CHAPTER NINETEEN

UNWELCOME NEWS

When I took Samson home on Wednesday evening it was raining and the window to his flat was closed. We went in through the main entrance and I pressed the doorbell to his flat – number 17. Bruno immediately started barking loudly on the other side and pounded down the hall, landing heavily against the back of the door. Adrian jumped back and I reassured him again that we wouldn't go in until the dog was safely shut away.

'Bruno!' Samson yelled at the top of his voice, banging his fists on the door and winding up the dog even more. I picked up Paula just in case someone opened the door before the dog was shut away. He was so big he would have knocked her flying.

Eventually someone dragged him away and his barks subsided. As we waited for the door to be opened Samson put down his backpack and took out the birthday card and presents we'd given to him, ready to show his family. It was his gran who opened the door.

'Look what I've got! Birthday presents!' he cried, holding them up for her to see.

'It's not your birthday, you silly bugger,' she said, leaning heavily against the wall for support.

'I know that!' Samson cried indignantly. 'But we pretended it was. I had jelly and ice cream and we played games and won prizes. They're in me bag.'

Most parents or grandparents would have said something like, 'That sounds great. Come in and tell me all about it.' But Samson's gran said, 'Are you coming in or what, you daft bugger? I can't be standing here all day. Me legs are killing me.'

I don't think she meant to be unkind, it was just her way, but I saw the look of disappointment on Samson's face. I was now expecting him to assume his usual tough exterior and run indoors shouting, without giving us a second thought, as he'd done before. But he didn't. He stayed where he was and looked up at me. 'Thanks for me party,' he said sweetly. 'It was nice of you to go to all that trouble.'

I could have cried. 'You're very welcome, love,' I said, and touched his shoulder. 'We all enjoyed it.'

Then, turning to Adrian, he said, 'Bye. Thanks for sharing your toys.'

'That's OK,' Adrian said.

Samson reached up to Paula who was still in my arms, wanting to say goodbye to her, so I set her on the ground. 'Bye, Paula,' he said, gently tickling her under the chin. She chuckled. 'Thanks for coming to me party.' I swallowed hard. All that bravado and underneath he was a kind-hearted, thoughtful child who had so much appreciated our pretend party. I felt guilty, and silently renewed my promise that if he ever needed a permanent foster home, I would look after him. It would be hard work, but I'd manage.

We weren't invited into the flat. Gran said to him, 'Now you've said goodbye, boy, you'd better get tidying ya room – ya social worker's coming tomorrow.'

He shrugged and disappeared down the hall.

'He's been fine,' I said to her.

'That makes a change,' she said, and shifting uncomfortably from one foot to the other she began to close the door.

We said goodbye and as we turned the door closed behind us. Bruno barked loudly from inside, which set off another dog in a neighbour's house. It was unlikely I'd hear the outcome of the social worker's visit, or what decisions were made regarding Samson's father and girlfriend, unless I looked after Samson again. Foster carers are told what they need to know about a child's situation while they are fostering them, but once they've left their care they're rarely given updates, which is a pity, as we often think about them and wonder how they're getting on.

We were now already halfway through the summer holidays and making the most of every day. John was due home in two weeks and the date was circled on the calendar on the wall in the kitchen, although we didn't need a reminder. The following day one of Adrian's friends came to play and stayed for dinner, and then on Friday I took the children swimming again. The week after followed a similar pattern of days out and time at home, and included a day trip to the coast with my parents. I hadn't seen Laura since I'd been invited to her house for tea to say goodbye to Gina. I assumed all was well. It had crossed my mind a couple of times to telephone her for a chat in the evening, but then the time had disappeared and it was too late to phone. Although I didn't have another foster child, I was on standby. A social worker had telephoned and said she was trying to bring a teenager into care but she'd run away. She'd asked if I could take her at short notice when they found her – they would bring her straight to me – and I said I could. I'd be told more once she was found and was with me.

It was early on the Saturday evening at the end of that week and I was in the living room with Adrian and Paula. We were on the floor playing Snap. Adrian and I were trying to teach Paula the game. She was too young really, but she wanted to join in. The telephone rang and I answered it in the living room. There was a short silence before a half-familiar voice said, 'Cathy, I'm sorry to disturb you. It's Geraldine.'

'Oh, hello,' I said, surprised. 'How are you? Is everything all right?'

'I'm sorry to bother you on a Saturday night,' she said, 'but I need your advice.'

'Yes,' I said, puzzled. 'I'll help if I can. Is it urgent? Or could I phone you back once the children are in bed?'

There was another pause before she said, 'I was wondering if I could come and see you. It would be easier to talk face to face rather than over the telephone.'

'Yes, of course,' I said, concerned. 'Is Laura all right?'

'It's partly about Laura, yes, but I'll explain when I see you.'

'All right. Would you like to come here this evening? About eight o'clock?'

'If that is convenient with you.'

'Yes. I'll have the children in bed by then. I'll see you at eight.'

'Thank you, Cathy,' she said stiffly, and hung up.

It was clear from her tightly controlled manner that she'd carefully planned what she needed to say. Given that she was not a person who easily shared her feelings or asked for help,

I appreciated that whatever she wanted to talk about must be very serious indeed.

I returned to sit on the floor and play with the children, but my mind wasn't on the game as I ran through the possible reasons for Geraldine wanting to see me. She'd said it was 'partly' about Laura, and I hadn't pressed her as I respected that she preferred to talk in person, which I understood. At seven o'clock, when we finished playing, I took Paula upstairs for her bath and bed, and once she was settled I fetched Adrian. As I lay propped on his bed beside him, having our little goodnight chat, I told him that Kim's grandma, Geraldine, was coming later, just in case he heard the door go and wondered who it was.

'Is she your friend then?' he asked, slightly surprised. I sometimes had a friend round in the evening.

'More like an acquaintance,' I said. 'She wants to talk to me about something – I don't know what exactly.'

'I hope Kim's mummy isn't in hospital again,' he said.

'I don't think she is or Geraldine would have said, but it's nothing for you to worry about.' Like me, Adrian was a bit of a worrier and could fret over things that shouldn't have bothered him.

'I won't worry,' he said cheerfully, snuggling down ready for sleep. 'Dad's phoning tomorrow and he'll be home in a week.'

'That's right. So you think about nice things while you go off to sleep and I'll see you in the morning.'

I kissed him goodnight and came out, then checked on Paula before I went downstairs. I gave the living room a quick tidy ready for Geraldine's arrival and then sat on the sofa. It was now 7.45 and still light outside. Toscha wandered in and settled beside me on the sofa.

At exactly eight o'clock I heard a little tap on the front door. I went down the hall and checked in the security spyhole before opening the door.

'I didn't use the bell,' Geraldine explained apologetically. 'I thought it might wake your children.'

'Come in,' I said. 'They're in bed.'

She was dressed smartly but reservedly as usual, in a knee-length skirt, button-up blouse and cardigan. Her short grey hair was neatly trimmed.

'I haven't seen you for a while,' I said, making conversation as I showed her through to the living room. 'How have you been?'

'Oh, me? I'm all right,' she said dismissively, as though her welfare was of no concern.

'Do sit down. Would you like a drink?'

'No, thank you. I won't keep you longer than I have to. I'm sure you have things to do.' She sat in one of the armchairs and I returned to the sofa. She had an air of businesslike formality about her.

'I'll come straight to the point,' she said, sitting upright and looking directly at me. 'Laura's had a setback.'

'Oh dear, I am sorry. She was doing so well. Is she in hospital?'

'No. She's at home, but she's been very upset and is now depressed again. She knows I'm coming to see you; so does Andy. We haven't worried Gina with it yet.'

I nodded. Clearly it was their decision what or when they told Gina, although I thought it should be sooner rather than later.

'The reason I've come to see you is to ask if it is possible to change social workers. I thought you might know, as you work with them. Are people allowed to change their social worker?'

'Well, yes, sometimes,' I said. 'Are you thinking of asking for Laura's social worker to be changed?'

She nodded stiffly. 'But we don't want to cause trouble and make things worse for Laura. Would it be held against her?'

'No. It shouldn't be. Can I ask why you are thinking of requesting a change of social worker?'

'We believe she's responsible for Laura's a setback,' Geraldine said.

I met her gaze. 'How?'

'What she says and the way she speaks to Laura is all wrong. Laura is sensitive at present, she's vulnerable, and the woman doesn't seem to understand that. It's not only Laura who thinks this; Andy and I do too. We thought the woman was going to help support Laura, but she's doing more harm than good. You know that Gina had a couple of blazing arguments with her a while back. Then Andy and I thought it was Gina who was in the wrong and had overreacted, but not any longer.'

'I see,' I said thoughtfully. 'Something certainly seems to have gone badly wrong for you all to feel this way.'

'Every time she speaks to Laura, Laura ends up in tears. And when she's not there Laura worries about what she's saying about her – the reports she writes and the meetings she has with her manager, which Laura isn't invited to. Laura says she feels her life is slipping out of her control again, because of this woman. She was doing so well. Do you think we have a good reason to ask for a change of social worker or will they say we're causing trouble?'

'I know of cases where there has been a change of social worker,' I said. 'Either because the social services felt it was appropriate, or the client requested it.'

'So it does happen?'

'Yes. Sometimes.'

'Do you think we should say it's a personality clash, rather than blaming the social worker?'

'I suppose it would be more diplomatic, although I think she needs to know how you all feel. She'll probably have no idea of the harm she's doing. Have you spoken to her about it?'

'No.' Geraldine shook her head.

'Would you feel comfortable discussing it with her?'

'I think that would be very difficult,' she said, her brow creasing.

'Then you will probably need to speak to her manager.'

'And we wouldn't be considered trouble-makers, for going behind her back?'

'No. You have valid concerns.'

'So if we request a change of social worker, can we ask for one by name? And if so, can you recommend one, or is that not allowed?'

'Not really,' I said. 'But I've worked with a lot of excellent social workers. What's happened here is unfortunate. If it's decided that a change of social worker is appropriate, it will depend on caseload and experience as to who takes over Laura's case.'

'I see,' Geraldine said, and wrung her hands in her lap. 'This is so difficult. Should we phone, write or make an appointment to see someone? Who do we ask for? Do you know the name of her manager?'

'No, I'm sorry, I don't offhand.' I hesitated and then said, 'Would it help if I telephoned the social services and found out who you should speak to? And confirmed what the correct procedure is?'

'Oh, yes. Would you? We'd be so grateful. We feel completely out of our depth. We don't want to say the wrong thing and make it worse.'

'Don't worry. I'll phone on Monday. But if they ask who it is in connection with, do I have permission to tell them?'

She hesitated. 'Yes, if it helps. I'll leave it to your discretion. Do what you think is necessary.'

'And Laura and Andy are happy for me to telephone?'

'I'm sure they will be. I'll ask them when I get back. Thank you so much, Cathy. I am grateful. I'll let you get on then.' Adjusting her cardigan, she stood ready to leave.

As I saw her out she thanked me again and said she'd phone as soon as she'd discussed what I'd said with Andy and Laura. She was going there now. I asked her to pass on my best wishes to Laura and to remind her that if she felt like dropping by I'd be very pleased to see her.

'I'll tell her,' she said.

Having seen her out, I closed the front door and returned to the living room, deep in thought. I could understood why Geraldine, Andy and Laura felt the way they did: viewing the social services as a vast, secretive, impenetrable organization with immense powers, ultimately to take your children away. Many feel this way, and until there is complete transparency in the system, with court cases accessible to the public, this view won't change. Sadly it seemed that Laura's social worker had compounded this perception. I suppose the family saw me, a foster carer, as a halfway point, a stepping stone, between them and the social services, and to a certain extent I was. Because of my role I had greater insight into the workings of the social services and possibly more accessibility. However, I didn't know whom I should contact to ask advice about a change of social worker; it wasn't something I'd ever been involved in before. Recently, I'd been working with two very good social workers, albeit for respite care only: Samson's and Shelley's. Of the two I'd found Shelley's more approachable. Shelley had spoken highly of her social worker, and I remembered she'd said she'd been very supportive of her when she'd been low after having Darrel. I decided she was the person to ask for advice and I decided I would telephone her on Monday, assuming of course that Andy and Laura agreed with Geraldine that I should phone.

They did. At nine-thirty, three-quarters of an hour after Geraldine had left me, Andy telephoned.

'Thanks, Cathy. Geraldine's told us what you've said and we'd like to accept your kind offer. Please go ahead, but could you emphasize that we're not making a complaint; we just feel Laura would benefit from a change of social worker.'

'I understand,' I said.

I then asked after Laura, and Andy said more or less what Geraldine had said. I finished by saying I'd let them know as soon as I'd spoken to someone at the social services on Monday.

'Thanks again,' he said.

I find that bad news never seems to come alone, and having heard that Laura had suffered a setback, I was shortly to receive more unwelcome news. On Sunday evening the children and I were in the living room; I was reading a story to them while we waited for John's weekly telephone call from

America. He always called about the same time on a Sunday and Adrian answered it. Aged five, this was the only time he was allowed to answer the phone, as I knew who it would be. He loved this small responsibility. 'Hello, Daddy,' he always said proudly, as soon as he picked up the handset, without waiting to hear his father's voice. Then John usually said, 'Hi, Son, how are you?' And they'd start chatting. Tonight, however, with John due home the following weekend, Adrian's excitement was bubbling over. He snatched up the handset and cried all in one breath, 'Hi, Dad, I'm going to see you soon! I can't wait.'

He went very quiet and I watched his little face fall, then he said quietly, 'Why not? You promised.'

Close to tears, he passed the handset to me. 'Dad wants to speak to you,' he said. 'He's not coming home next weekend.'

I put the phone to my ear. 'John?'

Both children watched me carefully as I listened to what John had to say. Paula wasn't old enough to understand what was happening, but she sensed the atmosphere had changed.

'I'm sorry, love,' John said. 'I know you're all disappointed. But the project I'm working on has developed a problem. I've had to cancel all leave and keep everyone on site until it's sorted out.'

'How long is that likely to take?' I asked, trying to adopt the sensible, adult approach.

'I'm hoping we'll get it fixed in a couple of weeks, but it could take longer.'

'And you have to be there?' I asked. 'Someone else couldn't manage it?'

'No. I'm in charge of this project, so it's my responsibility. I'm to blame, if you like. Trust me, I'd much rather be at home.' I heard the stress in his voice and knew he needed my support, not a guilt trip.

'I understand,' I said. 'I'll explain to Adrian, but he's bound to be disappointed.'

'I know. Let me talk to him again. I am sorry.'

I set my expression to an encouraging smile and passed the phone to Adrian. 'Daddy will be home before too long, he's just been delayed,' I said.

I couldn't hear what John was saying, but I could see from Adrian's expression that gradually, as his father spoke and reassured him, he accepted that the delay couldn't be helped and his dad would be home as soon as possible. He then brightened a little and told his father about some of the activities we'd done during the last week. When Adrian had finished talking to his father he passed the phone to Paula. She was able to say 'Hello' and 'Goodbye, Daddy', and in between she giggled and kept looking at the phone to see where his voice was coming from. John always finished by saying goodbye to Adrian and then me.

'Take care,' I said. 'And come home as soon as you can.'

'Of course I will,' he said.

That evening as I lay beside Adrian and we had our goodnight chat and hug, I reassured him again that his father would be home as soon as possible.

'I know,' he said. 'At least my daddy lives with us most of the time. Some of the kids at school don't have that.'

'That's right,' I said, pleased he was adopting a positive approach. 'And in a few weeks' time he should be home for good.'

CHAPTER TWENTY

WAITING IN

At 11.30 on Monday morning I settled Adrian and Paula in the living room with their toys and took the phone into the hall where I telephoned Shelley's social worker. It was the second time I'd tried to call her that morning. When I'd phoned her previously a colleague had said she was out of the office and would return around 10.30. I guessed she was very busy on a Monday morning, but now she answered.

'It's Cathy Glass. I looked after Darrel,' I said, feeling slightly guilty for bothering her with a non-urgent matter.

'Yes, of course, hello. How are you?'

'I'm fine, thank you. I'm sorry to trouble you, but I need some advice and I thought you'd be a good person to ask.'

'Is it about Shelley and Darrel?' she asked, a little concerned.

'No. Not at all. I'm really phoning on behalf of a friend.' I then quickly explained Laura's situation – her postnatal depression and psychosis, her admission to hospital, discharge and the problems she was now facing with her social worker, without giving any names. I finished with, 'Shelley mentioned you'd helped her after she'd had Darrel, so I thought you might be able to give me some guidance that I can pass on to the family on the best way to approach this.'

'I see, well, normally the social worker would be the person to approach in the first instance when a client has concerns, but it seems to have gone past that point, so they would need to speak to the social worker's manager. If you tell me who the social worker is I can tell you which manager the family needs to speak to.'

'Thank you. That's rather what I thought.' I told her the social worker's name.

There was a short pause. 'Does this refer to Laura and Liam?' she asked.

'Yes,' I said, slightly surprised.

'I know their social worker, we're in the same team and share the same manager. I'm sure she has no idea of the effect her words are having.'

'No, I'm sure she hasn't,' I said. 'And the family are keen that this isn't treated as a formal complaint. They might still have to work with her.'

'Yes, I understand, but our manager is very approachable. I'm sure she'll be able to help. Her telephone number is –' I wrote it down. 'I have a meeting with her this afternoon. Shall I tell her what you've said so she's expecting a call from the family?'

'I think that would be helpful. Thank you.'

'But you know, it's strange that they feel this way. From what I know of the case, Laura is doing very well.'

'She was,' I said. 'I don't know all the details.'

'All right. I'll speak to my manager. And please tell Laura not to worry. I'm sure we can work something out.'

'Thank you so much. I am grateful.' We said goodbye.

Before I made the next call – to Laura's home – I checked on Paula and Adrian, who were still playing, then I stepped into the hall again. I was half expecting Laura's telephone to be answered by Geraldine, but it was Kim who said a very polite, 'Hello, who's calling, please?'

'Hi, love, it's Cathy, Adrian's mum. How are you?'

'I'm very well, thank you. Did you want to speak to Mummy?'

'Yes, or Geraldine.'

'She's not here. Mummy is in charge. Granny Geraldine only comes here sometimes, when Mummy asks her to.' Which sounded positive.

'OK. I'd like to speak to Mummy then, thank you.'

'Mum!' Kim shouted. 'It's Cathy.' A moment later Laura came to the phone.

'Hello, have you spoken to the social services?' she asked slightly anxiously.

'Yes, just now. They told me to tell you not to worry, that something can be worked out.' She gave a long, heartfelt sigh; not so much from relief, I thought, but more as though it was all too much for her. 'Laura, would you prefer it if I called back later with the details when Andy is home?' I asked.

'No, I need to face this. I can't just hide.' I heard her sigh again.

'All right, if you're sure.'

'Yes, go ahead.'

'I've emphasized that you're not making a complaint but that you'd like to discuss certain issues relating to your social worker. As I thought, you need to speak to your social worker's manager. I have her name and number here.'

'Just a minute while I fetch a pen and paper.'

I waited, and when she came on the line again I gave her the manager's details. 'She's expecting your call,' I said.

'Is she?' Laura asked, now sounding alarmed. 'You told her I'd phone?'

'Not necessarily you. But I said one of your family would – Geraldine or Andy.'

'Oh yes, sorry. I see. I thought you meant I had to phone them. I couldn't do that right now. Or perhaps I should and push myself.' She sounded very tense, so different from the last time I'd seen her when we'd sat in her garden chatting and drinking tea.

'It's up to you who phones, but try not to worry,' I said. 'The social worker I spoke to was very helpful, and confident something could be worked out. You're not the only person to ever have had issues with their social worker.'

'Aren't I?' she said. 'She makes me feel like I am. If she'd just leave me alone I could get on with looking after Liam and Kim. I'm sure I'd do better then. As it is I feel like she's breathing down my neck the whole time, and one wrong move will put me back in hospital, and the children on the child protection register.'

'She didn't say that, surely?' I asked, horrified.

'No, but that's how she makes me feel.'

Cleary Laura's relationship with her social worker had broken down irretrievably, and I hoped the manager would act quickly before Laura lost any more confidence.

'So how are you and the family generally?' I asked, wondering if she'd like a chat.

'The kids are OK. I'm up and down and trying to stay positive,' she replied honestly. 'Sorry I haven't been to see you.'

'That's OK. Come when you feel like it.'

'I will. Thanks for phoning the social services. I'll tell Andy when he calls at lunchtime. He'll know what do to. I'd better go now and see to Liam.'

Laura didn't want to chat so we said goodbye. I felt very sorry for her. Although it appeared she hadn't gone back to those really dark days of psychosis, she did sound very down and anxious. I supposed that was the depression resurfacing. I'd done all I could to help, so, forcing aside my worries for Laura, I returned to play with the children.

Life is never dull as a foster carer, and crises in families that require social services' intervention can develop at any time, so carers have to be very adaptable. At around 12.30 that Monday the children and I were making the most of the good weather and the last week of the school holidays by enjoying a picnic lunch in the garden. When the telephone rang I went into the living room to answer it. I could still see the children from there. It was the social worker of the runaway teenager I'd been put on standby for, and after a pleasant, 'Hi, how are you, Cathy?' she told me that the girl, Tracy, had been found and she would bring her to me later that afternoon, together with the paperwork I'd need – essential information and placement forms. She didn't know what – if any – clothes or toiletries Tracy would have with her, so I reassured her that I had spares she could use. She couldn't give me an exact time of arrival, but guessed it would be in a couple of hours. She said she'd phone later when they were on their way. Tracy had been found at the home of a friend by the girl's mother. They lived two doors away from Tracy and she'd been hiding in her daughter's bedroom.

I returned to the garden and had to tell Adrian (and Paula) that we couldn't go to the park that afternoon as we'd planned because Tracy was on her way. To minimize their disappointment I said we would fill the paddling pool, which they loved to play in. But before I did I checked the spare bedroom and changed the duvet cover to one that would appeal to a teenager. Adrian and Paula then helped me to clear away the picnic and fill the pool. The water was cold but that added to their shrieks of delight. I joined in, paddling and splashing, although I was also listening out for the telephone that would bring further news of Tracy. I told Adrian that when they did arrive he and Paula would have to come indoors as I couldn't leave them unattended by the pool. However, the afternoon went by without Tracy arriving, so when they'd had enough of playing in the pool I emptied it, as I always did for hygiene and safety.

It was nearly five o'clock before the social worker telephoned again, and it wasn't good news.

'Tracy's done another runner,' she said. 'By the time we got to her friend's house she'd gone. Tracy's mother has given us a couple of addresses of other friends where she might be hiding, so we'll need to check those.'

'She's not coming today then?' I asked.

'Not sure yet. The police are going to visit the addresses soon. If she is found then they may bring her to you later this evening or tonight. They've got your address and telephone number.' Which I had to accept. But this meant that not only had I spent the entire afternoon on tenterhooks waiting for news of Tracy's arrival, but that this was now set to continue into the evening and night. I'm not always sure social workers fully appreciate just what carers go through when they are on standby waiting for a child to arrive. If you're a police officer or social worker involved in the case you know exactly what's going on, but the foster carers are often left sitting at home, unable to go out, with little to do but speculate and worry. And the nature of accepting emergency placements, as opposed to long-term fostering, means that this can happen at any time. I love fostering, but it can be very disruptive and makes planning ahead difficult.

Eventually, having heard nothing by eleven o'clock that evening, I went to bed, but I only dozed fitfully as I was aware that the telephone could ring at any time, or even the doorbell if the police just arrived with the child, which had happened before. At 6 a.m., after a restless night, I declared the night over and switched on my bedside radio. I had no idea if Tracy had been found and was on her way to me, or if she was still missing. At 6.30 I showered and dressed just in case she arrived. Then, once Adrian and Paula were up, I had to tell Adrian we were still expecting Tracy so we couldn't go out. Thankfully he was happy to play in the garden again and Paula just went along with her older brother. The morning passed with no news and then, just before midday, the telephone rang.

'I'm going to collect Tracy now,' her social worker said with a sigh. 'We should be with you by three o'clock.'

'Good,' I said, relieved. 'I'll see you later.'

She didn't offer details of where Tracy had been found this time, and I didn't ask. She sounded pretty fed up. Little wonder, I thought, with the run-around Tracy had given her. So the children and I settled in for another day of playing at home, which meant that effectively we'd been in waiting for Tracy for two days. However, by 4.45, when there was still no sign of her, I was frustrated and Adrian was asking if we could take his bike to the park. I waited until five o'clock, then telephoned the social services and asked to speak to Tracy's social worker.

'She's not in the office,' her colleague said. 'She's been out on a case all day. Can I help you?' I assumed the case was Tracy.

I gave her my name, said that I was a foster carer and I'd been expecting Tracy to arrive nearly two hours ago, but I hadn't heard anything.

'Is Tracy still going into foster care then?' she asked.

'As far as I know,' I said. 'I was told by her social worker to expect her at three o'clock. I've been waiting in all day,' I added for good measure.

'I'll see if I can get hold of Tracy's social worker,' she said. 'If I can I'll ask her to phone you.'

'Thank you.'

Another hour passed before Tracy's social worker finally telephoned. 'Sorry, I haven't had a chance to update you. It's been manic all day. Tracy is staying with her older sister for now, so we won't be needing the foster placement. I'll inform the office.'

'OK. Thanks for letting me know,' I said, with only a touch of sarcasm, and we said goodbye.

What a waste of time and resources, I thought. Apart from the police and social worker's time, I'd been on standby when I might have been looking after another child. There is always a shortage of foster carers. But as I said, you have to be flexible in fostering and sometimes bite your tongue. Now I was no longer needed for Tracy, my name would be put on the white-board again at the social services' office, but which child would arrive and when I didn't know. It's a sad fact that there is usually a bit of a lull in the number of children taken into care during the long summer holidays, and when the schools return and teachers start to notice bruises or a child behaving oddly or even disclosing abuse, the number of referrals rises. But for now I would make the most of the rest of the week – the last few days of the summer holidays.

'Who would like to go to the zoo tomorrow?' I asked Adrian and Paula.

'Meeeeeee!' Adrian cried in excitement.

'Meeeee!' Paula repeated, with no idea what she was agreeing to.

Adrian told her: 'They have grizzly bears with big teeth and claws, snakes that can strangle you, alligators and lions that eat you. Grrrr!' he said, clawing his hands and stalking her.

'Grrrrr,' she repeated, laughing, and not the least bit scared.

I sincerely hoped that I didn't receive a telephone call from the social services to say a child was in need of a home, for it's very difficult to say no, yet I couldn't bear the look of disappointment on the faces of Adrian and Paula if another outing had to be cancelled.

That evening, after the children were in bed and there'd been no phone call from the social services, I telephoned a friend of mine whose son was a friend of Adrian's (he went to his birthday party), and whose daughter was a similar age to Paula. I asked her if she'd like to join us on our trip to the zoo. She jumped at the opportunity as she had no other plans, and we made arrangements to meet in our cars at the end of my road at 9 a.m. The following morning when I told Adrian they were coming too, he was delighted, as I knew he would be – having a friend for company adds to the fun of any outing, even grocery shopping! Before we left the house that morning

I checked I'd switched on the answerphone so that if the social services did telephone they could leave a message. If there was an emergency placement then they'd have to find another foster carer. Today I was concentrating on my family.

My friend's car was already waiting at the end of the road and I parked behind her and got out. After a quick discussion on the best route to the zoo she said she'd follow me, as she wasn't sure about some of the route. The zoo was about a forty-five-minute drive away. We returned to our cars and headed off. As I drove Adrian kept watch through the rear window to make sure we didn't lose them, although of course I could see their car in my mirror, but it was part of the fun. Paula kept turning to look too, but being that much smaller she couldn't see over her car seat. The journey went well and when we arrived we parked in the zoo's car park, let the children out and then, armed with the strollers and bags containing nappies and so forth for the girls, we paid at the turnstile and amid great excitement went in.

The weather was perfect for a day that involved lots of walking outside – warm, but with some cloud cover so it wasn't too hot, although we still put sunscreen on the children. The zoo is set in acres of countryside so the animals are free to roam in large enclosures, which is much kinder than keeping them in cages and replicates their natural habitats as much as possible. Cars aren't allowed in the grounds so it's a safe place for children, and the boys ran ahead (although they knew they weren't to go out of our sight), while the girls toddled beside us. My friend and I chatted in between admiring the animals and discussing the facts we learned about them with the children. There were information boards dotted around the park by the enclosures, and I think we all learned something new. The apes, monkeys and chimpanzees were of course fascinating with their human-like characteristics, and we spent a long time just standing and watching them; they held eye contact with us, which was a bit unsettling. But when the female baboons turned around to expose their bright-red bottoms the boys fell about laughing, and the girls were pointing. Of course it's guaranteed with any visit to see animals that at some point a pair will become amorous. Today it was the goats' turn – one buck was very persistent and enthusiastic in trying to mount a doe, but she wasn't interested.

'Look, Mummy,' Adrian's friend said loudly. 'That goat wants to play piggyback but his friend won't let him.'

'I know the feeling,' a man beside us quipped. My friend and I laughed, but his wife told him off.

'They're trying to make babies,' my friend explained quietly to the boys.

The boys glanced at each other, looked embarrassed and then dissolved into laughter. The girls had no idea what was funny but laughed too.

We stopped for lunch in the zoo's café at one o'clock and then continued going round the rest of the enclosures. By five o'clock we'd seen most of the animals and everyone was exhausted; the girls were now asleep in their strollers, so we decided to head for the exit. We stopped off at the gift shop and bought a small souvenir each and then returned home in our convoy of two cars. At the top of my road we parted company, tooting our car horns and with all the children waving vigorously. We'd had a really good day out and despite feeling tired I felt refreshed from the change of scenery after two days at home.

As soon as we stepped into the hall I saw that the answer-phone light was flashing, signalling a message. 'Perhaps it's Daddy,' Adrian said hopefully.

'I doubt it. He'll be at work,' I said. He didn't usually phone during the week because of the time difference. But Adrian was still looking at the phone expectantly, so I pressed the play button. Samson's social worker's voice came through: 'Cathy, could you give me a ring, please?' Adrian immediately lost interest and went down the hall while I listened to the rest of the message. 'We're going to court next week for an order to bring Samson into care. I wanted to check that you are still happy to look after him. Could you phone when you are free, please?'

It was too late to telephone now – their offices would be closed – so I'd phone when they opened in the morning. Although I was still happy to look after Samson, I was sad that it had come to this and he had to be brought into foster care. It meant that, despite all the support the social services and other agencies had put into the family, their situation had deteriorated, and there was now no alternative but to bring him into care for his own good – assuming, of course, that the judge granted the order. Unlike under a Section 20 (of the Children's Act), also known as Accommodated, when parents agree to place their child in care voluntarily and there is no court case, the fact that the social services were going to court meant that Samson's family didn't agree with their decision and were fighting to keep him. And who could blame them? I knew Samson's home life wasn't perfect, but they were his only family, and to remove any child from home and split up the family is heartbreaking and a decision that is never taken lightly.

* * *

That evening when the children, tired from all the walking, were in bed asleep and I was thinking of going to bed soon, Shelley telephoned. 'I thought you'd like to know how the choir is going,' she said.

'Yes, please.' I sat up and shook off the sleep.

'It's great! I love singing with all the others and I've met someone! I'm dating!' I could hear the excitement in her voice and knew this was the real reason she'd telephoned.

'That's fantastic,' I said. 'I am pleased for you. Tell me all about him.'

'He's a really, really nice person, Cathy, and good-looking. I can't believe my luck. He hasn't met Darrel yet; I'm waiting until I'm completely sure of him. But I have met his parents. They're lovely too and they all sing. I think they liked me.'

'Is this the lad from the choir?' I asked.

'Yes. How did you know?'

'I think you might have mentioned him the last time I saw you.'

'Yes, possibly. I thought he was cool right from the start. I guess I was hoping he'd ask me out. He's two years older than me and he works for an IT firm, so he knows lots of stuff about computers. He has a car and he collects me from my flat and ...' Shelley continued telling me *all* about him: his work, hobbies, favourite food, tastes in and love of music, the football team he supported and that he went to church. When she'd finished I felt I knew as much about him as she did. I could tell it was serious and that she was falling in love.

'I'm going to tell Carol all about him when I see her on Sunday,' Shelley added.

'She'll be as pleased as I am,' I said. 'I'll look forward to meeting him when you're ready.'

'Oh yes, you and Carol will be the first to meet him. Well, my friend has already met him, but that's different because she babysits for me and he gives her a lift home after. I can't believe how my life has changed in the last six months! I'm so happy, Cathy.'

'You deserve it,' I said. 'You're a lovely person and by the sound of it he is too. You make a good match.'

'Thank you. He is really nice. But enough of me and what I've been doing. How are you guys?'

'We're all fine, thank you. Getting ready for going back to school. How's Darrel?'

'He's good. He starts school next week.'

We chatted for a while longer and then wound up. 'Give Adrian and Paula my love,' Shelley said.

'I will, and wish Darrel well on his first day at school. We'll be thinking about him.'

'Thank you. I'm more nervous than he is. It'll be strange not having him around during the day, but I'm sure he'll be fine.'

We said goodbye and I replaced the handset, still smiling and happy for her. Shelley was such a kind, good-natured, gentle person, she deserved all the happiness on offer. By the sound of it her young man was a genuinely nice guy, so I hoped their relationship would develop. I hadn't told her I'd spoken to her social worker earlier in the week, as it would have raised the question why, and of course my conversation about Laura had been confidential. I wondered if Andy or Geraldine had telephoned the social services and, if so, how they'd got on, but I wouldn't phone and ask them. If they wanted me to know they'd tell me, and before long I'd have my hands full looking after Samson.

CHAPTER TWENTY-ONE

LAST RESORT

I didn't have to telephone Samson's social worker in the morning as I'd planned to do; she phoned me as soon as she was at her desk, at 8.45. 'You got my answerphone message?' she asked.

'Yes. I can look after Samson,' I confirmed.

'Good. I need to show the judge that I have a suitable foster carer ready if the court grants the order. Can I confirm a few details with you? You're married, and you have two children. What are their ages?'

'Adrian is five and Paula is sixteen months.'

'And you'd be able to take Samson to school and collect him? He's been going to breakfast club, so he could continue with that if it helps.'

'Yes, that would help. I could take him first and then take Adrian after. We'll have to work something out for the end of the day.'

There was a pause as she wrote. 'At present Samson has supervised contact with his father once a week, on a Friday, at the family centre. We'll have to make separate contact provision for him to see his gran and possibly the aunts too. It would take place after school at the centre, so you'd be able to take and collect him?'

'Yes.' This was expected of foster carers and was one of their roles.

'If necessary, you'd be able to keep Samson long term?' she asked.

'Yes, although I'd need to check with my husband, but I can't see a problem. I'll mention it to him the next time he phones.'

She wrote again. 'And you can obviously manage his behaviour.'

'I will do my best,' I said. She gave a small laugh. 'Can I ask why you've decided to bring Samson into care?' I now asked.

'His gran's poor health and lack of mobility means she can't meet his needs or cope with his behaviour. There is no one else in the immediate family willing to take responsibility for him or look after him, so he's just been left to run riot. The police have been logging complaints from residents on the estate when he's been out at night causing trouble. Last week they picked him up with a gang of older youths armed with tools for breaking into houses. We're also concerned that no one in the family spotted the abuse by his father's girlfriend. It had been going on for some time. So generally the whole situation has deteriorated. We're going to court next Wednesday and, assuming the order is granted, we're planning to move him to you after contact on Friday.'

'All right, I'll be ready.'

'Thank you. I'll phone beforehand.'

With only three days before the start of the new school term, I checked Adrian's school uniform and games kit and that his book bag was ready. I'd already bought him new school shoes.

It's always a wrench returning to school after the long summer holidays, and while Adrian was looking forward to seeing his classmates again he was understandably anxious at the prospect of a new class teacher with different ways of doing things. I knew Paula would miss having him at home to play with, and I'd miss him too, as well as the relaxing routine of the holiday. The weather seemed to sense that the school holidays were drawing to a close and the autumn term was about to begin. On Saturday the temperature dropped and a chilly north-easterly wind began to blow, bringing rain. We spent the day indoors, and then on Sunday my parents came for dinner. We had a pleasant day, although they didn't stay late, as they knew we had to be up reasonably early for school the following morning.

Adrian took a long while to go to sleep that night; I think he was worrying about school, although he wouldn't tell me. Then on Monday morning he took ages getting dressed and didn't want his breakfast because he said he had a tummy ache. I knew it was a nervous tummy ache, so I gave him a big cuddle and reassured him that all his friends would be feeling the same way and once he was there he would be fine. I said we'd be thinking of him and that the day would fly by and before he knew it he would be home again. He managed a small, unconvincing smile, ate a little of his breakfast and then went very quiet as he brushed his teeth and put on his school shoes. The weather didn't help – it was raining again, so I had to find our raincoats and then fit the rain cover over the stroller, which Paula didn't like as it restricted her vision; she kept trying to kick it off. As a result we left the house later than we should have done and had to walk quickly. Not the best way to start the new school year!

Although we weren't late – the Klaxon hadn't sounded – we were one of the last to arrive in the playground. It was full of chattering parents and children sheltering under their umbrellas, which was probably why I didn't spot them straight away. Then I heard two female voices call, 'Hi, Cathy!' and 'Over here!' I looked over to see Fran and her daughter and, to my surprise, Laura, with the pram and Kim, waving to me.

I began towards them but the Klaxon sounded, so I made a detour to the entrance. Because it was raining the children didn't have to line up in their classes; they could go straight in. As I said goodbye to Adrian a friend joined him in the queue to go in and Adrian immediately brightened as they began talking. 'Have a good day,' I said to the both of them. Adrian smiled and gave a little wave, which was a relief.

Paula now began agitating and kicking the inside of the rain cover, wanting to get out. 'No, you have to stay there. It's raining. Baby Liam's over there.'

I crossed the playground to Fran and Laura. Their children had now gone into school and they were standing under Fran's umbrella waiting for me. Laura, like me, didn't have an umbrella but had her hood up, as it's virtually impossible to manoeuvre a pram or stroller while holding an umbrella.

'How are you? Good to see you,' Fran said, tilting her umbrella to one side so we could cheek kiss.

'I'm fine. Lovely to see you both.' Then to Laura I added, 'What a nice surprise.'

'I surprised myself!' Laura joked, and laughed easily.

'Did you have a good summer?' Fran asked me.

'Yes, very relaxing. And you?'

'We went camping in France. Three weeks. Bliss. I wish I was there now.' She pulled a face and looked up at the sky.

'Rather than stand here getting wet, why don't you both come back to my place for coffee?' Laura suggested. 'We can talk there.'

'I'd love to,' Fran said. 'But I've got the plumber coming in half an hour to quote for a new boiler. Another time.'

'I'm free,' I said.

'Good,' Laura said. 'And you're in luck – Mum was with us at the weekend and made one of her cakes.'

'Even better,' I said.

'I'm jealous,' Fran joked.

We left the playground together and then Fran said goodbye and went on her way.

'How is Liam?' I asked, glancing into the pram. I couldn't see much of him because of the rain cover.

'He's doing very well. Putting on weight. You'll notice a difference; he's grown so much.'

'Baby Liam!' Paula cried from under the rain cover and gave it another kick. The rain had eased now to a light drizzle, so I stopped and drew back the top part of the cover so she could see out.

'Baby Liam!' she cried, much happier now. Pushing herself up in the stroller, she tried to peer into the pram, but it was too high.

'You can see Liam when we go to my house,' Laura said to her.

'We're going to Liam's house,' I confirmed to Paula.

Now she was free of the cover and had the promise of seeing Liam, she was happy to stay in the stroller rather than walk. Laura and I made polite conversation as we walked.

'Is your husband home now?' she asked. I must have mentioned a while back that he was due home at the end of August.

'No, unfortunately not, he's been delayed. A technical hitch with the project he's working on.'

'Oh dear. What a disappointment.'

'It was, but he's hoping to be home in a couple of weeks. The time will soon pass.'

'It will. I can't believe Liam is over six months old already.'

We continued making polite conversation, small talk on safe, general, non-probing subjects: the weather, the children, and the new classes they were in. I asked her how Gina and Geraldine were. I didn't ask how she was feeling – I couldn't think of a way of phrasing it that didn't make it sound blunt or intrusive. Laura looked well, but then she had done the last time I'd seen her, before her setback. That's the problem with mental health; it's often hidden, not like a broken arm, which is obvious. But of course ignoring Laura's health or that she'd had issues with her social worker was like ignoring the elephant in the room. She must have felt it too, for once we were in her hall and she'd closed the front door and was removing the waterproof from Liam's pram she said, 'You know, Cathy, it's OK to ask me how things are. I won't go to pieces and embarrass you.'

'I'm sorry,' I said.

'Don't be. I know it's difficult. Let's settle the children. I'll make us a drink and tell you what's been happening.'

Fifteen minutes later we were all in her living room, with Liam in his bouncing cradle being kept amused by Paula, who was showing him a selection of toys from a box Laura had brought in. She had a bottle ready for Liam when he needed it and on the coffee table was a beaker of water and a biscuit Paula had wanted. Laura and I were sipping coffee and tucking into Gina's delicious walnut and butter-icing sponge cake – another recipe I'd be asking for. Paula had tried a little of mine but hadn't liked the ground nuts.

'Thank you for telephoning the social services,' Laura began, setting her cup in its saucer. 'It was a great help. Andy was going to phone you to thank you, but I told him I'd be seeing you in the playground.'

'That's OK. I'm pleased it helped,' I said.

'It did, a lot. I've been given a new social worker, but what really helped me was when the one I had telephoned and apologized. She admitted that once it had been pointed out to her she could see that the way she'd approached some aspects of my case could have been handled differently. You see, Cathy, she kept giving me advice and referring to meetings she'd had with other professionals involved in my case, so I felt they were taking over and running my life. It was like when I was really ill and Geraldine took over. My confidence went and I felt useless. I began overthinking everything again, questioning everything I was doing. There's this internal dialogue going on in your head, telling you you're a waste of space and you'll never cope. Everything the social worker said seemed to make it worse, and then I started to have the distant, far-away feeling I'd had before when I was ill, like I was not fully there and was watching myself in a movie. If that makes sense.'

'It sounds dreadful,' I said. I'd stopped eating my cake and was concentrating fully on Laura. It was the first time she'd talked candidly about what she'd actually experienced, and I began to have an insight into just how frightening it must have been for her.

'I was nowhere near as bad this time as I was when I was very ill,' she continued. 'But there were enough reminders to make me scared. I knew where it could go if I didn't say something and get help. I felt I was being dragged towards the edge of that cliff again. It's a very scary place, Cathy, a dark and dangerous place, and I knew I mustn't ever go there again. Before, when I was really ill, I used to sit in here huddled up at one end of the sofa and cry silently for hours and hours.' She shuddered. 'I kept the curtains closed so the room was always dark. It seemed safer, but I began to feel as though the walls were closing in and crushing me and I couldn't breathe. I felt I was being crushed to death.

'And poor little Liam,' she said, glancing towards him. 'I thought he hated me – when I was really bad, psychotic, before I went into hospital. It seems ridiculous now, but the way he looked at me and wouldn't cooperate seemed to confirm it. When I tried to feed him he'd turn his head away sometimes, and would scream if I changed his nappy or bathed him. I know all babies do that, but when I was in that dark place I thought it was because of me. At night he wouldn't settle for me, but he would for Geraldine and Andy, so I thought he'd be better off without me. Now, of course, I realize he was probably picking up on my anxiety. But at the time I thought I was such a bad and wicked mother that I'd been punished by giving birth to the devil's child.'

'Oh, Laura,' I said. 'You poor thing.'

'Thankfully he was unaware of it,' she said stoically. 'But when I started having issues with that social worker and began to slide again I knew I needed help. Geraldine and

Andy saw me in tears and I was able to tell them how I was feeling. As soon as I'd told them, and we had a plan of action to try and change social workers, I started to feel a bit better. I felt I was taking control again. Then after Andy spoke to the manager and the social worker phoned and apologized, I felt vindicated. It wasn't all my fault, and a huge weight lifted from my shoulders. Even if I hadn't been given a new social worker, I think I would have got by – once she'd acknowledged there was a problem and it wasn't just me. I haven't met the new social worker yet, but she sounded nice when she phoned. I think you know her.' She gave the name of Shelley's social worker.

'Yes,' I said, smiling. 'You're in safe hands there.'

'I feel I am,' Laura said, finally picking up her cake again. 'I know I'm going to be just fine, thanks to you.'

'Thanks to you,' I said firmly. 'You're a great mum. Your children are very lucky to have you, Laura.' And I felt my eyes fill.

I stayed for a second cup of coffee and a slice of cake and then left with a copy of the recipe and a big hug from Laura, in the happy knowledge that she and her family were going to be all right. They had come through a very difficult time but were now looking forward to a brighter future, their family stronger from the experience they'd shared. Sadly, this wasn't true for Samson, who at present was blissfully unaware that very soon he would be packing more than a backpack and going away for a lot longer than a few days' respite, possibly for good. I felt for him having to leave his family and endure all the changes that lay in store, but at least now that I knew it was almost certain he would be arriving on Friday I could plan ahead, unlike with an emergency placement when there is very little notice.

That afternoon I changed the duvet cover and matching pillowcase again in what would shortly be Samson's room, putting on one suitable for a six-year-old boy. It was light grey with images of action heroes – Spiderman, Superman and so on. I took down the posters of cute, cuddly animals and then gave the room a good dust and hoover, as it had been standing empty for a while. That evening after dinner I told Adrian that it was very likely Samson would be coming to live with us on Friday and I asked him how he felt about it.

'OK,' he said. 'But he won't be allowed to bring Bruno, will he?'

'No, although he's going to miss him.'

'Perhaps he could have a photo of him,' Adrian suggested. 'Like the children have of their parents.'

'Good idea.' I always encouraged the children I fostered to bring some photographs of their family with them, and Bruno was part of Samson's family.

Although Adrian seemed OK about having Samson come to live with us, I would be keeping a close eye on them, especially in the early weeks while Samson was settling in, as well as making sure all the children received their fair share of attention. While Samson's behaviour on respite hadn't been too bad, I knew it could be very different when a child came to live long term with a carer. Angry, hurting and confused at having to leave their family and wanting to test their carer's commitment, their behaviour can deteriorate rapidly and become very challenging. Then they adjust to being in care and their anger begins to leave them. They decide you've passed their test and have proven that no matter what they throw at you, you will still care about them, and they turn the corner and settle down. Well, that's the theory, at least.

On Tuesday, after taking Adrian to school, I drove into town and bought some new posters for Samson's bedroom: of the moon, a robot, a shark leaping from the water, a large male lion roaring, and one showing the times tables, which I knew he was struggling to learn at school. I also bought a poster each for Adrian's and Paula's bedrooms so they didn't feel left out. On returning home, Paula came with me to Samson's room and 'helped' me decide where the posters should hang. There was already a clock on the wall and a child's calendar, which were useful for a child of any age. Satisfied that the room was welcoming and ready for Samson, I came out and closed the door.

I knew I'd have to establish a routine for Samson that would include time for learning as well as play. We couldn't hold sports days and pretend birthday parties every evening and weekend, although I would of course give him a proper party when it was his birthday, which was some months away yet. I would also need to put in place guidelines for when and how long he watched television and played on his PlayStation, which I assumed he would want to bring with him. He would still be allowed these, of course, but as a recreation, something to do in his spare time, not as a tool for babysitting or keeping him quiet. I'd have to check the PlayStation games for their suitability. If they weren't age appropriate, which, from what he'd told me, I assumed many of them weren't, then I'd put them away until he was older and inform his social worker I'd done so. I could foresee Samson kicking off big time if I did have to put away some of the PlayStation games, but it would be irresponsible of me as a foster carer and a parent to allow him to view inappropriate material in any form, on the PlayStation, on television or in magazines.

I knew Samson's school work was a long way behind what it should be, especially his literacy skills, and I would be helping him to catch up, a little at a time. Adrian was learning to read and he was in the routine of reading to me for a while every evening, as well as doing any homework set by the school, before he played or watched television. But of course it's easier to establish a routine when you've had your child since birth, whereas Samson would have to relinquish some of what he was used to before accepting my guidelines. It was for his own long-term good, although I doubted he'd see it that way. But I'd take it gently, one step at a time. You can't make too many changes all at once or the child can withdraw or rebel. I was also mindful that Adrian, a year younger, was well ahead of Samson academically, and I'd need to make sure Samson didn't feel this, as it could undermine his confidence. As far as I knew, Samson didn't have learning difficulties and his lack of progress was due to neglect at home, so he should be able to catch up. I'd know more about his abilities and his background when his social worker gave me the placement information on Friday.

On Wednesday morning as I showered and dressed my thoughts went to Samson's gran, who at this moment was rising and getting ready for three days in court. I didn't know if anyone else from the family would be going, but my heart went out to her. She wasn't in good health and going to court is an anxious and gruelling ordeal for anyone, even more so for someone of her age, and of course she was fighting to keep her only grandchild. What must she be feeling!

I walked back from school that morning with Laura and I mentioned that I was expecting a new child on Friday, although I didn't give any details. I saw her face grow serious and she went very quiet. 'You know, Cathy,' she said after some moments, concentrating on the pram, 'that really scares me, hearing you say that. The poor family, having their child taken away. That moment when you have to say goodbye and hand your child to another person ... I don't know how they cope.'

'Neither do I,' I said quietly.

CHAPTER TWENTY-TWO

A REPRIEVE

On Thursday morning my thoughts turned again to Samson's gran and how she was coping as she faced her second day in court. The adversarial nature of our court system in care proceedings meant that his gran and any other family members responsible for Samson would be in court, represented by a solicitor and barrister who would argue their case for Samson not going into foster care. If the child's parents are not living together then they are likely to have a solicitor and barrister each, the child often has their own legal representation, and the social services has a legal team. In addition to the judge there is a court recorder, an usher and other court staff, although journalists and the public are not allowed in, which is why these proceedings are sometimes referred to as taking place behind closed doors. But like any court there is a correct procedure, which must be strictly adhered to, as statements are scrutinized and witnesses called to give evidence. While solicitors do their best to explain procedures to their clients, it can still be daunting, confusing and complex, especially for someone like Samson's gran, who presumably had never been involved in care proceedings before. It's also very nerve-racking to have to stand in front of a court, swear an oath, give evidence and then be cross-examined by a barrister.

I wasn't expecting to hear from Samson's social worker until Friday when the judge had made his or her ruling. I'd planned to take Paula to the mother-and-toddler group on Thursday afternoon as I had been doing the previous term. She enjoyed the contact with the other children and I enjoyed the company of the other mothers and one father. However, mid-morning on Thursday I received a telephone call – or rather an SOS – from Chris, another foster carer I knew.

'Cathy, could you do me a big favour and look after Elspeth for an hour or so this afternoon? I've been up all night with raging toothache and I've made an emergency appointment at the dentist for one-thirty.'

'Yes, of course,' I said. 'You poor thing.' We arranged for her to bring Elspeth to me just after one o'clock.

Fosters carers often network in the area in which they live, for company, emotional support and to help each other out. It's difficult as it is to attend appointments with a small child, but it's even more so for a foster carer when babysitters have to be identified to the social services in advance. You can't, for example, simply ask a random friend to help out in an emergency as you would with your own child.

Elspeth was the two-year-old girl Chris had been fostering for over a year, and after lunch I explained to Paula that she was coming to play for a while. She tried to say 'Elspeth' and was still practising when they arrived. It had been a couple of months since I'd last seen Elspeth, and in that time she'd grown and was now more adorable than ever. With her mop of loose black curls, large dark eyes and chubby little cheeks she looked like a life-size doll. 'This is Elspeth,' I said to Paula.

'Elf,' she said, smiling at her.

Chris didn't have time to come in so I wished her good luck and she kissed Elspeth goodbye.

'Bye,' Elspeth said, waving.

'Bye,' Paula repeated, also waving.

Two little cuties. Chris smiled as she left, despite the pain she was in.

Six months older than Paula, Elspeth (or rather Elf) chatted away to Paula and kept her amused, when she wasn't chasing the cat. Elspeth didn't have any pets at her house, so Toscha was a novelty. She was fascinated by the way she cleaned herself with her paw and purred when stroked. Chris was only gone for an hour and returned with a prescription for antibiotics and another appointment in ten days' time, when I said I'd look after Elspeth again if necessary. She thanked me and stayed for a quick cup of tea before we both had to leave and go our separate ways to collect our children from their schools. I knew the care plan for Elspeth was originally for her to return to her mother, but that was looking increasingly less likely as the poor woman kept dropping out of the methadone programme she was in and returning to heroin. I knew that before long the social services would have to decide if going home was feasible and, if not, they would place Elspeth for adoption. Sad though this would be, it's unfair to leave a child in care indefinitely and deny them a chance of a permanent family of their own.

On Friday morning my thoughts turned again to Samson's gran and they continued to do so as the day wore on. By early afternoon I knew the judge would have probably heard all the evidence and would be delivering his or her judgment. I thought Samson's gran (and other family members) were probably resigned to their fate by now and would just want to get the inevitable over and done with – to hear the decision and prepare to say goodbye to Samson.

I collected Adrian from school, gave Samson's room a final check and then made dinner. I was expecting his social worker to telephone at any time, but by 5.30 when she still hadn't phoned I assumed she'd been too busy and would simply arrive with Samson after contact, which finished at six o'clock. I knew how hectic it was for social workers after a court hearing when they had to bring a child into care. I'd no idea what personal possessions Samson would be bringing with him, but if necessary he could use the spare clothes I kept until he had some of his own, either from home or bought by me. Hopefully his gran would pack his favourite toys, which would help him settle in.

When the phone rang at 5.45 I was relieved to hear Samson's social worker. 'Sorry I haven't been in touch sooner,' she said. 'This is the first opportunity. It's been non-stop.'

'I can imagine,' I said.

'I doubt it. We didn't get the order. Samson's not coming into care. Not now, at least.'

'Oh,' I said. I didn't know whether to feel relieved or disappointed – I felt a bit of both.

'The judge wants more support put into the family, with a review in three months' time. I'm not sure what else we can do, but we have to accept and abide by the ruling. The hearing had its moments, though. The first day was a fiasco. The whole family turned up: aunts, uncles, cousins I'd never heard of, his gran, his father – no sign of the mum. They brought the dog with them too, which they tied up outside the court.'

'Oh no!'

'You could hear it barking from inside the courtroom. The judge wasn't impressed and said it was cruel to leave it tied up all day, and also it was terrorizing those coming into and leaving the building. He told them not to bring it back the next day.'

I had to smile; having met Bruno, I fully appreciated the scene.

'But Gran's barrister made a good case for Samson staying at home, with more support. So that's what we're going to do, starting with fumigating the flat.'

'Pardon?' I said, thinking I'd misheard.

'They've got bed bugs. Gran told the judge she'd been asking the council for weeks to fumigate the flat, but nothing had been done. She pulled up her top and showed him her bite marks. The family laughed, but they were bad, and the judge criticized us for not doing anything about it sooner. I've just contacted pest control now; they're fumigating the flat next week. I hope Samson didn't bring any bugs with him when he stayed with you.'

'So do I!' I said, grimacing and involuntarily scratching my arm.

'Check the room he slept in. Especially the bedding and curtains. They are easily transported on clothes and in luggage and can reproduce very quickly. Do you know what they look like?'

'Yes, I think so. I've seen pictures.'

'So, Cathy, that's it really. Samson will continue to have supervised contact with his father once a week, and we'll look at what other support we can put into the family. I expect you'll be asked to have Samson again on respite.'

'That's fine if I haven't got another child,' I said.

'I've put your name back on the board again. I'm going home now. I'm exhausted. Have a good weekend.'

'And you.' We said goodbye.

I could tell she was disappointed at the ruling, as indeed to some extent I was. All that planning and organizing had come to nothing. Clearly the social services had believed that bringing Samson into care full time was the right course of action or they wouldn't have applied for an order, but now they had to comply with the judge's decision, whether they agreed with it or not. What would happen in three months' time would depend on the progress the family had made in meeting Samson's needs, but for now he could stay at home and I had to readjust to that, as would his social worker. I went into the living room where Adrian and Paula were playing with Lego and I told them that Samson wouldn't be coming to live with us after all.

'Oh,' Adrian said, surprised. 'Why not?'

'The judge has decided he should stay with his gran, although he may come to us again on respite.'

'That's good for him and his gran then,' Adrian said perceptively.

'Yes, it is. Very good,' I said. 'Can you watch Paula for a few minutes? I need to check Samson's room – I mean, the spare room.'

Adrian nodded. He was responsible enough that I could leave him with Paula while I went upstairs for a while. It still seemed to me to be Samson's room with the bedding and posters I'd chosen with him in mind. I went in and began searching for any uninvited guests: little brown bugs that turned red after feeding on human blood and caused their host a lot of itching and painful swelling. I checked the walls first, especially the corners, for while bed bugs feed on their hosts at night in bed they can live anywhere in a room. Although the bedding was freshly laundered I carefully pulled back the duvet, watching for any signs of life, and removed the cover and thoroughly checked it inside and out. Then the pillowcase, sheet and mattress protector. I turned the mattress and examined it on both sides but it was clear. I'd have been surprised if I had found bugs, as I regularly change the bedding, vacuum and thoroughly clean the room, so even if Samson had brought any with him they should have been disposed of in the cleaning. Lastly, I checked behind the curtains, the drawers and wardrobe, and they were clear too, but just to be perfectly sure I'd vacuum the room again tomorrow when I had time. As I refolded the bedding I looked around the room. I'd invested so much time in preparing and customizing it for Samson's arrival. It seemed a sad place now, lonely and empty, as though in losing its purpose it had lost its soul. But even well-laid plans can and do change abruptly, and accepting this, adjusting and moving on is all part of fostering.

My name was on the whiteboard again at the social services as being free to foster, so it was possible I could have a child placed with me over the weekend as an emergency. The following morning, as soon as Adrian and Paula were up, I thoroughly cleaned the spare room again. I didn't know the age or sex of the child I might be asked to foster, so for the time being I left up all the posters and remade the bed with the superhero duvet cover I'd put on fresh for Samson.

As it turned out my preparations didn't go to waste this time. Although I didn't receive a call to take a child as an emergency over the weekend, on Monday morning I was surprised to receive a phone call from Samson's social worker.

'Hello again,' she said, sounding more upbeat than she had on Friday. 'Did you have a good weekend?'

'Yes, thank you. Did you?'

'Wonderful. I slept for most of it.' She gave a small laugh. 'The reason I'm phoning is that Samson's flat is being fumigated tomorrow, Tuesday, and while it's OK for them to go back into the flat once the chemical has dried, Gran has asked if Samson can be looked after for the night, just to be safe.'

'Yes, sure,' I said. 'His room is still ready from Friday.'

'That's great. Thank you. I'll tell Gran to pack an overnight bag for him to take to school with him tomorrow morning. Then you can collect him from after-school club at five o'clock and take him straight home with you.'

'Yes, that's fine.'

'On Wednesday morning take him to breakfast club with his bag, and he'll go home at the end of the day as normal.'

'That works well for me,' I said.

'Good.' She gave me the name and address of the school, which I wrote down. 'Thanks, Cathy.'

I was pleased to be looking after Samson again, even if it was only for one night, although I'd be checking his bag to make sure he hadn't brought any bed bugs with him. I knew from an article I'd read previously just how quickly an infestation can occur and how difficult it was to get rid of.

When I saw Laura in the playground that afternoon she asked why I hadn't got another child with me, as I'd told her I was expecting a child to arrive on Friday. I said only that the judge hadn't granted the social services the Care Order, and she was surprised. 'So they don't get it automatically?' she asked.

'No. They have to prove their case.' She looked puzzled. 'If there are concerns about a child,' I explained, 'and the parents don't agree to placing the child in care voluntarily, the social services have to apply to court for a Care Order. They can't just take a child away.'

'I see,' she said. 'Well, that is reassuring. I assumed the social services had complete authority. I didn't realize a judge could overrule them.'

'I think a lot of people believe that,' I said. 'I've heard similar said before, but the social services have to prove to the judge that there are sufficient grounds to remove a child. If there aren't then the child remains at home and the social services usually continue to monitor the family.'

'I see,' she said again. Then as we walked home together Laura said, 'I think that child's family will try harder in the future, now they've had the shock of nearly losing him.'

'It does happen,' I said. 'A wake-up call. Although you have to remember that not everyone has the support of a loving family, as you and I do. It can be very difficult for some families to get their lives back on track. You'd be shocked at just how alone some people are. And some people haven't had good role models when they were growing up, or were treated badly. These factors can have a huge impact on the way a person treats their own children.'

Laura nodded. I didn't know how much of this was relevant to Samson's situation, but it was true generally. Although there were a lot of members in Samson's extended family, they appeared to let his gran get on with raising Samson without helping or supporting her. And Gran herself sometimes seemed cold and uncaring.

'Well, I hope that child's family can change,' Laura said. 'I know I would do anything to keep my kids.'

That evening I explained to Adrian (and Paula) that Samson would be coming to stay for one night and outlined the arrangements for collecting him from school the following day and returning him on Wednesday morning.

'Why don't I go to breakfast club?' Adrian asked.

'There is no need. I don't have to leave the house early to go out to work.'

'Does Samson's gran work?' he asked. He knew something of Samson's family from what Samson had told him and from what he'd picked up by going to his flat.

'No, she doesn't,' I said. 'But it helps her if he has breakfast at school, and I think he likes it.'

'Is that why he has to stay for after-school club as well?' Adrian asked. 'To help her?'

'Yes,' I said.

'Samson said it was to get him out from under her feet.'

'I guess that is helping her then,' I said with a smile.

The following day the arrangements worked perfectly. With Samson staying late at after-school club, I had plenty of time to collect Adrian and then drive to Samson's school where I parked in a side road and we waited until it was time to go in and collect him. A noticeboard outside the school gate said that the after-school club was held in the main hall, so we followed the other parents in. The children were ready with their jackets on, waiting to be collected.

'That's her!' Samson yelled as we entered the hall, making

everyone turn to look. He ran over with his school bag on one shoulder and a large holdall on the other.

'Hi, Samson, good to see you again,' I said. He high-fived Adrian and then Paula. I showed the person in charge my foster-carer ID and we left.

'We've got bed bugs,' Samson announced proudly.

'Really?' Adrian said, impressed, not knowing what these were.

Samson told him. 'They live in your bed and while you're asleep they crawl all over you and suck your blood.'

'Not *your* blood,' I reassured Adrian, who was looking worried. 'We haven't got bed bugs.'

'We have!' Samson declared, as though it was an achievement. 'Gran told the judge and showed him where they'd eaten her alive and sucked out all her blood like a vampire.' I thought Samson had been watching too many horror films again, but it was interesting that his gran had told him she'd been to court. I wondered what else she'd told him.

'Bed bugs are only very small,' I reassured Adrian. 'They take a tiny bit of blood, like a mosquito. But they're nasty and make you itch. They have to be got rid of.'

'We're having them exterminated,' Samson said as we walked to the car. 'Like the daleks. Exterminate! Exterminate!' Raising his arm, he fired at us in a dalek-like extermination and Adrian and then Paula fired back. It was good to see him again, and in a way I felt sad that he wouldn't be staying for long.

Once home, I settled the children with some toys in the living room while I took Samson's holdall outside, onto the patio. I opened it and, one item at a time, shook out his clothes, watching for any sign of wildlife. I was impressed by the amount he'd brought with him this time. It was far in excess of the contents of the backpacks he usually brought. Now he'd remembered pyjamas, a dressing gown, wash bag containing a face flannel, toothbrush and paste, a towel, clean underwear, a set of casual clothes and a change of school uniform for the morning, all neatly folded and packed. Having shaken out all the contents of the holdall, I turned the bag over and gave that a good shake too. Relieved that nothing ran out, I quickly repacked the bag and returned indoors, placing it at the foot of the stairs ready to be taken up on my next trip. I returned to the living room where the children were still playing nicely. I thought Samson seemed a lot calmer tonight.

'Who packed your bag?' I asked him casually.

'Gran,' he said. 'She said she had to do it to make sure I had everything I needed.'

'Excellent,' I said. So perhaps Laura was right and the shock of nearly losing him had given her a wake-up call.

When we were having dinner and his behaviour continued to impress me I praised him. 'Good boy. You're doing very well,' I said.

'Thanks,' he said with his impish smile. 'Gran says I have to behave or the social worker will come and take me away forever. I'm not allowed out on the estate at night any more since I got in trouble with the police. And I've got to stop cheeking the teachers at school, but that ain't easy. It gives me a headache trying to be good all the time, but I don't want to be taken away.'

While I wasn't sure I agreed with threatening a child with being taken away if they didn't behave, if it worked for his gran, who was I to criticize?

After dinner I heard both boys read from their school books and then I left them playing while I took Paula up to bed. I couldn't have done that when Samson had first come to us on respite; I'd had to watch him the whole time. Once Paula was settled I returned downstairs to the living room where the boys were now sitting side by side on the sofa. Was it my imagination or were they looking a little guilty, as though they had a secret?

'What's going on?' I asked lightly.

They giggled, nudged each other and then Adrian said, 'Samson's got a pet. Can you guess what it is?'

'That's easy,' I said. 'I've met Bruno. He's a big dog.'

Both boys laughed raucously. 'No!' Adrian said. 'He's got another pet. A new one. Guess what it is.'

I thought the last thing Gran needed was another mouth to feed, for even small pets need a lot of care and looking after.

'Is it a cat?' I asked.

'Noooo!' they chorused together and laughed conspiratorially.

'A rabbit?'

'Noooo!'

'A gerbil?' I suggested.

'Noooo!'

'A snake, spider, alligator, elephant, giraffe?' I said in a rush, also laughing.

'Noooo!' they yelled.

Then Adrian turned to Samson. 'Go on, show her. She won't mind.'

I felt a stab of anxiety and misgiving as Samson dug his hand into his trouser pocket, took out a matchbox and began to open it.

'No, just a minute!' I cried, going over. 'Don't open it yet. What's in there?'

'It's his pet bug,' Adrian said, grinning.

'What sort of bug?'

'A bed bug,' Samson declared. 'Don't tell Gran. I've saved him from being exterminated. He's called Bruce.'

'Bruce Lee, martial arts fighter,' Adrian qualified.

My first impulse was to grab the matchbox and throw Bruce as far as I could down the garden, or stamp on it, but that would have upset Samson. I needed a more subtle approach.

'Samson,' I said, eyeing the closed box carefully. 'It was kind of you to save the bug.'

'Bruce,' he corrected.

'It was kind of you to save Bruce, but do you know what would happen if he escaped into the house? Very soon there would be hundreds and thousands of bed bugs sucking our blood and making us itch, just like they do at your home.'

Having heard this, Adrian lost some of his enthusiasm and shifted away from Samson.

'But Bruce is my friend,' Samson said.

'In that case, the kindest thing to do would be to let him go in the garden.'

'What if I make sure he doesn't escape?' he asked, unwilling to give him up.

'It's not fair to keep him in that tiny box,' I said. 'He'll die without air or water. I think we should find a new home for him in the garden. I know just the spot! Come with me and I'll show you. It's a special place only a few of us know about.'

My enthusiasm combined with the hint of secrecy captured Samson's interest, as I thought it would. Clutching the box carefully in one hand he slid off the sofa. 'Come on then, where is this place?' he asked.

'We'll need to put on our shoes first – it's at the very end of the garden,' I said, lowering my voice to maintain the air of mystery. The boys followed me down the hall to where our shoes were paired and we carried them to the back door and put them on. Paula was asleep upstairs, but we wouldn't be long.

It was still light outside and I led the way across the patio, down the lawn and to the shed at the bottom of the garden, like an explorer on an adventure. Just behind the shed, standing on a brick, was an upside-down plant pot, under which I kept the key to the shed. Not for security but so I could find it. 'This is the secret place,' I said, crouching down. They crouched down too, and I carefully lifted up the pot. A few ants scurried away.

'This will be his new home,' I said. 'He'll be safe here, and he's got the whole garden to play in rather than that little box.'

'I'll leave the box under the pot,' Samson said. 'That can be his bed.'

'Excellent,' I said. I moved the key to one side to make room for the matchbox and Samson carefully placed it beside the key and then slid it open to reveal Bruce, a large bed bug, reddish-brown from previously gorging on someone's blood. I resisted the urge to shudder. 'He'll be safe here,' I said, and carefully lowered the pot.

'Night, Bruce,' Samson said.

'Night,' Adrian and I chorused, and we returned indoors. Crisis averted, although I would check Samson's school bag and jacket to make sure he didn't have any other 'pets' concealed in matchboxes.

CHAPTER TWENTY-THREE

GOING HOME

The following morning Samson wanted to check on Bruce, so I said that after breakfast, once everyone was ready for school, we could have a look. I guessed the bug would be long gone, so I told Samson I thought he would be playing in the garden.

'Bugs don't play,' he scoffed. 'They suck people's blood.'

But of course when we looked the matchbox was empty.

'Mum was right,' Adrian said, impressed. 'Bruce is playing in the garden.'

And just for a moment Samson looked as though he might believe him, and perhaps he did.

The talk from Samson that morning in the car as I drove him to school was about exterminating, and not just bed bugs. Samson had watched far too many gruesome films about people being exterminated – by axe-wielding psychopaths, out-of-control robots, flesh-eating aliens and an array of other evil forces. I hoped that while Samson's gran was upping the level of care she provided for him she would also begin censoring what he was allowed to watch. His head was full of macabre nonsense and scenes of violence, so much so that he was becoming desensitized to horrors that would normally shock or deeply affect a child (or adult), which would be no good for his psychological or emotional development, now or in the future.

I took Adrian and Paula with me into Samson's school to see him to breakfast club. He gave his overnight bag to a member of staff for safe keeping and we said goodbye and that we hoped to see him again.

'Look after Bruce!' he called as he went to collect his breakfast.

'We will!' Adrian and I replied.

We returned to the car and I took Adrian to his school. By the time I returned home I'd been out of the house on the school run for an hour and a half. It was a sample of what it would be like if Samson came to live with us, although I knew other carers who spent even longer in their cars doing the school run. It's generally considered better for a child when they go into care, less unsettling, if they stay at the school they are familiar with and where their friends are, but it can mean long journeys.

That morning Samson's social worker telephoned to see how his overnight stay had gone and I was able to tell her lots of positives. She was pleased and made some notes, but laughed when I told her about Bruce the bug. I didn't know if or when we'd see Samson again, as it would depend on when he needed respite and if I was looking after another child and had room to take him.

As it was a pleasant September day I was planning on making the most of the last of the good weather before autumn set in and taking Paula to the park that afternoon. However, all that changed when the telephone rang again. It was a different social worker and she needed an emergency placement for a small child.

'Hayley is three,' she said hurriedly. 'She's at the police station. Her mother was arrested this morning at the shopping centre, drunk. Can you collect Hayley as soon as possible? The police are holding the mother and will release her when she is sober.' It's an offence to be drunk while in charge of a small child.

'Yes,' I said. 'I'll leave straight away. Will she be staying with me overnight?'

'Not sure yet. It will depend when the police think the mother is fit to go.'

'Do we know anything about the child?' I asked. 'Does she have any allergies?'

'I don't know. The family has never come to the attention of the social services before. I'll ask the police to ask the mother about allergies. They can tell you when you arrive.'

'Thank you.' This was important information that would have been included on the placement forms, along with other essential information, if the move had been planned.

As soon as I'd replaced the handset I began helping Paula into her jacket and shoes, and then put on mine. 'We're going in the car to the police station,' I told her as we left the house. 'To collect a little girl.'

'Baby?' she asked.

'No, she's three. She's coming to play with you for a while.'

The police station was about a ten-minute drive from my house. I parked in a side road close to the main entrance. Holding Paula's hand, I walked with her round to the front of the building and up the steps where I pressed the bell to be admitted. My pulse had stepped up a beat with anxiety and concern for the child. Inside I showed the duty officer behind the desk my ID and I said I was a foster carer. I didn't have to say any more.

'Yes. The social worker said you were on your way,' he said. 'Hayley is being looked after by one of our WPCs [woman police officer]. I'll take you through.'

We followed him down a short corridor and into an office where the WPC was sitting with Hayley on her lap, drawing pictures to keep her amused.

'This is Cathy, the foster carer,' the officer said, introducing us before returning to the front desk.

'Time for you to go now, poppet,' the WPC said gently to Hayley, lifting her from her lap. 'I have to do some work. Cathy's going to look after you.'

'Where's Mummy?' the poor child asked, looking very frightened.

'She's staying with us for a while,' the WPC said kindly. 'We'll look after her until she can come and collect you.'

'Do we know when that will be?' I asked.

'Once she's sober,' the WPC replied a little brusquely, clearly not impressed by the mother's behaviour. Then looking at me, 'I asked her mum if Hayley had any allergies and she said she didn't.'

'Good.'

She brought Hayley over to me and I took her hand. She was a pretty child with long fair hair, petite features and blue eyes – which were now wide with fear. 'This is Paula,' I said, hoping this would help put her at ease.

'I want my mummy,' she said, rubbing her eyes and close to tears.

'I know, love. You'll see her later,' I reassured her.

I felt her hand clench mine and hold it very tightly as though she feared I, too, might leave her. With Hayley on one side of me and Paula on the other, I followed the WPC into reception where she saw us out.

'We're going in the car to my house,' I told Hayley as we began towards my car. 'You'll be able to play with Paula.'

'Where's Mummy?' she asked again, her little brow creasing.

'You'll see her later.'

'I want Mummy.'

'I know you do, love.'

I opened the rear door of the car and strapped Paula into her seat and then Hayley into Adrian's, adjusting the straps so that they fitted her correctly.

'All right, love, try not to worry,' I said, seeing the fear in her eyes. But clearly that was asking a lot of a small child who'd gone shopping with her mother, had been taken away by the police and was now having to come home with a stranger. 'You'll see Mummy again soon,' I said, hoping I was right, and I closed the car door.

Hayley didn't say a word on the way home but stared wide-eyed through her side window, mute with fear. I kept glancing at her in the mirror and offering her words of reassurance, but without success. Paula was looking at her anxiously too. Once home, I parked on the drive and helped both girls out of the car. 'Is Mummy here?' Hayley asked as we approached the front door.

'No, love. You'll see her later. This is my house.' It was all I could say.

Indoors, I asked her if she wanted to go to the toilet and she shook her head. I told her that when she did she should tell me and I would take her. I showed the girls into the living room and got out plenty of toys that I thought would interest Hayley, but she put her thumb in her mouth and just sat on the floor looking at them, despite my encouragement to play. Ten minutes later she wet herself – not surprising given the stress she must have been under. I reassured her, changed her into dry clothes from my spares and put her own clothes in the washing machine. I tried again to engage her in play, as did Paula, but she had no interest in any toy or activity we showed her, and she didn't want a hug. It was pitiful to see her so unhappy, and when it was time for me to make lunch I took both girls with me into the kitchen. Hayley managed two mouthfuls of lunch and then wet herself again. I reassured her and changed her into more spares. The only words she spoke all afternoon were 'Mummy?' 'Where's Mummy?' or 'I want my mummy.' It was heartbreaking.

I finally gave up trying to engage her in play and sat both girls on the sofa where, with an arm around each of them, I read stories until it was time to collect Adrian from school. I explained to Hayley where we were going. 'Mummy?' she asked again hopefully.

'Not yet, love.' I wondered if her mother had any idea of the distress her irresponsible behaviour was causing her daughter.

We walked to school and Adrian wasn't completely surprised to see me in the playground with another child, as it had happened before with an emergency placement. I introduced Hayley, but despite Adrian saying a very friendly, 'Hi, how are you?' she just looked at him, lost and bewildered.

Laura saw us and waved, but stayed behind in the playground talking to Fran.

Hayley held my hand very tightly all the way home, and once there she wouldn't let me out of her sight. She came with me into the kitchen while I made dinner and then wet herself again. I changed her into her own clothes, which were now dry. I think she was toilet trained, for she was old enough and hadn't come in a nappy, but acute stress can cause loss of bladder and bowel control. It was an indication of just how traumatized she was by the day's events. If she had to stay overnight I knew I would be up most of the night settling her. With no idea what time her mother would be released from police custody, or indeed if she would be released that evening, I continued with our usual routine as much as possible while looking after Hayley. At 5.30, just as I was about to serve dinner, the telephone rang and I answered it in the kitchen. I don't think I've ever been so pleased to hear from a social worker in my life.

'Cathy, the police are going to release the mother in an hour,' she said. 'Is it all right if I give her your address so she can come straight to you and collect Hayley?'

'Yes, of course,' I said.

'I'll let them know now, thank you. The mother is called Catherine.'

It wasn't for me to ask what had led to the mother's heavy drinking, but the social services must have been satisfied that Hayley wouldn't be in danger if she returned home or they would have asked me to keep her longer while they investigated.

'Mummy coming?' Hayley asked hopefully as I replaced the handset.

'Yes, love.'

'Mummy coming?' she asked again, unable to believe that her nightmare was finally coming to an end.

'Yes. She's coming here to collect you after we've had dinner.' I settled her at the table, called Adrian and Paula, and served dinner, of which Hayley ate a very small amount.

It's always difficult meeting a foster child's parent(s) for the first time, as I'm sure it is for the parents to meet the foster carer. I try not to form preconceptions, but I'll admit they can creep in. However, any idea I had about Hayley's mother vanished at seven o'clock when I opened the front door. Slightly built, late thirties, quietly spoken and well dressed, she was close to tears.

'Cathy?' she asked, her face creasing just as Hayley's had.

'Yes. Catherine?' She nodded. 'Come in. Hayley will be so pleased to see you. She's with my son and daughter in the living room.'

I didn't have to show her through, as Hayley, having heard her mother's voice, had run into the hall. 'Mummy! Mummy!' she cried. With a mixture of absolute relief and excitement, she rushed to her mother.

Catherine dropped to her knees so that she was at her daughter's height and, encircling her in her arms, held her close. The tears she'd been holding back fell. 'Oh, love, my precious, I'm so sorry. I've been so stupid. How can you ever forgive me?'

They clung to each other and cried openly. Adrian and Paula, worried by what they could hear, came into the hall. 'It's OK,' I reassured them. 'You go and play. Hayley will be all right soon.' Adrian took hold of Paula's hand and led her back into the living room.

I gently touched Catherine's shoulder. 'Would you like to come and sit down and I'll get you a drink.'

'Thank you.' I helped her to her feet. Hayley still had her arms wrapped around her mother's neck and her legs tightly around her waist.

I took them through to the kitchen-cum-diner and drew out a chair at the table for Catherine to sit down. Hayley was on her lap. I placed a box of tissues within reach. 'What would you like to drink?'

'Water, please.'

I poured a glass of water and placed it on the table, then pulling out a chair I sat beside them. Hayley was still clinging to her mother for all she was worth. 'Has she had a drink?' Catherine asked, taking a tissue from the box.

'Yes, and a little bit of lunch and dinner. But not much.'

'Thank you for looking after her,' she said, wiping her eyes. 'I feel so ashamed. Now I'm sober I can't believe what I've done.' Fresh tears fell.

'We all make mistakes,' I said, touching her arm.

She shook her head in despair and couldn't speak for emotion, but now Hayley was with her mother she was starting to look a bit better and her confidence was returning. 'Don't cry, Mummy,' she said, wiping the tears from her mother's cheeks. Which of course made Catherine cry even more.

I waited until she was able to speak. 'Thank goodness I didn't have to stay at the police station overnight,' she said.

'I would have looked after Hayley,' I reassured her.

'I know, that's what the police lady said. Thank you.' She wiped her eyes again and looked at me. 'I want you to know I don't normally behave like that. It was completely out of character. I can't justify what I did, but I did have a good reason.' I looked at her and waited while she composed herself again. 'Last night my husband left me,' she said. 'Just like that. After ten years of marriage, he told me he'd fallen in love with his secretary. I mean, what a cliché! He said they couldn't help it, but it had just happened, like it wasn't his fault and he wasn't responsible. He said it was best for everyone if he left. Best for him, more like it!' Catherine's voice had risen and I could see that Hayley was looking at her anxiously.

'Perhaps Hayley would like to go and play with Adrian and Paula while we talk,' I suggested. But she snuggled closer to her mother, not wanting to be parted from her.

'It's all right. I won't go into all the details,' Catherine said. 'I just want you to know I'm not a bad mother. I love my daughter more than anything and would never harm her. But what he said was such a shock. I was up all night and I began drinking. I don't know how but I got through nearly two bottles of wine and by this morning I'd hatched a plan to shame him and his secretary. I went down to the shopping mall with Hayley. He's the manager of the department store there. He wouldn't see me, so I started shouting and causing a fuss, telling everyone what he'd done. The store security called the police, and the rest you know.' I nodded sympathetically as she held Hayley close and kissed the top of her head. 'This is going to take a lot of getting over,' she said more calmly. 'But at least we've got each other.'

'Yes,' I agreed. 'You have.'

'Can we go home now, Mummy?' Hayley asked in a small voice.

'Yes, of course, we'll go now.'

I offered to take them home in the car – they lived about two miles away – but Catherine said they would be all right on the bus, so I saw them to the door. Catherine thanked me again for looking after Hayley, and then said that if ever I saw them in the town would I please not mention what had happened, as she was so embarrassed. I reassured her I wouldn't and I wished them well for the future. I knew that if Catherine and her husband were divorcing then she'd have a lot of sorting out and adjusting to do, but I also knew she wouldn't make the same mistake again. Having the police involved, and her daughter taken into care, even though it was only for a day, had obviously shocked her deeply. Hopefully some good would come out of it, for sometimes we need a jolt to allow us to re-evaluate our lives and see what really matters.

I stood for a few moments at the front door after they'd gone, aware of the fresh, slightly autumnal air. The sun had set, the birds had gone to bed and the night was still. Most people were home now and only the occasional car passed. A lone dog barked in the distance. For tonight, at least, it seemed that my spare room would remain empty, although I knew it wouldn't be long before another child arrived. Somewhere out there, maybe not far away, was another family in crisis, with a child or children who would shortly need foster care. Perhaps it would be the child of someone like Laura, who was ill but didn't have a family network to help her through. Or maybe someone like Shelley, who had no parents, or someone like Catherine, whose error of judgement had unintentionally placed her child at risk of harm. Or possibly the next child I fostered could be someone like Samson, who would be part of my family long term and would need firm and consistent boundaries as well as love, care and attention. Or maybe, and most upsettingly, it would be a badly abused or neglected child, when I would put on a brave face as I bathed their bruises and reassured them they were safe, and then later in the solitude of my bedroom I would cry myself to sleep. I didn't know who my next child would be, but for tonight at least I felt satisfied that I'd done my best for the children I'd looked after – Darrel, Samson, Hayley and even little Elspeth. They were all home now with their families, and Laura was with hers. And for a foster carer there's no better ending than that.

EPILOGUE

Laura continued to make good progress, and Kim and baby Liam flourished. I saw them regularly on the way to and from school and sometimes we got together with other mums for a coffee. Laura didn't have any more setbacks and at the end of twelve months the social services ended their monitoring, although Laura still attended a support group where she'd made friends. I saw Gina a couple of times when she visited and we always had a good chat. I also saw Geraldine if she was helping out and collecting Kim from school. She just about managed a small nod in my direction, but then that's Geraldine. Her heart is in the right place, and it wouldn't do if we were all the same.

Adrian, Paula and I went to see Shelley sing with her choir at their Christmas concert, and it was beautiful. The hall was gaily decorated for Christmas with garlands and a tall tree that glittered with silver lights. The singing was perfect, ethereal, a choir from heaven. The songs were a mixture of traditional Christmas carols and popular children's Christmas songs, some of which the audience were invited to join in with. During the concert we saw Darrel sitting with another family and I rather guessed it might be

Carol. After the concert the audience could mingle while enjoying a drink and a mince pie, which gave Shelley the chance to introduce us to Carol and her adult children. I immediately warmed to them and Carol said they were all looking forward to having Shelley and Darrel at Christmas. Shelley also introduced us to her young man, Michael, and his parents, although I'd already guessed who he might be from the way he kept looking at Shelley while they were singing. He came across as a charming, sincere person who clearly thought the world of her, as did his parents. He also appeared caring of and committed to Darrel, which was so important. I didn't ask if I could expect to hear wedding bells soon, but I wouldn't be surprised, and Shelley deserved happiness and security after her unsettled early life. Adrian and I were still humming Brahms's 'Lullaby' at night sometimes and Paula was picking up the tune too.

The next time Samson needed respite care I was already fostering another child and didn't have the room, so he had to stay with a different carer. It was a pity, and it cemented the plans John and I had previously discussed in respect of extending the back of the house to create more room downstairs and another bedroom upstairs. The matchbox Samson had so carefully placed under the plant pot by the shed stayed there all winter, as I didn't have the heart to throw it away – the little reminder of Samson and his pet bed bug Bruce!

John's homecoming was delayed again and he finally arrived home in the middle of October, in time to attend my degree award ceremony. Unfortunately, a week later he had to work away again, but that's another story. So, too, is the story of the child I'm looking after now, who like all the other children I've fostered is being so brave and trying not to cry.

A true little hero. But then they all are, and I admire them greatly.

For the latest updates on these children and those in my other fostering memoirs, please visit www.cathyglass.co.uk.

SUGGESTED TOPICS FOR
READING-GROUP DISCUSSION

What were the reasons for Geraldine and Andy not consulting a doctor earlier when it became clear Laura was unwell?

Can there ever be any justification for not consulting a doctor about a mental-health issue?

Is there still a stigma attached to mental illness? If so, why do you think this is? What could be done to change this?

Cathy is very careful when dealing with Laura's family not to cross the boundary between being friendly and neighbourly and being intrusive and nosey. Does she get it right or should she have intervened earlier and alerted the social services?

Do you think Cathy, as a foster carer, reacts differently to Laura's situation than perhaps the average person might?

Shelley tells Cathy that she is not introducing her boyfriend, Michael, to her son Darrel until she is 'completely sure of him'. What do you think she means by this, and what might her reasons be?

Based on what you know, was the social worker's decision to apply to court for a Care Order for Samson the correct one? Why? If you had been the judge would you have refused or granted the Care Order? What extra support could have been given to the family?

The update on Cathy's website, www.cathyglass.co.uk, shows that Samson became his gran's carer until she died. Does knowing this change your view as to whether or not Samson should have been returned home as a child?

It could be said that Catherine, who was drunk in charge of a child, was treated harshly by the law. Do you think arresting her was the correct action? Were there any alternatives?

The ending of the book gives satisfactory resolutions for all those involved. Is there any other information you would have liked to see included?

Cathy Glass

One remarkable woman, more
than **150** foster children cared for.

Cathy Glass has been a foster carer for
twenty-five years, during which time she has
looked after more than 150 children, as well
as raising three children of her own. She was
awarded a degree in education and psychology
as a mature student, and writes under a
pseudonym. To find out more about Cathy
and her story visit www.cathyglass.co.uk.

Girl Alone

An angry, traumatized young girl on a path to self-destruction

Can Cathy discover the truth behind Joss's dangerous behaviour before it's too late?

Saving Danny

Trapped in his own dark world, Danny doesn't understand why his parents are sending him away

Cathy must call on all her expertise to deal with his challenging behaviour, and discovers a frightened little boy who just wants to be loved.

The Child Bride

A girl blamed and abused for dishonouring her community

Cathy discovers the devastating truth.

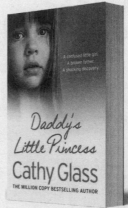

Daddy's Little Princess

A sweet-natured girl with a complicated past

Cathy picks up the pieces after events take a dramatic turn.

Will you love me?

A broken child desperate for a loving home

The true story of Cathy's adopted daughter Lucy.

Please Don't Take My Baby

Seventeen-year-old Jade is pregnant, homeless and alone

Cathy has room in her heart for two.

Another Forgotten Child

Eight-year-old Aimee was on the child-protection register at birth

Cathy is determined to give her the happy home she deserves.

A Baby's Cry

A newborn, only hours old, taken into care

Cathy protects tiny Harrison from the potentially fatal secrets that surround his existence.

The Night the Angels Came

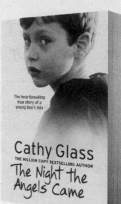

A little boy on the brink of bereavement

Cathy and her family make sure Michael is never alone.

Mummy told me not to tell

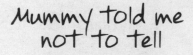

A troubled boy sworn to secrecy

After his dark past has been revealed, Cathy helps Reece to rebuild his life.

I Miss Mummy

Four-year-old Alice doesn't understand why she's in care

Cathy fights for her to have the happy home she deserves.

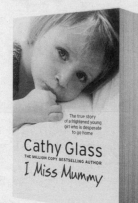

The Saddest Girl
in the World

A haunted child
who refuses to speak

Do Donna's scars run
too deep for Cathy
to help?

Cut

Dawn is desperate
to be loved

Abused and abandoned,
this vulnerable child pushes
Cathy and her family to
their limits.

Hidden

The boy with no past

Can Cathy help Tayo to
feel like he belongs again?

Damaged

A forgotten child

Cathy is Jodie's last hope. For the first time, this abused young girl has found someone she can trust.

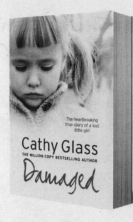

Inspired by Cathy's own experiences...

Run, Mummy, Run

The gripping story of a woman caught in a horrific cycle of abuse, and the desperate measures she must take to escape.

My Dad's a Policeman

The dramatic short story about a young boy's desperate bid to keep his family together.

The Girl in the Mirror

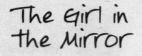

Trying to piece together her past, Mandy uncovers a dreadful family secret that has been blanked from her memory for years.

Sharing her expertise...

About Writing and How to Publish

A clear and concise, practical guide on writing and the best ways to get published.

Happy Mealtimes for Kids

A guide to healthy eating with simple recipes that children love.

Happy Adults

A practical guide to achieving lasting happiness, contentment and success. The essential manual for getting the best out of life.

Happy Kids

A clear and concise guide to raising confident, well-behaved and happy children.

Be amazed
Be moved
Be inspired

———